Nigeria: Renewal from the Roots?

The Struggle for Democratic Development

• Titles published by Zed Books in association with ACDESS •

Africa within the World: Beyond Dispossession and Dependence (1993)

South Africa and Africa: Within or Apart? (1996)

Nigeria: Renewal from the Roots?
The Struggle for Democratic Development (1997)

Nigeria: Renewal from the Roots?

The Struggle for Democratic Development

by

Adebayo Adedeji, Onigu Otite,
'Kunle Amuwo, Samuel Egwu, Inya Eteng, Sina Kawonise,
Nnamdi Ofondu, Aja Okorie, and Nuhu Yaqub

Zed Books
London and New Jersey

in association with

African Centre for Development
and Strategic Studies (ACDESS)
Ijebu-Ode

Nigeria: Renewal from the Roots? was first published by
Zed Books Ltd, 7 Cynthia Street, London N1 9JF, UK, and
165 First Avenue, Atlantic Highlands, New Jersey 07716, USA,
in association with the African Centre for Development and Strategic
Studies (ACDESS), PO Box 203, Ijebu-Ode, Nigeria, in 1997.

Cover design by Andrew Corbett
Laserset by Long House Publishing Services, St Vincent, WI
Printed and bound in the United Kingdom
by Biddles Ltd, Guildford and King's Lynn.

A catalogue record for this book is
available from the British Library.

ISBN 1 85649 509 4 Cased
ISBN 1 85649 510 8 Limp

Contents

About ACDESS

JULIUS K. NYERERE*

There is no poverty of ideas about what Africa's problems are, nor how to deal with them – either within or outside the continent. But it was thought that there was a lack of opportunity to express, debate and test African leadership which is dedicated to thinking about and for Africa's future.

It is to fill that gap that ACDESS was established. Its task is that of providing a firm foundation of ideas tested against African realities, on the basis of which Africa can develop and pursue its own strategies.

ACDESS is not intended to become another academic institution, although independence of thought and high intellectual capability are essential to its role. The purpose of ACDESS is to provide a Centre where many ideas flow together, fertilize each other and challenge each other, while the policy relevance of research remains pre-eminent. And no one will be responsible for its work and output except itself – so that all African peoples, institutions, and governments will be able to use it, and consider its ideas and arguments, while the approval of no government or institution will shape the outcome of its research.

ACDESS is an expression of confidence in Africa and Africans, and in the future of our continent despite the frequently depressing present. Africa's history is not only one of slavery, exploitation and colonialism; it is also a story of struggle against these evils, and of battles won after many setbacks and much suffering.

The current problems and challenges are immense. Africa's relative backwardness in science and technology and the legacy of its long (and continuing) history of external domination, mean that the challenges facing Africa are as great if not greater today than they were in earlier periods. But so far we have managed to survive as Africans, with our own cultures and approach to life. We can do so now, and it is important that we do so.

As Africans in Africa we still have a great deal to contribute to the world. And our future cannot be determined without us. Either we acquiesce in a future determined for us by others, or we seize control of it ourselves.

It is hoped that ACDESS will play a useful part in helping Africa to draw strength from its own past, and its potential in human and natural resources, in order to build the future of Africa on the basis of self-respect, self-reliance and freedom.

* Mwalimu Nyerere is the president of the Board of Trustees and Overseers of ACDESS. Excerpts from the Preface of: *Africa Within the World: Beyond Dispossession and Dependence* (Ijebu-Ode and London: ACDESS and Zed Books, 1993).

Preface and Acknowledgements

This is ACDESS's first effort, as it were, at dirtying its hands and going to the backwoods to observe what is happening at the grassroots level in Nigeria. These Nigerian case studies of the growth and dynamics of popular participation will be the start of a series of studies of grassroots organizations and civil society in other African countries, in the hope that a discernible continental picture based on empiricism rather than speculation and/or wishful thinking may emerge. Nigeria has been selected as the first country to be studied partly in recognition of its relative importance in Africa – the giant of Africa, as Nigerians claim – and partly because it is host to ACDESS. The 1993 abortion of the democratic process and the resulting deterioration in the economic and social conditions of the people, further intensifying political instability and human insecurity, more than qualify it as the first candidate for research and strategic study.

The crisis which engulfed most African countries in the 1980s might have begun as an economic one, but its accelerating intensity could not but erode social and political structures as well. Particularly in rural communities, some of those structures were based on age-old traditions, which are more often than not still viable in their delivery of social functions and values. There are, however, other such structures which were taken over from colonial times and are either irrelevant to the day-to-day priorities of the vast majority of the people or likely to be seen as irritating and oppressing.

The intensification and generalization of the crisis has triggered an increased questioning of structures (of the old and the not so old) and is bringing forth a vast array of manifestations of an intuitively democratic nature: farmers' associations seeking to gain control over credit schemes; women farmers requesting free access to land and protection under the law; youth and trade union organizations demanding a say in the direction of local and national policies. While most of these organizations came into being in order to pursue defensive goals (against various forms of economic exploitation and disenfranchisement), individual experiences of their members as well as their collective impact are gradually beginning to alter the character of civil society, in particular its role *vis-à-vis* the post-colonial state. Social movements of this nature may thus play an increasing role in defining what democracy at the level of rural communities means. Studying and widely discussing the roots, structures and impact of people's organizations is thus of great importance for the growth of democracy and democratic culture. It is also essential for our understanding of the nature of governance and public service delivery, while providing a clue as to why it is proving difficult to launch a sustainable, democratically-determined development process.

These Nigerian case studies were conducted in seven communities in four regions: the North, East, South-west and Middle Belt of Nigeria. Each of the seven resulting studies has provided a solid assessment of the historical development of the impact of grassroots organizations. A comparison of the case studies complements the conclusions drawn from the historical assessment while increasing the level of precision with which results can be formulated.

At the time the research was initiated Nigeria appeared to be on the road to democracy after nine years (1984–93) of yet another military dictatorship. The Babangida military administration had taken the country through a very tortuous stop–go transitional process which in spite of all the hiccups culminated in elections to the National Assembly in 1992 soon followed by the presidential elections of 12 June 1993. Unfortunately, the process was aborted by the annulment of the results of the presidential elections. The public outrage which followed this unprecedented act forced General Babangida to 'step aside' after handing over to a handpicked civilian interim administration, which was soon toppled and replaced by yet another military dictatorship headed by General Sani Abachi in November 1993. The new government lost no time in disbanding all democratic institutions: the two political parties – the Social Democratic Party (SDP) and the National Republican Convention (NRC) – the state legislatures and the National Assembly. A new five-year transitional programme has since been put in place by the Abacha regime. That programme includes the creation of new states and new local government areas. On 1 October 1996, six new states and 183 new local government areas were created. Also on that date the government approved the formation of five new political parties in replacement of the two they had abolished. These new parties are: the United Nigeria Congress Party (UNCP); the Democractic Party of Nigeria (DPN); the Grassroot Democratic Movement (GDM); the National Centre Party of Nigeria (NCPN); and the Committee of National Consensus (CNC).

These developments have made these studies on the struggle for democratic development at the grassroots level in Nigeria most opportune and pertinent.

The seven communities studied displayed rather diverse cultural backgrounds and socio-economic conditions. All but one of these seven local government areas (LGAs) are predominantly rural: Ethiope East LGA in Delta State; Afijio LGA in Oyo State; Dekina LGA in Kogi State; Mbaitoli

LGA in Imo State; Ohaozara LGA in Abia State; and Wurno LGA in Sokoto State. The exception is the predominantly urban area of Ijebu-Ode LGA in Ogun State.

The scholars who undertook the studies have been drawn from various universities in the country. Not only do they speak the local languages but they are also intimately familiar with the modes of social organization in the societies concerned. The overarching interest of the study is to determine whether traditional and modern modes of social organization have the capacity or the potential to revitalize the political, social and economic system in rural communities in various regions of Nigeria, and thus contribute not only to the redefinition of social cohesion in the country but also to the definition of a truly post-colonial state. The growth of democracy and a sustainable democratic culture in Nigeria depends on strengthening civil society and its popular grassroots organizations. An in-depth study of the nature and characteristics of these organizations is an essential first step in the process.

It is clear that ACDESS's initiative has been inspired by the African Charter for Popular Participation in Development which, since its adoption in Arusha, Tanzania, in February 1990, has been hailed as Africa's Magna Carta. Indeed, the international conference at which the Charter was prepared was my last major initiative as head of the Economic Commission for Africa. Since in my speech closing the conference on that historic day of 16 February 1990, I urged that all participants must give life to the Charter at the national level, no one should be surprised that ACDESS has chosen, as one of its five priority programmes, *Modes of Social Organization: Case Studies of Rural Communities of Popular Participation in the Democratization Process*. As the person who had successfully piloted the African Charter through the meetings of the Assembly of Heads of State and Government of the Organization of African Unity (OAU) and the General Assembly of the United Nations Organization in 1990, I could not be expected to do less.

The ECA under my leadership was the architect of the holistic human-centred development paradigm at a time when the dominant orthodox strategy was marginalizing the people and rending the fabric of society. Focusing on macro-economic aggregates, debt servicing and balancing the books by rolling back demand rather than expanding and diversifying supply, the dominant development paradigm was things-oriented rather than people-centred. In those days, our viewpoint that nations cannot be built without popular support and the full participation of the people, and that the African economic crisis cannot be resolved or human and economic conditions improved without the full and effective contribution, creativity and participation of the people, was considered heretical. And many otherwise intelligent and well-meaning Africans, who have been brought up to underestimate the power of ideas while being overawed by the idea of power, particularly financial power, joined the chorus.

Fortunately, since 1990 there has been an ideological shift. No one now disputes the centrality of popular participation and the human factor as the only viable development paradigm for Africa. But regrettably there are still many countries in our continent where despotism, authoritarianism and kleptocracy are prevalent, where the message of the African Charter is being honoured more in the breach than in the observance. Put simply, the Charter reinstates the centrality of the human being in all development processes: political, economic, social and cultural. It reasserts the self-evident truth that the foundation for self-reliant and self-sustaining processes of development is people's participation. In other words, that no society which excludes the generality of its people from participating fully in and contributing to national directions and policies, which denies its people their basic human rights and individual freedom, and which does not guarantee its citizens individual and collective security, can achieve self-reliance and self-sustainment. In a society where there is a pervasive lack of democracy, popular mobilization and public accountability are invariably non-existent. The African Charter has therefore been perceived right from its adoption as the framework for a new political, economic and social order in Africa. Indeed, our slogan at the Arusha conference was 'Putting the People First'.

In order to review and expand upon the results of the seven case studies and to explore well-substantiated answers to issues raised, ACDESS organized two workshops in December 1994 at Ijebu-Ode, its headquarters. These brought together over 70 community leaders, organizers of local development projects, academics and senior professionals with vast experience in national and international administrations. Participants intensely debated field experiences in the seven LGAs studied by the ACDESS research team and identified lessons to be drawn from the past five years of effort to bolster popular participation in development and democratization in Nigeria. At the end of the process, strategic and operational implications were spelled out.

ACDESS wishes to acknowledge not only the support of the Friedrich-Ebert Foundation for the research work in rural communities throughout Nigeria, but also the assistance of the United Nations Economic Commission for Africa (ECA), in particular its focal point on popular participation within the Division for Public Administration, Human Resources and Social Development, and of the African Development Bank whose generous grants-in-aid have been an important source of co-financing. ACDESS's continued indebtedness to UNDP must also once again be publicly acknowledged. In addition to its general support for institutional building, it made available the services of Ms Jumi Familoni (Nigeria/USA) for a period of three months as a TOKTEN expert. The ultimate input came, however, from the researchers and participants in the workshops who shared their rich and diversified individual experiences and concluded that there is indeed a way forward towards a dynamic and caring society, and towards a responsive and responsible state in Nigeria.

Adebayo Adedeji
ACDESS, Ijebu-Ode

Contributors

Adebayo Adedeji: Founder and Executive Director, African Centre for Development and Strategic Studies (ACDESS), Fellow of the Nigerian Economic Society and Fellow of the African Academy of Science.

'Kunle Amuwo: Lecturer, Department of Political Science, University of Ibadan, Nigeria; ACDESS Associate Fellow, 1993.

Samuel Egwu: Lecturer, Department of Political Science, University of Jos, Nigeria; ACDESS Associate Fellow, 1993.

Inya Eteng: Professor, Department of Sociology, University of Port Harcourt, Nigeria.

Sina Kawonise: Lecturer, Department of Sociology, Ogun State University, Ago-Iwoye, Nigeria; ACDESS Associate Fellow, 1993.

Nnamdi Ofundu: Lecturer, Department of Political Science, University of Lagos, Nigeria; ACDESS Associate Fellow, 1993.

Aja Okorie: Professor of Agricultural Economics, University of Swaziland, formerly Hallsworth Research Fellow, School of Economic Studies, University of Manchester, Uniter Kingdom and Professor, University of Benin, Nigeria; ACDESS Associate Fellow, 1993.

Onigu Otite: Dean, Faculty of Social Sciences and Professor of Sociology, University of Ibadan, Nigeria: ACDESS Associate Senior Fellow, 1993.

Nahu Yaqub: Dean, Faculty of Social Sciences and Administration and Head of Department of Political Science, Usmanu Danfodiye University, Sokoto, Nigeria; ACDESS Associate Fellow, 1993.

Abbreviations

ACB	African Continental Bank
ADU	Afijio Descendants' Union
BBC	British Broadcasting Corporation
BLP	Better Life Programme for Rural Women
CB	Community Bank
CBN	Central Bank of Nigeria
CCF	Cooperative Community Farm
CCS	Cooperative Consumers' Society
CD	Community Development
CDA	Community Development Association
CDC	Community Development Council
CDD	Community Development Department
CDS	Centre for Democratic Studies
CID	Criminal Investigation Department
CMS	Cooperative Multi-Purpose Society
CMU	Cooperative Multi-Purpose Union
COWAD	Community Women and Development
CPC	Community People's Congress
CTCS	Cooperative Thrift and Credit Society
CTCU	Cooperative Thrift and Credit Union
DA	Development Area
DC	Development Council
DFRRI	Directorate of Food, Roads and Rural Infrastructure
DPO	Divisional Police Officers
ECA	(United Nations) Economic Commission for Africa
EFA	Education for All
EMS	Express Mail Service
EPI	Expanded Programme of Immunization
EU	European Union
FMCS	Farmers' Multi-Purpose Cooperative Society
FRCN	Federal Radio Corporation of Nigeria
ICDA	Isoyin Community Development Association
IDA	Ijebu-Ode Development Association
IDA	Ilora Development Association
IDYA	Ilora Development Youth Association
ILO	International Labour Organization
k	*kobo*
kg	kilogram
KVA	kilowatt-ampere(s)
LG	Local Government
LGA	Local Government Area
LGEA	Local Government Education Authority

MAMSER	Directorate of Social Mobilization, Self-Reliance, Economic Recovery and Social Justice
MCS	Multi-Purpose Cooperative Society
₦	*Naira*
NACB	Nigeria Agricultural and Cooperative Bank
NBCB	National Board for Community Banks
NCWS	National Council of Women's Societies
NDE	National Directorate of Employment
NEC	National Electoral Commission
NERFUND	National Economic Reconstruction Fund
NGO	Non-Governmental Organization
NIGEP	Nigerian Guinea-worm Eradication Programme
NITEL	Nigerian Telecommunications
NOA	National Orientation Agency
NOM	National Orientation Movement
NPC	National Population Commission
NPC	Northern People's Congress
NPP	Nigerian People's Party
NRC	National Republican Convention
NTA	Nigerian Television Authority
NURTW	National Union of Road Transport Workers
OCB	Obanta Community Bank
OECD	Organization of Economic Cooperation and Development
OGACDC	Ogun State Association of Community Development Councils
OYSADEP	Oyo State Agricultural Development Programme
PBN	People's Bank of Nigeria
PRO	Public Relations Officer
ROTSAC	Rotating Savings Club
SAP	Structural Adjustment Programme
SDP	Social Democratic Party
TDU	Town Development Union
UBA	United Bank for Africa
UBN	Union Bank of Nigeria
UNDP	United Nations Development Programme
UNICEF	United Nations Children's Fund
UPN	United Party of Nigeria
VDC	Village Development Committee
VDO	Voluntary Development Organization
VPC	Village People's Congress
WAI	War Against Indiscipline
WAIC	War Against Indiscipline and Corruption
WIA	Women in Agriculture
WIN	Women in Nigeria
WUCOMAT	Wurno Construction Materials Factory
YC	Youth Council

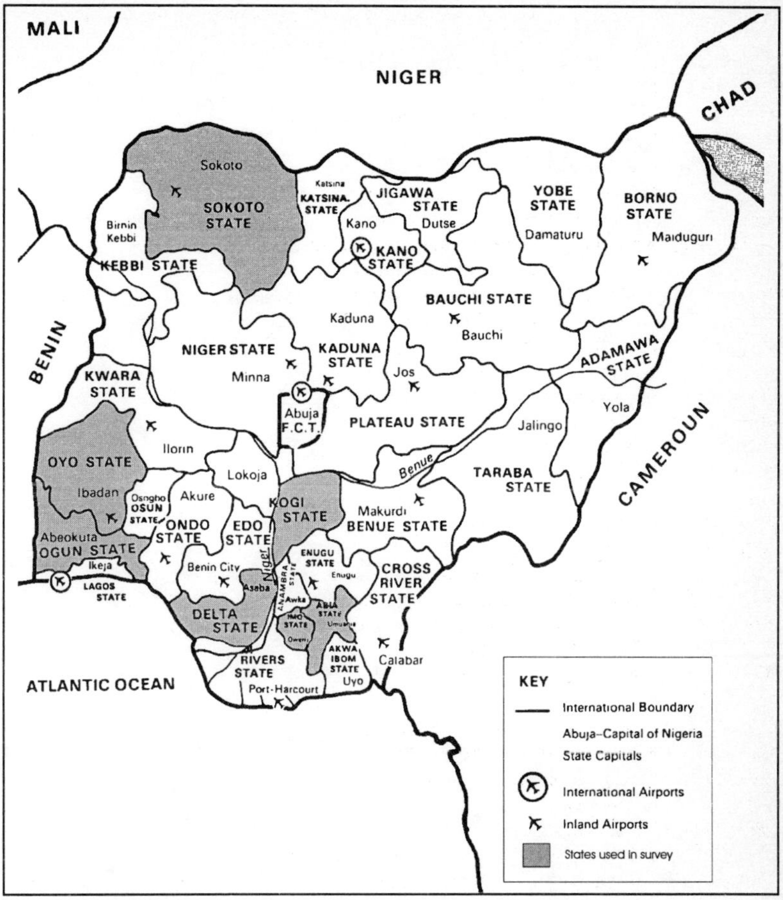

Map of Nigeria

I

Theoretical Perspectives

1

Popular Participation, Democracy and Development: Is there a Dialectical Linkage?

ADEBAYO ADEDEJI

Democracy: means or an end?

Francis Fukuyama's article 'The End of History' in *The National Interest Journal*[1] in the summer of 1989 provoked a great deal of controversy. But his hypothesis is very straightforward. With communism collapsing in more or less the same way that other political systems, such as monarchy and fascism, have disappeared, liberal democracy remains as the only system of government which still enjoys legitimacy throughout the world. Consequently, he contends, the struggle for supremacy as to which system of government is best is over, with liberal democracy constituting the 'end of mankind's ideological evolution' and 'the final form of human government'.[2] All other forms of government are characterized by grave defects and irrationalities that have led to their eventual collapse. Only liberal democracy is free from such fundamental contradictions and remains the only coherent political aspiration that spans different regimes and cultures around the globe.

Further, Fukuyama has no hesitation in establishing a linear relationship between liberal democracy and what he calls the liberal principles in economics – the free market – as he asserts that 'there is no question but that the world's most developed countries are also its most successful democracies'.[3] In other words, liberal democracy is not only an end in itself but also a means of achieving the objectives of neo-classical economics – marketization, reduced state intervention, privatization and globalization.

Yet it is now generally recognized that the neo-classical economic paradigm is the bedrock of inequity and worsening inequalities, and the most potent force for the marginalization and alienation of the people and their grassroots organizations. This attempt to establish a linear linkage between democracy and development is an oversimplification of political history and a most inadequate explanation of the phenomenon of democracy. While the process of economic development will inevitably result in large-scale social transformation which may create material conditions for democracy, there is no automatic linkage. Democracy has almost never been chosen for economic reasons.

After all, the first major democratic revolutions of the United States and France took place before either country had achieved economic take-off. It was rebellion against colonial predators and oppressors (in the case of the US) and a despotic and exploitative oligarchic system of governance (in the case of France) that pushed them onto the path of democracy. Their opting for human rights and fundamental freedoms was in no way conditioned by their pursuit of the neo-classical economic paradigm and the industrialization process. The goals – inalienable rights of all members of the human family as the foundation of freedom, justice and peace and the guaranteeing of life, liberty and the pursuit of happiness – were perceived as being worthy of pursuit by any civilized society or by any society that makes any pretence at being civilized.

Indeed, during the process of industrial revolution, the backwash effects of market forces promoted and exacerbated both regional and interpersonal inequalities. Living standards for the masses were kept low in order to create the large-scale saving and capital formation which was necessary for rapid economic development. And given the accelerated population increase of the eighteenth and nineteenth centuries, and the technical advances in agriculture during the same period, the supply of labour became so large that the holding down of wages was accomplished simply by releasing the market forces. The state in those days was an oppressor state whose primary function was to serve as a means of supporting the cumulative process tending towards inequality. The state usually became the tool for advancing the interests of the rich and mighty while stopping or inhibiting the efforts of the poor and powerless. Thus the anti-state and anti-organization bias of the classical economists was to foster the interests of the emerging entrepreneurial class. The conventional wisdom was that while inequalities were a necessary condition for progress, the lack of political democracy made its continuation possible.

Little wonder that Aneurin Bevan, in a lecture on 'Democratic Values', not only stressed that 'democracy as we know it today is a product of the twentieth century' but also added poignantly that:

> It is highly doubtful whether the achievements of the Industrial Revolution would have been permitted if the franchise had been universal. It is very doubtful, because a great deal of the capital aggregations that we are at present enjoying are the result of the wages that our fathers went without.[4]

A similar irony was noted recently by the Prime Minister of Malaysia when, in a speech delivered at the European–East Asia Forum in Hong Kong in October 1992 he stated that:

> in the former Soviet Union and the East European countries, democracy was introduced along with the free market. The result is chaos and increased misery. Not only have the countries broken up, mainly through bloody civil wars, but there is actual recession and more hardship for the people than when the Communists ruled. One may ask whether democracy is the means or the end. Democracy at all costs is not much different from Communist authoritarianism

> from the barrel of a gun .... In a number of East Asian countries, while democracy is still eschewed, the free market has been accepted and has brought prosperity. Perhaps it is the authoritarian stability which enabled this to happen. Should we enforce democracy on people who may not be able to handle it and destroy stability?[5]

Unlike Prime Minister Mahathir, many people do indeed subscribe to the view that democracy is an end, not just a means. There simply is no clear link between democracy and the pace of economic development. While some forms of government clearly are destructive to launching and sustaining the economic development process, others, including some undemocratic systems, all seem capable of delivering a good economic performance. The South-East Asian economic miracle has not been achieved through the democratization process. Instead, the emphasis has been, *inter alia*, on (1) the installation of effective systems of public administration and achieving good governance; and (2) systematic intervention by government in the development and transformation process through multiple channels. Examples of such intervention are targeted and subsidized credit to selected industries; low deposit rates and ceilings on borrowing rates to increase profits and retained earnings; protection of domestic import substitutes; subsidies to declining industries; the establishment and financial support of government banks; public investment in applied research; and the development of export marketing institutions. They have also taken full advantage of their cultural heritage. The cohesiveness of their societies and the herd instinct of their investment communities are two well-known examples.

The pro-authoritarian analysts argue that the high rate of private domestic investment, arising from a corresponding high rate of domestic saving, which constitutes the bedrock of the Asian miracle, would have been impossible to achieve under a liberal democratic system. This argument enjoyed widespread support for generations until the collapse of communism recently. After all, there is no other road to economic development than a compulsory rise in the share of the national income which is withheld from consumption and devoted to investment. To achieve this requires a policy of austerity which requires frugality in the living standards of the mass of the people. This becomes a most difficult task to accomplish in societies where democratic forms of government are adopted. To quote the late Aneurin Bevan again,

> it is not easy in some parts of the world where life is exceedingly primitive to entrust to all the people the power of democratic selection, and then to ask them to forgo some immediate delights. It is not easy.[6]

That was why, in the present-day advanced countries, effective political suffrage was restricted by various devices to the upper income strata until late in the development process. But that type of 'restricted democracy' is no longer acceptable in today's world. A country is either democratic or not.

What is democracy?

But then, how does one judge whether a country is democratic or not? In other words, what is democracy? Today, when there is almost universal support for democracy and sound governance, such questions may provoke the laughter of derision. Yet they are capable of different answers.

Nowadays, democracy is more often than not identified with the ballot box and a pluralistic political party system. Indeed, some well-known theorists have gone as far as defining democracy as the 'competitive struggle for the people's vote'.[7] There has been so much emphasis on elections that even dictators can now claim to be democratic because they have gone through the motion of holding rigged multi-party elections. The ease with which the international community has conferred its seal of approval on any semblance of free and fair elections in Africa has validated the equation of democracy with elections and multi-partyism.

This phenomenon has been described as 'low intensity democracy'[8] – a compromise between pseudo-democratic institutions and dictatorships enjoying little popular support. By ensuring that the democratization process is channelled within the formal bounds defined by the state and embodied in political parties, elections and parliaments, low-intensity democracy keeps in power a coalition comprising conservative politicians and the segment of the business community most intent on preserving its manifold privileges. Naturally, because such regimes have a mantle of respectability bestowed on them by the international financial institutions, they are readily and cynically manipulated by them. It is needless to add that low-intensity democracy is perceived by the people as illegitimate, as mere scheming with no real change in power structures and with negligible positive effects on their lives.

Democracy in Africa to be sustainable needs therefore to go well beyond the Western model with its divisiveness, its winner-takes-all approach or zero sum game, and its relatively narrow base in terms of popular participation. For the majority of people in the Western democracies, the system offers no built-in participation as political machineries have usurped power and structures. The Western model, currently engulfed in a structural crisis, is largely unable to address the needs of developing countries.

Similarly, while increasingly it is understood that democracy cannot be decreed or brought about in an authoritarian manner, military regimes in Africa go through the pretence of democratizing their countries. The military is anything but democratically managed. It is a disciplined force ruled by command. There is therefore nothing in the background of military dictatorships that qualifies them to be the mentors of democracy, nor for that matter the installers of effective systems of public administration and good governance. More often than not, military regimes muzzle free speech and stifle freedom of association and of the press. They rule by coercion rather than by consent; by command rather than by consensus; and by alienating the populace rather than by mobilizing and motivating them. And yet they expect the democracy they install – usually the low-intensity brand of democracy – to survive and thrive!

Democracy as a sub-set of popular participation

For democracy to survive, grow and thrive in a society it must derive from and be inspired by a deep-rooted culture of popular participation. Popular participation is in essence the empowerment of the people to involve themselves in creating structures and in designing policies and programmes that serve the interests of all and contribute optimally to the development process. Consequently, popular participation involves (1) the opening up of the political process to accommodate freedom of opinions, tolerate differences and accept consensus on issues; (2) ensuring the full participation of all the people and their organizations and associations; and (3) creating necessary conditions for such an empowerment. This requires an evolving political system in which all sections of the society participate.

In other words, popular participation is the *fons et origo* of a people-centred development vision that embraces the transformation agenda and is likely to achieve Africa's second liberation – its freedom from poverty, hunger, disease, ignorance and environmental degradation; and its emergence as a self-reliant and dynamic political economy, fully integrated and no longer marginalized, but rather participating actively in the comity of nations. Popular participation, being at the heart of a people-centred development paradigm, looks up to justice, sustainability and inclusiveness as the defining principles of authentic development. Development – be it political, economic or social – becomes a people's movement rather than a foreign-funded initiative. Government's primary role is as an enabling one: to provide people with the opportunity and environment for self-development.

Popular participation, in the final analysis, brings about a new synthesis of the fundamental objectives of political, economic, environmental and social change. Since governments by nature give priority to the interests of those who control power, it is only through popular participation, through the political empowerment of the people, that just, sustainable and inclusive communities can emerge. Only thus can the right of the people to a voice in making the decisions that influence their lives, both at family and community levels, be assured. And only under such circumstances does sovereignty reside in the people and the authority of the state truly derive from the people.

It is clear that democracy in terms of the ballot box, the pluralistic party system and parliament is only a sub-set of popular participation. Because the role of the people and their popular organizations is central to the realization of popular participation, they have to be fully involved and committed at all levels of social organization – at the family level, at the workplace, in all organizations and, indeed, in all walks of life. In this human-centred holistic paradigm there are no marginalized or vulnerable groups. The role of women and youth is central and it is a fundamental requirement that a special and continuing effort should be made to eliminate gender biases. This can be assured through the extension and protection of people's basic human rights and particularly through the vigorous implementation of the Universal Declaration of Human Rights, the African Charter on Human and People's Rights, the Convention on the Rights of the Child, the International Labour Organization (ILO) Convention concerning freedom of association and protection of the right to organize, and the Convention on the Elimination of all Forms of Discrimination against Women.

It cannot be overemphasized that popular participation is not just a manipulative and bureaucratic matter of attending meetings, shouting slogans and voting. It goes well beyond these. It centres on effective participation, not just involvement, in the decision-making processes at all levels, in the formulation of policies and programmes, in the allocation of resources, in the execution of projects and in the monitoring of performance. It includes the equitable sharing of the benefits of development as well as holding the leadership accountable for their actions. This is why popular participation necessarily posits people's power alongside state power and insists that the sovereignty of the state should be the popular sovereignty of the people. Hence one of the imperatives of popular participation is a manifestly democratic political culture.

The African Charter for Popular Participation for Development spells out the roles, duties and responsibilities of each of the principal actors – the people and their organizations, non-governmental organizations (NGOs) and voluntary development organizations (VDOs), women's organizations, organized labour, youth and students and their organizations, government, the international community and the media and mass communications systems.

At the level of the people and their organizations, the roles, duties and responsibilities include:

- The establishment of autonomous and democratic grassroots organizations to promote participatory self-reliant development and increase the output and productivity of the masses;
- The development of the capacity of the people to participate in debates on policy issues – economic, social and political policies;
- The promotion of education, literacy, skill training and human resources development as a means of enhancing popular participation;
- The shaking off of the lethargy and traditional beliefs that are impediments to change and progress.

The NGOs and VDOs which, for their part, are driven by a commitment to shared values in the pursuit of their mission, are themselves required to be fully participatory, democratic and accountable. In addition to their traditional humanitarian activities they should provide increasing support for the productive capacities of the poor and for promoting an environmentally sound pattern of local development. NGOs and VDOs – African and non-African – should develop and/or strengthen institutional structures at the national and regional levels; establish national forums for honest and open dialogue between themselves and governments; and establish networking arrangements for the dissemination of successful popular participation and grassroots experience so as to create a multiplier effect.

In order to ensure that the participation of women is advanced and strengthened, popular women's organizations should be democratic, autonomous and accountable. They should continue to strengthen their capacities as builders of confidence among women, and in particular strive for the attainment of policies and programmes that reflect and recognize women's roles as producers, mothers, active community mobilizers and custodians of culture.

Similarly, trade unions must be democratic, voluntary, autonomous and accountable organizations initiating, animating and promoting mass literacy and training programmes. They should defend trade union rights, particularly the right to strike, and assist in the formation of workers' cooperatives, promote workplace democracy and give special attention to effective and democratic participation of women members at all levels of trade unions.

Full democratic participation in society by youth and students and their organizations should be encouraged through the elimination of major impediments to youth participation such as frequent bans on youth and student organizations, police brutality against unarmed protesting students, detention and harassment on campuses and the frequent arbitrary closure of educational institutions. Nigeria and other African countries will need to adopt a charter on youth and students' rights which includes the rights to education, employment, free public expression and organization.

It goes without saying that popular participation is not only dependent on the nature of the state itself but, more particularly, on the ability of government to respond to popular demand. Unless governments yield space to the people, popular participation will be difficult to achieve. As is frankly admitted in the Charter,

> too often the social bases of power and decision making are too narrow. Hence the urgent need to broaden these; to galvanize and tap people's energy and commitment; and to promote political accountability by the state to the people. This makes it imperative that a new partnership between African governments and the people, in the common interest of societal and accelerated socio-economic development, should be established without delay.[9]

This urgency is indisputable if, with the Charter, we believe that

> nations cannot be built without the popular support and full participation of the people, nor can the economic crisis be resolved and the human and economic conditions improved without the full and effective contribution, creativity and popular enthusiasm of the vast majority of the people ... neither can Africa's

perpetual economic crisis be overcome, nor a bright future for Africa and its people see the light of day, unless the structures, pattern and political context of the process of socio-economic development are appropriately altered.[10]

Democratically-determined development: a second sub-set of popular participation

A democratically-determined development is a consequence of a human-centred holistic paradigm. The economic empowerment of the people is its *conditio sine qua non*. This means, in specific terms,

1 Land reform for better access and entitlement to land for productive use;

2 The enhancement of the role of women as agents of change and the modernization of the food production sector;

3 The creation and strengthening of rural financial institutions;

4 Easy and ready access to credit by the rural communities (particularly women) without the requirement of collaterals;

5 The use of selective nominal interest rates as an instrument for increased mobilization of domestic savings, reduction of speculative activities and shifting resources to productive activities;

6 The satisfaction of critical needs, investment in human capital, particularly education and health, and the integration of women in the development process so as to increase productive capacity and productivity, and through these the standard and quality of life;

7 The legislation of a clear framework of ownership and participation of the different socio-economic groups such as rural cooperatives, trades and artisans in order to promote popular participation in production, marketing and development, and to strengthen the informal sector with a view to its ultimate integration into the development process;

8 The establishment of community development institutions, especially indigenous NGOs and civil society institutions promoting self-help programmes, thus enabling the use of direct community labour on a voluntary basis for the provision of rural infrastructure; and

9 The fostering of greater mass participation in decision making, policy formulation, execution and monitoring, thus developing the confidence of the people in themselves, in their own societies and in their government. This, in turn, would lead to the development of a greater sense of commitment to development, and a readiness to make sacrifices for it.

A democratically-determined development process immerses the entire populace in the struggle for socio-economic transformation and in turn transforms the people themselves by changing and significantly modifying their values, their attitudes to work, saving and investment, their sense of self-reliance and human dignity and, above all, their perception of citizenship. Participation in citizenship constitutes the basis of all other forms of participation in development.

> Divorced from participation in citizenship, the concept of popular participation in development becomes a mere administrative strategy – a callous manipulation of the innocent and [the] ignorant even if the end result might be a 'successful project' – but the end can never morally justify the means. Sadly, much of the current jargon about popular participation is based on the administrative desire for project success and effectiveness.[11]

In this connection, it must be recognized that popular participation is a process not an event. Its growth is more often than not inhibited by many obstacles. Powerful vested interests, usually driven by personal greed, erect numerous obstacles to block the routes to people's political and economic power.

These obstacles can be legal, bureaucratic, social and/or distributional. In many African countries, the legal system is unjust. Often arbitrary and capricious, it favours those with economic clout or political influence. Equality before the law, which implies transparency, accountability and fairness, is conspicuously absent. Some countries place unabashed, open restrictions on the participation of women and religious and/or ethnic minorities. Even workers are denied basic rights. In these countries the people are shackled by innumerable regulations and controls requiring all sorts of permits and licences. Many old anti-participatory values and prejudices persist. Worst of all is the maldistribution of the means of production, particularly land, capital and skill.

In Africa, as in other developing regions, one of the most significant assets is land. Yet it is usually maldistributed. For example, the present distribution of land in South Africa

> is criminally grotesque. The average size of white farms is a staggering 988 hectares (2,470 acres) as against the average of 161 hectares in the United States and Canada. The average size of the farms of black farmers is barely one hectare ... The government's land reform scheme, even when it has been implemented fully, will be the beginning of the process of turning South Africa downside up and reversing the epoch-long bias against the vast majority of the people.[12]

Changing the power equation requires the organization of a countervailing force. The civil society with independent peoples' organizations – genuinely grassroots, voluntary, democratically administered, self-reliant and rooted in the tradition and culture of the society – is the only answer. It will ensure community empowerment and self-development and thus offers the most important source of countervailing power.

Before we conclude this section of the chapter, it may be appropriate to address the question of the effect of marketization on popular participation in general and the democratically-determined development process in particular. Will the markets allow the people to participate effectively in the development process? What is the impact of the markets on the distribution of income and other development opportunities, and on economic empowerment? Are the markets really free and accessible to all the people? Are there people-friendly markets? Is this not a contradiction in terms?

Indeed, the basic message of neoclassical liberal economics is that if you 'free' the market from the yoke of government regulation, and if macroeconomic policies are conducted properly by the authorities, the economy will grow steadily, reflecting the universal power of the market as the most efficient mechanism yet devised for the exchange of goods or services – impersonally matching supply and demand, bringing together buyers and sellers, employers and workers, and constantly setting and resetting prices so that the economy works at peak efficiency. Indeed, this perception of the market derives from the abstract model of Walrasian general equilibrium, based on the assumption of perfect competition on both supply and demand sides, perfect divisibility of all resources and products, and free factor moblility.[13] The problems of asymmetric information, monopoly, deception or fraud do not exist because there is an omnipotent hand managing the market. But such a market exists only in the imagination of the classical economists. In any case, the neoclassical liberal market is limited to physical goods. Transactions of stocks such as land and human capital do not seem to fit this framework so smoothly.

For all their vaunted efficiency at matching buyers and sellers, markets are usually associated with increasing inequality and poverty as well as large-scale unemployment. In addition, most markets suffer from three types of distortion: (1) distortions in the workings of the market themselves; (2) disparities (lack of education, skills or assets) among the people who enter the markets; and (3) failure to reflect external costs and benefits. This last is the villain of the piece and the cause of conflicts between private profit and social benefit.

One major source and guarantee of economic empowerment is employment. Employment empowers people (1) economically, by giving them purchasing power for goods and services; (2) socially, by offering them a productive role that enhances their dignity and self-esteem; and (3) politically, by enabling them to influence decision making in the workplace and beyond. Unfortunately, throughout the world a high level of unemployment has become the norm. But the situation is much worse in sub-Saharan Africa where double-digit unemployment figures are prevalent. Without doubt there is a threat to social cohesion when people, particularly the educated youth, lose all hope of jobs. So serious is the unemployment situation that resort has to be made to the informal sector. According to United Nations Development Programme (UNDP) estimates, nearly two-thirds of the urban workforce are in the informal sector.[14] The neoliberal economic paradigm has the most disempowering effect in Africa and other developing countries as it fosters growth without employment. Even in the European member countries of the Organization of Economic Cooperation and Development (OECD), unemployment has increased more than threefold from 3 per cent in the mid-1970s to over 10 per cent in the mid-1990s. In addition, job security has been deteriorating.

All these factors have made a democratically-determined development process more distant than ever. And yet we are in the age of the globalization of democracy and the democratization process. Precisely at the moment when the principles of democracy and popular participation have gained universal validity, a sense of increasing alienation has begun to erode confidence in the process. This alienation manifests itself in the sense of powerlessness shared by a large segment of the population, not only in societies which are undemocratic, but also in 'democracies' themselves.

The globalization of democracy – like the globalization of the capitalist market economy, the global penetration of science and technology, the internationalization of the state and the universalization of nationalism – is a dynamic produced by modernity. All these dynamic modern processes have resulted in the paradox that their full-fledged development has brought about self-defeating contradictions. But the countervailing force to all this development lies in the strengthening of civil society, the people's movement which can, over time, generate enormous synergic dynamics to ensure that political and economic empowerment of the individual citizen becomes a permanent reality and that increasingly a sustainable process of democratically-determined development is achieved. Democracy and the kind of development that flows from it are therefore two sides of the same coin and can only be delivered through popular participation.

Governance and public service delivery

The quality of governance is a crucial factor in determining the relationship between the people and their governments. Good governance is required to build an effective relationship between people and their governments and it is essential for creating an enabling environment for sustainable development. Whenever good governance prevails, the government is responsive to popular demand: this puts it in a position to galvanize and tap people's energy and commitment. Good governance promotes political accountability by the state to the people and establishes a new partnership between the government and the people which cannot but enhance the general welfare of the populace and peace and order in the polity.

Good governance is characterized by adherence to the rule of law, respect for human rights, political openness and tolerance, pervasive and effective personal security and maintenance of law and order, governmental accountability and transparency, and a decentralized power structure and decision-making process. In other words, good governance requires:

> the politics of consent and consensus, the politics of conviction and commitment, and the politics of compassion and accountability. Consensus politics is involving people in the process by which policies are developed, listening to what they have

> to say and adapting the approach of the leadership and government in the light of all these. By so doing, government is most likely to win the consent of the majority of the people, if not of all, to such policies and, with that consent, conviction in the rightness of the courses being pursued and commitment to see them through successfully. The politics of consensus and consent, conviction and commitment, and compassion and accountability are the practical corollary of a concern for a nation as a whole, not just for a particular group.[15]

Good governance is only realizable in a participatory democracy. To expect it under a military dictatorship – such as has prevailed for more than three decades in Nigeria – is a heroic assumption. Centralization of power and a command structure and system are the hallmark of the military. It is therefore simple-minded to expect a military government to be adherents and practitioners of the democratic system of governance, of building consensus and winning people's consent. Indeed, by their very nature, the politics of consensus and consent, conviction and commitment and compassion and accountability are alien to a dictatorship, particularly a military dictatorship.

Little wonder that countries that have long been under this type of governance (Nigeria and Zaire are now the classical examples) are groaning under gross mismanagement, massive capital flight, corruption, unproductive uses of resources, poor resource mobilization, distorted priorities and lack of basic human rights. The authoritarian imposition of unpopular and irrelevant structural adjustment programmes in Nigeria and elsewhere in the 1980s was possible only because of lack of democracy and popular participation. As I have written elsewhere:

> In the absence of political power for the people, and moreover, due to the lack of control over power and of public accountability, displays of tyranny proliferate – motivated by the unwillingness to accommodate the plurality of democracy and the disdain of truth. Tyranny not only moulds its own delusion but also drapes itself in an infallible armour as well as convinces itself of its self-appointed messianic ardour.[16]

It is needless to add that good governance is not necessarily guaranteed by multi-party elections, although elected governments should be better motivated than authoritarian ones to practise it. In a country where low-intensity democracy prevails, however, the quality of governance may not be much different from that prevailing under a military dictatorship. In fact, it can be worse because such regimes are not only illegitimate and coercive, but also divisive and polarized, pursuing a zero sum political game where winners take all and losers are not only excluded from power but run the risk of being exterminated.

The most universal criticism of African governance is that of non-delivery of services and lack of capacity. As has been pointed out rightly by Reginald Green:

> Even when accountability is seen as passable, corruption as bothersome rather than appalling and oppression as limited and unusual, capacity is criticized.... A national accounts committee is crucial but to an ordinary person an explanation

of what a local health unit did and how community contributions were used is likely to be a much more immediate and frequent concern. Similarly, an active, accessible, user-friendly 'bobby on the beat' and a magistracy are of higher priority to most people than issues of due process or contractual certainty in courts of appeal. [17]

A United Nations Children's Fund (UNICEF)/UNDP Study on *Pay, Productivity and Public Service in Africa*, undertaken in 1995 by a three-man team led by me with Professor Reginald Green as the rapporteur, has showed glaringly how desperate the growing inability of the civil service to deliver public services has become. Behind the decline – quantitatively as well as qualitatively – in public service provision are many factors: persistent economic crises, reduced real revenues and increased domestic and external debt service, aggravated by external conditionality formations and levels of remuneration. The officials most seriously affected are the front-line personnel – school teachers, health workers and paramedicals, agricultural extension officers, craftspeople, etc. These account for about three-quarters or four-fifths of the entire strength of an African civil service. Until they are at their posts, in attendance and at work, the problems of inadequate supplies of basic social services, human investment and infrastructure services will remain. But this condition cannot be met unless they are paid living remunerations. In all the countries covered by UNICEF/UNDP, real remunerations for most civil servants have fallen by at least half, and in two countries especially – Mozambique and Tanzania – by at least three- quarters.

The consequences of sustained falls are severe, particularly as the levels of civil servant remuneration were not high initially. In the 1960s and 1970s they were barely sufficient for supporting the family, but since 1980 they have fallen progressively so that today they are very much below the household absolute poverty line for a majority of public servants, particularly front-line professionals, para-professionals and artisans. The cumulative effect of this persistent deterioration has been that (1) too many staff are unqualified; (2) attendance at work is consistently low relative to the nominally required forty-hour week; (3) even when in attendance staff may be 'at work' for themselves rather than attending to their jobs; and (4) pervasive corruption ranging from the collection of user fees by officials (postal clerks, receptionists, guards, teachers, nurses, constables, tax collectors), driven by sheer survival more often than by greed, to the more blatant greed-driven corruption. Since service delivery depends on these cadres of public servants, their remunerations must of necessity be adjusted urgently to a level above the poverty line, particularly as no one, including the World Bank, seriously argues that any alternative basic supplier of these services exists or will emerge to replace the state in poor countries with poor majorities.

Finally, there is lack of capacity: the ability to strategize, prioritize, articulate and carry out state functions (whatever range and instruments are chosen). In recent years, public administration structures have been increasingly burdened by the ever-growing concern and preoccupation with short-term crisis management, virtually to the exclusion of long-term strategies. In addition, the increasing role of foreign experts and managers from international financial institutions in national economic decision making in Africa has further undermined indigenous capacity. As Reginald Green has pointed out correctly,

> an accountable state delivering law and order plus freedom to criticize but demonstrably incompetent on strategic policy and unable to deliver on programmes is not providing good governance nor will its citizens perceive it to be.[18]

Democracy in a divided society: what prospects?

The last places where one can expect popular participation and democracy, an ongoing process of democratically determined development, good governance and an efficient and effective public service delivery system are countries and societies embroiled in armed conflict, civil strife and severe and paralyzing political crises. And yet Africa is full of these. The continent seems to be perpetually at war with itself.

Table 1.1 shows that 14 African countries were engaged in armed conflicts and/or civil strife while another 14 countries faced political crises in 1996. Indeed, within the month of January 1996 alone military *coups d'état* took place in Sierra Leone and Niger. And early in April the fledgling peace in Liberia broke into a conflict of unprecedented savagery. Ethnic, racial, religious and social conflicts underscore security and stability as imperative objectives to pursue. They also pose a fundamental dilemma for the nation state: how can particularistic and often antagonistic group identities be reconciled with the overarching objective of popular participation? How can democracy become sustainable in a divided society? How can ethnic conflicts be controlled in order to facilitate the growth of a democratic culture?

The tragedy of Africa is that since independence one country after another has been shaken by political convulsion and violence. Political instability and conflicts have become the most dominant, all-pervasive factor in the contemporary social history of Africa. This was frankly acknowledged in the Khartoum Declaration on the Human Dimension of Africa's Economic Recovery in Development, in these words:

> the political context of promoting healthy human development [in Africa] has been marred for more than two decades by instability, war, intolerance, restriction on the freedom and human rights of individuals and groups as well as overconcentration of power with attendant restrictions on popular participation in decision making.[19]

Not only has the establishment of viable and integrative political order eluded many African countries, but insecurity, at both the societal and the individual personal levels, has become the norm. A number of countries have come close to being destroyed by civil wars, or bad governance, or both. As I have argued,

> the operation of the law of cumulative causation in Africa has been such that

TABLE 1.1
Countries with armed conflict/civil strife or severe political crises in Africa in the first quarter, 1996

Armed conflict/ civil strife	Severe political crisis	More or less normal political situation
Algeria	Cameroon	Benin
Angola	Congo	Botswana
Burundi	Djibouti	Burkina Faso
Kenya	Egypt	Cape Verde
Lesotho	Ethiopia	Central African Republic
Liberia	Gambia	Comores
Morocco	Ghana	Côte d'Ivoire
Rwanda	Madagascar	Eritrea
Sierra Leone	Malawi	Equatorial Guinea
Sudan	Mozambique	Gabon
Somalia	Niger	Guinea
Chad	Nigeria	Guinea Bissau
Togo	Senegal	Libyan Arab Jamhariya
Uganda	Zaire	Mali
Western Sahara	Zambia	Mauritania
		Mauritius
		Namibia
		São Tome & Principe
		Seychelles
		South Africa
		Swaziland
		Tunisia
		Zimbabwe

political instability and the weakness or ineffectiveness of many governments have resulted in the aggravation of the continent's economic vulnerability, stagnation and decadence which, in turn, has exacerbated its economic backwardness and is resulting in severe societal strains and stresses which in some cases are close to total breakdown.[20]

The situation in Nigeria since independence in 1960 is typical. During the past nearly four decades the country has been shaken repeatedly by political convulsions and violence. There have been six successful *coups d'état*, if what happened on 17 November 1993 and brought General Sani Abacha to power can be so classified instead of being seen as an extension of the 1985 coup. The Abacha regime is the country's tenth government since independence, if the interim national government of Ernest Shonekan, declared illegal by a court of law, is included (the military junta that replaced it endeavoured by military fiat to confer legitimacy upon it by purporting to set aside the decision of a properly constituted court of justice). Nine governments in 33 years gives the average of a government every three years and nine months. But, like all averages, this picture is deceptive because two governments (Gowon's and Babangida's) together lasted for 17 years. The average for the remaining seven governments is therefore 2.2 years. And between 1967 and 1970, for a period of thirty months, Nigeria was in the throes of a civil war. What a chequred political history!

As I said in a lecture on 'The Rehabilitation and Restitution of the Nigerian Political Recovery as a Prerequisite for a New Economic Order:[21]

> Nigeria has earned itself a top place on the top league table of politically unstable countries in the Third World. It has by now beaten the Latin American countries to it. In 1993 it had three different Administrations.... The scramble for power has been the undoing of the country. Politicians as well as the military have indulged in it - with the cumulative effect that no viable and integrative political and economic order has been established and that most of what has been built up since independence has been destroyed by bad governance and dismantled by ever-recurring political instability.... More than ever before [national] unity is shaky. In fact, rarely has the nation ever been more vulnerable. The social fabric is in danger of being torn apart as the vast majority of Nigerians have been pushed to the margins of existence. The State has been privatized. Instead of being dynamic, resilient and full of opportunities, the Nigerian economy is stagnant, dependent and largely unproductive.

It was in this politial and socio-economic context that the seven empirical case studies were undertaken to show how the masses of the people through their grassroots organizations are coping and responding to the situation. What chance has popular participation in a conflict-ridden and divided society? What opportunities are there for democratic renewal from the grassroots? And what is the dialectical relationship between popular participation, democracy and development?

Notes

1 Francis Fukuyama, 'The end of history', *The National Interest*, 16 (Summer 1989), pp. 3–18.
2 Francis Fukuyama, *The End of History and the Last Man* (New York: Avon Books, 1992), p. xi.
3 *Ibid.*, p. xv.
4 Aneurin Bevan, *Democratic Values*, Fabian Tract No. 282 (London: 1950).
5 Quoted in José María Maravall, 'The myth of the authoritarian advantage', *Journal of Democracy*, 5, 4 (October 1994), pp. 17–18.
6 Aneurin Bevan, *op. cit.*
7 Seymour Lipset, 'Reflections on capitalism, socialism and democracy', *Journal of Democracy*, 4, 2 (1993), pp. 46–7.
8 Adebayo Adedeji, 'Economic reform and democracy: an alternative for Africa', *Journal of Democracy*, 5, 4 (October 1994), p. 128.
9 Economic Commission for Africa (ECA), *African Charter for Popular Participation in Development* (Addis Ababa: ECA, 1990), p. 21.

10 *Ibid.*, pp. 17–18.
11 ECA, 'Underlying principles for enhanced dialogue, cooperation and interface between governments and people's organizations', *Studies in Participatory Development*, 4.
12 Adebayo Adedeji (ed.), *South Africa and Africa: Within or Apart?* (London: Zed Books; CapeTown: SADRI Books; Ijebu-Ode: ACDESS, 1996), p. 223.
13 UNDP, *Human Development Report 1993* (New York and Oxford: 1993), pp. 21–9.
14 *Ibid.*, pp. 21–9.
15 Adebayo Adedeji, *The African Alternative: Putting the People First* (Arusha: 1990), p. 10.
16 Adebayo Adedeji 'Nigeria, shivering and hovering on the brink', text of public lecture delivered in Lagos on 8 July 1994.
17 Bade Onimode and Richard Synge (eds), *Issues in African Development – Essays in Honour of Adebayo Adedeji at 65* (Ibadan: Heinemann Educational Books (Nigeria) Plc; Ijebu-Ode: ACDESS, 1995), pp. 272–3.
18 *Ibid.*, p. 272.
19 Adebayo Adedeji, Sadiq Rasheed and Melody Morrison (eds), *The Human Dimension of Africa's Persistent Economic Crisis* (London: Hans Zell Publishers, 1990) p. 380.
20 Adebayo Adedeji, 'Africa and the Africans and their historic challenge', Convocation Lecture of the Eighth Convocation Ceremony of the University of Calabar, Nigeria, 3 December.
21 Delivered in Lagos on 14 January 1994 at the 12th Delegates Conference of the Chartered Institute of Bakers of Nigeria.

2

Models in Popular Organization and Participation

INYA A. ETENG

Popular mass organizations in Nigeria have their origin in the social and cultural history of the country. Traditionally, they have developed along sex, age and specialized occupational lines, and have been predominantly communal and simple-commodity formations of pre-capitalist times. Through them, pre-colonial communities routinely organized community development and social welfare activities. Their purposes were manifold: guarding and protecting the community's boundaries and its productive forces against external encroachment; ensuring equitable distribution of resources and opportunities as a means of fostering community self-sufficiency; protecting the community's religious values and practices and its sacred places and artefacts; promoting the mental, physical and reproductive health of the people; fostering consensus, solidarity, and socio-cultural identity; regulating social relations; mutual sharing of labour, assets and information; and providing assistance to dependants and the poor.

Popular mass organs have also developed as institutions for confronting economic and political injustice throughout the colonial period and in more recent times. The Iseyin-Okeiho and Egba Risings of 1916 and 1918, respectively, the Aba Women's Riot of 1929–30, the Agbekoya Revolt of 1968–9, the Bakolori Revolt of 1980, the Etchie Incident of 1990, the Ogoni and similar revolts by communities in the southern oil-bearing enclave since the 1990s, strongly indicate the potency of mass movements emanating from popular organizational participation.

Popular organizational participation is increasingly regarded as a means of furthering the democratization process in today's Nigeria. Therefore, what forms participation assumes, and the types of popular organs within which it takes place, need systematic analysis. Popular organizational participation is a reflection of the continuing desirability of democracy and this chapter reviews the two broad types of popular organs and the participation modes they engender; the operational problems each organization type encounters are identified, and possible solutions to these problems are discussed. The point is finally made that effective mobilization – a major component of the popular mass participation process – is possible when the required preconditions are adequately and appropriately mass-oriented.

Popular organizational participation and the desirability of democracy

The critical mainstay of the history of mankind is the struggle for liberation and freedom between opposing social forces.[1] Indeed, our contemporary world has been characterized by an unprecedented quest for democracy. Historical experience strongly indicates that, overall, popular organizations, which often develop into historical social movements under propitious circumstances, have proved to be most appropriate and effective for this human enterprise. This is the more so, to the extent that these social instruments guarantee voluntary and democratic membership participation, as evidenced in prospects for self-organization, self-mobilization, self-development and self-defence.

A strong correlation, therefore, historically and implicitly exists between popular organizational participation and the democratic agenda for human liberation and social development. The political education manual of the Directorate for Social Mobilization, *Towards a Free and Democratic Society*, accordingly defines popular organization as:

> ... voluntary associations which citizens set up in order to promote their common welfare..... They are popular because their members freely support their formation and activities. They are not imposed on the people from outside. Anything which people freely support and fully participate in, is usually referred to as popular.

Bullock and Stallybrass define populism as

> The promotion of political ends ... by appealing to the people to exercise pressure on governments.... Populism identifies the will of the people ... puts this 'will' above all other social standards and mechanisms....[2]

Populism is accordingly people-directed, either by championing their cause, or by misdirecting popular inclinations to serve personal ends, as demagogues do by appealing to people's base sentiments in pursuit of undisclosed ends. Popular organizations as defined here, however, are genuinely people-oriented associations.

The thematic categories subsumed in this definition are critical for understanding and appreciating the democratic and developmental import of popular organizational participation.

First, these organizations are, in the main, voluntary: they are, therefore, freely formed and not externally imposed on members. They are thus grassroots organizations.

Second, their aims – goals and objectives – are self-motivated: they are essentially inspired and designed to promote and defend the common social welfare interests and values of members. They are thus basically *cui bono* organizations, even while serving the interests of the wider commonwealth.

Third, these organizations are more or less self-reliant and self-sustaining, though not necessarily self-sufficient: they are, therefore, freely supported and sustained by their freely participating members, to achieve self-motivated ends.

Fourth, they are popular: their organizational set-ups have general currency and relevance, and therefore they are suitable to the common experience of the members. Their *modi operandi*, equally, are freely chosen, easily understood, and appropriate for the available means of the majority of the membership: they thus have common approval and appeal.

By their very nature and internal dynamics, therefore, popular organizations are strongly linked to, and supportive of, the democratic agenda. Indeed, the assumptions underlying the desirability of and the persistent clamour for democracy enable us to appreciate the instrumental role of popular organizations in the democratization process. Democracy is assumed to facilitate the organization of the people into relatively autonomous and independent groups, none of which can, or should, dominate the other. Each of the groups is subject to agreed rules of political competition for state power. Democratic participation fundamentally enables the civil society to 'tame' the state, and to channel state instruments to serve the public good, thus ensuring public accountability and popular sovereignty.[3]

Furthermore, because popular organizations generally promote popular democratic participation, they are also supportive of human development and emancipation. This is largely because, in certain respects, democracy is practically synonymous with social development and liberation, themselves important human values. Consistent with these central values, democracy is basically oriented towards changes in the creative energies of man, woman and society. It embodies the idea of continuous improvement in humankind's and society's capacity to control and manipulate the forces of nature for their own benefit. By implication, democracy involves the inherent genius of human beings for self-improvement through creative production, reproduction and social transformation. This creative genius implies increasing skill, confidence, self-discipline, spontaneity and responsibility. Finally, popular democratic participation counters the individual's alienation from society, enables the legitimation of governmental authority, and ensures commitment to the creation of new, humane values on the basis of a collective ethos, tolerance, trust, dialogue, consensus, patriotism and loyalty to the nation and the government-in-office.[4]

The existence of popular organizations therefore implies the desire for democracy, social development and liberation. To what extent this is the case is reflected in the following brief discussion of types and models of popular organizational participation in contemporary Nigeria.

Models of popular organizational participation

The findings of a nation-wide survey of non-governmental grassroots associations (NGGAs) by the Directorate of Food, Roads and Rural Infrastructures

(DFRRI) in 1990–1, clearly indicates that contemporary Nigeria consists of an ever-increasing number of these organizations. There are evidently diverse types with overlapping structural features. This makes their classification into neat and mutually exclusive categories and models problematic.

Going by their internal organizational structure, goals and objectives, and modes of operation, however, the following types of popular organization tend to stand out: (1) promotional organizations; (2) protective/defensive organizations; (3) non-governmental (but not grassroots) organizations; and (4) 'human rights' bodies. Given a more stringent classification, however, NGOs can be subsumed easily under the 'promotional' type, while 'human rights' bodies can be grouped logically under the 'protective/defensive' type.[5] The basic structural features, operational dynamics and membership participation modalities with respect to these two models of popular organization are summarized below.

Promotional organizations

This broad category covers such popular organizations and networks as: small mutual self-support networks, village welfare associations, resource mobilization and investment societies and cooperatives, community self-help organizations, and non-governmental organizations (NGOs).

SMALL MUTUAL SELF-SUPPORT NETWORKS

These are typically narrow, inward-looking neighbourhood-welfare and pre-cooperative groupings which essentially operate at the primary, subsistence and informal level. They generally attempt to enhance the well-being of their membership in normal and favourable circumstances. As small-scale, mutual self-support networks, they thrive on mutual sharing of labour, assets, and information. They are highly informal, frequently invisible to outsiders, and generally small in size.

Each member has claims on others in the network, especially in terms of labour demand, shortage of assets, or special social needs. Formal rules and formal leadership are generally non-existent. All services are rendered, therefore, on the basis of mutual understanding and consensus. Accordingly, the networks are relatively flexible and unencumbered, and provide opportunities for mutual exchange of political, socio-cultural and market information. There is strong group consciousness among members.

The networks are sustained to the extent that members fulfil their mutual obligations to one another, and participation in the networks is contingent on the benefits derived. In the absence of commitments, the networks are considerably weakened, and may even cease to exist. Permanent economic crisis in Nigeria, however, has ensured their continuous existence. Members really need them to survive.

VILLAGE WELFARE ASSOCIATIONS

Although these associations are often informal, or quasi-formal, they are nonetheless quite visible, middle to large in membership size, and well represented all over rural and urban Nigeria. Those that are urban-based still have their roots in the rural villages where their parent bodies are established and annual congresses are held. Their democratic values and beliefs are markedly entrenched in their constitutions, minutes, organizational structure and daily practices.

Owing to the increasing challenges and demands of the country's extremely austere circumstances, these associations are assuming a multi-purpose orientation in their objectives and activities, directed towards mobilization, self-help community development, cooperative ventures, social welfare, solidarity and identity maintenance. These social concerns necessarily assure membership and groups of continuous viability, sustainability, integrity and stability. The associations also play a key role in the regeneration of traditional social values of communalism and mutual reciprocity, we-consciousness, respect for elders and the social division of labour. They also assist households in times of sickness, bereavement or other setbacks, while carrying out a host of other welfare activities for their memberships: financial support, medical insurance, residential accommodation, unemployment insurance, socio-political and cultural education, socio-psychological succour and information sharing. Thus, given the virtual absence of state-organized social welfare schemes in the country, the socio-economic, political and social-psychological relevance of these voluntary associations for individual members, the community and the society is indeed incalculable.

RESOURCE MOBILIZATION AND INVESTMENT SOCIETIES

The growth of savings and credit associations in Nigeria is related to the importance of the informal sector in the economy and the role played by the small-scale operators, as well as to the tenacity of the Nigerian peasant subsistence economy. There has been an insatiable need for simple, quick and efficient savings and credit mobilization in the prevailing economic circumstances, including the inappropriateness of the banking system to satisfy popular requirements.

There is also an indeterminate but large number of registered and unregistered cooperatives in contemporary Nigeria. These may be production-oriented, distribution-oriented or multi-purpose. Some are membership-exclusive, based on age, sex, religion, ethnicity, community of origin or type of economic venture. Others are class-specific, with membership restricted to those belonging to specific socio-economic classes or occupations. Others are multi-class, with membership cutting across socio-economic classes, ethno-religious groups, political affiliations, sex and age. Although multi-purpose cooperatives are increasing in numbers in the country, the most popular variants are the distributive/marketing cooperatives.

Community self-help organizations

These are, in the main, commonwealth organizations. Thus, in terms of internal structure and organization, these bodies are essentially community-based, comparatively formal, oriented towards community development, multi-purpose, and relatively fewer than informal structures and other voluntary associations. Community development associations (CDAs), by whatever name, which have sprung up since the 1970s, are typical examples. Generally, these organizations have proved to be instruments of reactive community development and social welfare promotions. They are essentially reactive, in the sense that they have generally responded defensively to changes imposed by external capitalist forces. Consequently, they undertake projects which governments fail to execute. They also organize community surveillance and security, and promote conflict management and resolution. Major areas of their activities are identified as follows:[6]

1 Promotion of social services: education, health, housing, recreation, cultural facilities.

2 Development of community infrastructures: roads, bridges, culverts, water, electricity, drainage.

3 Social mobilization: literacy campaigns, political awareness campaigns, public health information, family planning information, tax payment campaigns, fund-raising campaigns, law and order/community security activities.

4 Articulation of community interests: social, economic, political, cultural.

5 Promotion of rural economic production: increased productivity, employment, income generation, savings, and investment distribution.

6 Intermediation between the community and other development agencies from within and without.

7 Promotion and dissemination of development and social welfare communication and information.

Non-governmental organizations

Virtually all popular organizations are, by definition, non-governmental, and accordingly are important segments of the civil society, but we may define NGOs in Nigeria as being voluntary and engaged in developmental, social welfare and philanthropic activities. Rural-based NGOs include local and foreign private organizations which are often extensions of multi-purpose rural organizations or small independent unions working with peasant organizations.

At the rural level, urban-based NGOs provide expert advice and economic and health inputs to individual peasants and grassroots groupings, promote resource conservation and family planning, and assist women individually and collectively. At the urban level, these NGOs include local and foreign-linked social clubs and fraternities, as well as private business, social, religious, educational, cultural and environmental bodies which tend to combine social welfare and promotional activities with philanthropic commitments.

Protective/defensive organizations

The main purpose of these organizations is to defend and protect the major interests and central values of their members, their organizations *per se*, their households, their communities and other individuals and groups within the civil society who are deemed to be oppressed or potentially threatened by the ruling class and its surrogates acting through the state and the government in power. Such organizations come into existence not only when the existing power structure is authoritarian and repressive, but also when the economic system seriously threatens the general well-being of the organizations' members and the society at large.

Such organizations perceive the external environment, or the segments of it within which they operate, as highly unstable and constantly hostile and threatening. Dealing with environmental uncertainties thus becomes a consuming passion.

Assumed defensive functions are performed at the rural village level on behalf of the entire community by such specialized professional bodies as traditional herbalists' and hunters' associations, and by voluntary organizations acting as executive arms of the village community associations, such as: village/town/cultural unions, youth associations, age grades, hunters' associations, religious associations, cult associations and vigilante groups. At the level of the larger society, these defensive organs include: labour (working class and professional) unions, market associations, transport unions, women's associations, student organizations, political parties, private media and civil rights bodies.

Frequently communities, too, have organized themselves against internal and external feuds, encroachment, loss of communal property (land or water resources, for example), inadequate compensation and other difficulties. Threats may be posed by dominant élites, hostile neighbours, government, or private business interests. When communities do organize as such, they constitute defensive collectivities.

In almost all cases, defensive organizations – local or national – manifest a sense of unease, repulsion and fear, arising from the felt or perceived threat of exploitation and expropriation (loss of ownership and control of essential means of survival), disempowerment (socio-political and cultural marginalization) and external domination. This accounts for their members' spirited attempts to defend their 'territory', resource base, infrastructure, communication network, ideological position or cherished cultural heritage against 'invasion'.

To ensure a high degree of effectiveness, these organizations tend to establish a strong, credible and level-headed leadership, well-maintained communication networks, a reasonably regular funding system, a relatively watertight security and surveillance system, concrete, tangible, feasible and agreeable goals, a credible geographical spread, a highly conscientized, loyal and committed membership, and flexible and adaptive organizational structures and strategies. Some of these organizations are capable of metamorphosing into social movements.

In contemporary Nigeria civil rights bodies exemplify typical defensive popular organizations. They are indigenous, voluntary, multi-class, nationwide, issue-oriented and ideologically radical organizations; some have international connections and virtually all have complex intra-national networks. They have emerged and multiplied especially during the country's long period of military rule, characterized by extreme economic hardship, unprecedented corruption, sharp class distinctions, mass disempowerment, social violence, state terrorism, gross human rights derogation, hunger and mass alienation.

Their main objective is to fight relentlessly for the promotion and sustained enforcement of human rights, the rule of law, due process, equity, justice and fair play in the country. They deal more with larger social issues of governance and political empowerment and less with 'personal problems'.[7] They have fought continuous legal battles against persistent state terrorism and violence against the Nigerian civil society, as manifested in security surveillance, harassment, physical incarceration, summary detention and violent killings committed against civilians by state security and law enforcement agents. They have also taken issue with a series of draconian government decrees and specific socio-economic and political policies and programmes, such as Nigeria's structural adjustment programme (SAP) and the transition programme, which have been clearly anti-people. The civil rights organs have also fought against frequent university and newspaper closures, summary dismissals of public officials, bannings of popular mass organizations, the desecration of the Nigerian legal system, and the continued imposition of military rule against the sovereign will of the Nigerian masses.

Problems of popular participation

The vast majority of Nigerians consider democracy to be highly desirable. The clamour for its installation is therefore intense, persistent and interminable among members of various popular organizations. But the process is fraught with problems due to the inherent risk of reversion to dictatorship, and even fascism, in the event of the failure of the democratic process. As the unfolding consequences of the annulment of the 1993 presidential election have demonstrated, the failure of the democratic agenda does indeed lead to unimaginable economic crisis, gross inequality, social violence and state repression. Nigerian popular organizations thus face the riddle of their failure: objectively and subjectively they symbolize the quest for popular democratic participation, yet in concrete reality the feasibility and sustainability of democracy, with its maximum accruable benefits, have continued to elude them.

In the search for the feasibility of democracy in Nigeria, popular organizations must come to grips fully with the endemic conflict and contradictions inherent in the country's class system. Indeed, the feasibility issue is whether the prevailing class system operating within the country's dependent capitalist social formation is capable of promoting and sustaining popular sovereignty, people's human rights and people's socio-economic rights.[8]

The country's ruling class of petty and comprador bourgeoisie has continuously and virulently undermined effective popular participation at virtually all levels of the society. In consequence, popular organizations have persistently and excruciatingly faced two sets of related problems: (1) problems related to the operational capacity of these organizations themselves; and (2) problems due to certain features of the larger environment in which the organizations operate.

Operational problems of promotional grassroots organizations

Most of the promotional grassroots organizations are based in rural village communities constituting various local government areas (LGAs) as currently structured. Regardless of the existence of these LGAs and their direct funding by the federal centre, the whole of rural Nigeria and the urban small-scale and informal sectors, where most of these popular mass organs predominate, are essentially at the periphery of the nation's control and decision-making structure. Their operational problems largely arise from the susceptibility of this underdeveloped periphery to continuous expropriation, disempowerment and marginalization. The operational problems afflicting these promotional popular organizations are summarized below:

CAPACITY PROBLEMS

1. Poor organizational and managerial arrangements and processes;
2. Limited resources;
3. Inability to access and utilize available information;
4. Poor articulation and definition of goals, objectives, programmes and projects;
5. Poor, non-credible and often dishonest leadership;
6. Limited membership participation and commitment;
7. Poor or limited mobilization capacity;
8. Parochialism, exclusiveness and unhealthy inter-organization competition, leading to inability to benefit fully from economies of scale

contingent on cooperative/coordinated mobilization and joint programme/project execution.

9 Leadership cult and consequent subversion of popular democratic participation; and

10 Lack of systematic rationalization and streamlining of the activities of CDAs.

ENVIRONMENTAL PROBLEMS

1 Escalating demand for community facilities and services;

2 Widespread poverty engendering rural–urban migration;

3 General social inertia;

4 Government policies which stultify the capacity and activities of NGGAs and their role in development and democratization;

5 Limited, even obstructing, role of LGAs in community development and popular participation;

6 Inter-community conflict over such issues as control of development resources, external aid and community status;

7 Conflict between organizational demand on members' participation and members' preoccupation with survival;

8 Depleting communal resource base; and

9 Limited and often destabilizing role of the community élite and voluntary associations in developmental and democratization processes.

Operational and environmental problems of defensive popular organizations

Problems of defensive organizations tend to vary in terms of organizational structure, operational base, central focus and target. Those based in rural communities generally face similar problems to those encountered by their promotional counterparts and outlined above. Quite often, as observed earlier, these village-based promotional associations (like youth and women's organizations) and the communities themselves mobilize defensively and protectively against threatening external forces. When this occurs, they normally encounter operational difficulties arising from their direct confrontation with the state and other national and international power groups, as do urban-based defensive popular organizations, like civil rights bodies, the Nigerian Labour Congress and the Academic Staff Union of Universities. Current confrontations between oil-bearing communities, on one hand, and the federal government and foreign oil corporations, on the other, are cases in point.

As has been emphasized, by definition popular organizations generally champion popular causes and promote mass democratic participation. Consequently they contend, almost routinely, with anti-popular forces at various societal levels. Nigeria's history since independence has been one of uninterrupted conflict between progressive pro-democracy forces and a permanently self-serving, anti-democratic ruling class in control of the country's dictatorial state and governments in power.

The results thus far have been minimal, however, judged in terms of acquiring political power, or effectively influencing the state to pursue sufficiently mass-based, people-oriented policies and programmes.[9] This glaring ineffectiveness is a function of several operational problems which constantly afflict these defensive organizations without exception. These problems are summarized below.

CAPACITY PROBLEMS

1 Lack of ideological clarity;

2 Multiplicity of similar organizations, and the problem of inter-organizational competition, factionalism, disunity and low collective mobilization;

3 Undue emphasis on liberal-bourgeois 'rule of law' and 'due process', often at the expense of radical political mobilization;

4 Preference for reactive *ad hoc* decisions in place of a holistic long-term corporate planning perspective aimed at the drastic structural transformation of the society;

5 Limited resources;

6 Restricted national spread due to the influence of parochial, primordial and anti-nationalist forces;

7 Poor, non-credible or dishonest leadership; and

8 Poor or limited mobilization capacity.

ENVIRONMENTAL PROBLEMS

1 Prevalence of conflicting ideological positions and differential levels of political consciousness;

2 Pervasive poverty;

3 Cumulative and pervasive effects of a multiplicity of visible and covert ruling-class and state-sponsored anti-democratic forces all competing for popular membership recruitment;

4 Inhibitive influence of mass indiscipline;

5 Poor infrastructural and communication systems; and

6 The virtual non-existence of systematic and comprehensive scientific data on various aspects of popular democratic participation, and

the extremely underdeveloped research in this important area in contemporary Nigeria.

Enhancing popular democratic participation

All mass organizations and other progressive social formations and elements should forge permanent fraternal links nation-wide among themselves, without prejudice to their relative autonomy, for purposes of (1) advancing common ideological-conceptual-programmatical perspectives on issues related to the national question; (2) sharing organizational and survival experiences and strategies; (3) tapping fully the diverse advantages of group solidarity; (4) developing consensus on basic issues of national development; (5) mutually promoting and sustaining the material interests of the broad masses of Nigerians; (6) collectively defending and reinforcing one another's rights to popular mass organization and participation; (7) generating operational funds and other resources; (8) promoting mass political education on popular democracy, with special emphasis on the meaning and implications of fraternity (popular sovereignty), liberty (human rights enforcement), and equality (socio-economic rights); and (9) promoting and sustaining national unity. These are indeed central values inherent in social democracy.[10]

To further consolidate these fraternal links, and enhance the prospects of achieving these goals, popular pro-democracy forces should, out of sheer historical necessity, mobilize nationally toward the formation of a mass party. The ultimate, long-term goal should be the capturing of state power, the socio-democratization of civil society, and the humanization of political culture. Meanwhile, the popular organs should align themselves to ensure that their members, strategically representing a large segment of civil society, especially the most disadvantaged and vulnerable, are increasingly elected into key organs of state power at all levels of governance.

Conclusion

The desirability of democratic participation is one thing, its feasibility – more critical and problematic – quite another. Two broad strands of operational problems which constantly inhibit effective democratic participation and development in these popular organizations have been summarized above; they include a set of environmental and capacity problems. To enhance the operational capacity of these organizations, wide-ranging recommendations have been provided, dialectically suggested by the problems themselves.

Socio-democratic participation, within popular mass organs and at the national level of the political process, is both an end in itself and a precondition for national development and mass liberation. Either way, effective nation-wide mobilization of the masses through their popular organs is absolutely necessary. Various Nigerian governments have attempted unsuccessfully to mobilize the masses through operations such as the National Orientation Movement (NOM), War Against Indiscipline (WAI), the Directorate of Social Mobilization (MAMSER), and now the National Orientation Agency (NOA) and its War Against Indiscipline and Corruption (WAIC). The failure of these programmes underscores the fact that (1) those engaged in mass mobilization lacked popular credibility and legitimacy; (2) structures and programmes for mass mobilization have been less than ideal for this purpose; (3) the socio-economic, political and cultural environment within which popular mobilization has taken place has not reflected actual or realizable potentials of social justice, equity, liberty and fraternity; (4) the goals of mobilization have not been clear, concrete and agreeable to the Nigerian masses being mobilized; and (5) the effects of mobilization have continuously exacerbated exploitation, expropriation, poverty, disempowerment, social marginality, apathy and alienation of the masses. To be increasingly effective, therefore, popular organizations must strive to eliminate these and related aberrant tendencies, on one hand, and the operational problems identified, on the other.

Notes

1 Karl Marx, *The Communist Manifesto* (1848), *KMSW*, p. 222.
2 A. Bullock, O. Stallybrass, S. Trombley and B. Eadie, *Fontana Dictionary of Modern Thought* (Fontana, 1988), p. 474.
3 P. A. Nyong'o, 'Democratization processes in Africa', *AAPS Research Agenda*, 1 (1992).
4 O. Nnoli, 'Values and political development: towards achieving a participatory political culture', paper presented at the National Orientation Agency (NOA) Workshop on National Mobilization, Enugu, 1994.
5 I. A. Eteng, 'Popular organizations in transition mobilization: some participatory models', paper presented at the Rus Communication Ltd National Workshop on Mobilization of Popular Organizations Towards the Success of the Transition Programme, Jos, 1993.
6 E. O. Akeredolu-Ale, Lagos Zone Report, preliminary draft, Directorate of Food, Roads and Rural Infrastructures (DFRRI) Survey of NGGAs in Nigerian LGAs, 1991.
7 C. Wright Mills, *The Sociological Imagination* (New York: Oxford University Press, 1959).
8 O. Nnoli, 1994, *op. cit.*
9 F. Akingbode, 'Selected Nigerian popular organizations and their operational dynamics', paper presented at the Rus Communication Ltd National Workshop on Mobilization of Popular Organizations Towards the Success of the Transition Programme, Jos, 1994.
10 O. Nnoli, 1994, *op.cit.*

3

Modes of Social Organization: Their Implications for Popular Participation

ONIGU OTITE & SINA KAWONISE

Indigenous and Euro-American social and cultural elements coexist in contemporary African societies. This constellation of influences has far-reaching implications for popular participation and democratic processes in different societies in Africa. It is perhaps nowhere more evident than in Nigeria, a country with a relatively large land area inhabited by over 370 ethnically and culturally distinct peoples. A study of popular participation in such a heterogeneous society has its own significance not only by contributing to data for theory building but also by providing an empirical background for formulating policies and strategies which are relevant for grassroots organizations because they increase the level of popular participation in economic and socio-political development.

The above thrust has recently become the major concern of policy makers and scholars in the social sciences and humanities both within and outside the continent. In Nigeria it has particular relevance because, although the country has enormous human and material resources which can be exploited for development, using both indigenous and modern technologies and systems of organization, it has yet to attain any appreciable level of advancement. The need has been identified for the opening up of state structures and institutions for people's participation in politics and in their own government and development. Increased popular participation is one viable means of avoiding the under-representation and the marginalization of people – women, men, children, literates and illiterates in English – and of preventing their alienation from their own labour wealth and development.

What is popular participation?

Popular participation is the involvement of people in activities and decisions regarding the designing and implementing of social, economic, political, and other strategies, as well as policies and processes which affect their lives and their development. Popular participation thus concerns people as individuals or groups and associations as essential elements in the process of development. In this regard, the African Charter for Popular Participation in Development asserts:

> As an instrument of development, popular participation provides the driving force for collective commitment for the determination of people-based development processes and willingness by the people to undertake sacrifices and expend their social energies for its execution. As an end in itself, popular participation is the fundamental right of the people to fully and effectively participate in the determination of the decisions which affect their lives at all levels and at all times.[1]

Thus popular participation refers to the empowerment of the people, both politically and economically, to take steps towards their own development. It requires the involvement of the people's associations, their local communities, the government or the state, and non-governmental organizations (NGOs) in the provision of infrastructures (for example) to facilitate the people's participation in their local and national affairs.

It is apparent that popular participation cannot be conceptualized in a 'pure' form. It must be seen as a catalyst with an operational and empirical content. According to Adebayo Adedeji, it involves 'the dialectics of democracy, accountability, and development'.[2] Adedeji has made interrelated observations in this connection:

> First, the pervasive lack of democracy or popular participation in Africa is basic to Africa's persistent poverty so that the current economic crisis is also essentially a political crisis with respect to the contradiction between state power and people's power. Second, without democracy, there can be no effective political accountability, and without accountability, there can be no sustained development.[3]

Given the above, it is obvious that popular participation is not only central to the dialectical linkage which brings democracy, accountability and development together; it is also a crucial element in the realization of each of these ideals. It is noteworthy that participation is usually taken as the defining element of democracy. According to Imam, democracy is the 'people's right to participate fully in the discussions and decisions on issues that affect them and to take control of their own lives'.[4]

As an important condition of democracy, participation is also a significant measure of the democratic nature of any socio-economic and socio-political organization. In specific instrumental terms, popular participation imbues the people with a greater commitment to democratic values, encourages greater group or associational solidarity, and serves as a platform for training in democratic leadership and the selection process.

Popular participation is linked as closely to accountability as it is to democracy. The concept of accountability rests on the assumptions that power is divisible, that legitimacy is based on consent and that power is held by leaders in trust for their followers. It is obvious from these assumptions that popular participation is central to accountability; for without a sustained interest in public affairs, without institutional mechanisms for monitoring and appraising the policies and actions of political leaders, and without formal and informal checks on their power and their management of the national purse as well as financial and other resources, the risk is ever present that leaders and those in positions of authority will serve their selfish interests to the neglect of the collective interests and aspirations of the people.

Popular participation, which involves democracy and accountability, is also a requirement for development. Whatever the degree of concentration of material resources in any particular country or community, there cannot be any appreciable development without the active participation of the people. In this sense, popular participation is a catalyst for development. It requires people to identify, mobilize and manage natural and material resources for development. But the people themselves are also the recipients of the gains of development. This means that people are the agents, through popular participation, as well as the beneficiaries of development. Thus development must be humane; it must have a human face. Otherwise the people could easily be alienated from their own products and development, making them less active as agents of development. This point also suggests that, for development to be sustainable, the people's culture, value systems, ideas and concepts of progress and social advancement must be recognized and taken into account.

Popular participation and modes of social organization

There are two analytically and empirically distinct spheres of popular participation. These are the indigenous and the new Euro-American, so-called 'modern' spheres. The latter is a derivative of colonialism which followed much earlier European adventures and trade and economic missions to Africa. Although these contacts became formal in Nigeria and the west coast of Africa by the fifteenth century, it was with the establishment of colonial administrative structures after 1900 that the 'two publics' started to manifest themselves as primordial cultures and civic cultures.[5] While the former is the domain of indigenous cultures and social structures which are ethnically bound, the latter deals with the emergent nation-wide culture. Also, while the former in their contemporary situations flow from pre-colonial indigenous cultures and are 'modernizing' or reshaping while coexisting with one another in an encapsulating national society, the latter exists as a single emerging culture for the whole nation.

In Africa, two main types of indigenous social organizations have been identified by social anthropologists. These are the 'centralized' and the 'uncentralized' socio-political systems which correspond to 'state' and 'stateless' societies. Although these labels have been subject to criticisms and refinements since 1940 when they were developed,[6] in essence the categories have been maintained. Thus the Bini, Hausa, Itsekiri, Kanuri, Nupe, Urhobo, Yoruba and many other indigenous societies in Nigeria are organized around a central apex institution in which the incumbent actor –

a traditional ruler such as the Emir, the Oba or the Ovie – is regarded as the symbol of his nation. Popular participation in these societies occurs in various social fields defined by hierarchy, kinship, community, town and village arrangements. There are also associations such as age grade organizations or craft guilds which cut across and also integrate the society or major sections of it. There are descent group, family and ward organizations which determine access to such economic assets as land, ponds, pasture and water. In all these respects, popular participation is emphasized in relation to problems of economic survival and to individual or group status – for example, in the Bini palace associations and the Nupe or Hausa patronage–clientage relationships in the political sub-system.

The second major indigenous socio-political arrangement is typified by the Igbo (except Onitsha, Nri, Aboh, Osamari and Oguta)[7] until the colonial warrant chief's position was created; by the Tiv before the colonial creation of the Tor Tiv in 1947; and by other societies in which no central socio-political institution exists or existed to articulate the people's overall political interests as an apex symbol. Instead, segmentary units, such as villages or village groups and descent-kinship units, provide the overall maximal organization within which popular participation takes place. Age group grades and elders' councils are fields of popular participation which aim at just local governance, sectional integration, segmentary opposition and defence and group development. Various associations of a politico-economic nature exist and provide opportunities for people to validate their local citizenship.

In both types of socio-political organization, common cultural traits exist as contexts within which popular participation takes place. These include well-known systems of moral sanctions, altruism, familyhood as a way of life, humane frameworks, and close social networks. Formal and informal associations for popular participation in the indigenous sphere continue to reflect those cultural features despite the demands of the civic culture of the emerging Nigerian society.

The Nigerian society encapsulates the various indigenous societies and cultures.[8] It is plural and ethnically heterogeneous, as well as being a composite of a variety of values and traits, following cultural invasions which accompanied Arab and Euro-American colonialism and neo-colonialism. Here, there is hardly any moral scruple in individual and group behaviour, and generally no standard or system of moral sanctions is evident in the emerging society. Society is characterized by opportunistic exploitation for selfish or close group survival and materialistic gain. Popular participation through associations of various types reflects the ideals and demands of this Nigerian society. Workers' and transport unions, cooperative societies, town development unions, farmers' associations, multi-purpose societies, traders' and market women's associations, credit and thrift cooperative societies, bakers' associations, mechanics' and drivers' unions: all are examples, along with political parties, of the multiple arenas of popular participation in the contemporary Nigerian society.

Thus the various spheres of popular participation in contemporary Nigeria are either indigenous or non-indigenous, and some are both. They involve primordial and secondary associations. Some of the associations, such as those based on the age grades and age groups, pre-dated colonialism, while others, such as the *Egbe Omo Ibile,* were developed in reaction to the colonial situation and as responses to intra- and inter-ethnic relations in the new society.

Two important features of the indigenous and non-indigenous cultural and institutional coexistence or dualism in Nigerian society must be noted because of their effect on popular participation. First, there are cultural and organizational survivals from pre-colonial times. For example, the Moslem practice of purdah restricts the lives of categories of wives to secluded or walled compounds. Such women may get betrothed and married at as early as 12 years of age, and their participation in open societal activities is limited. In this culture, mothers who engage in craftwork or in household cooking, baking, or frying of foodstuffs send their children to hawk or market their products. Women are generally excluded from political and other activities.

Such practices affect contemporary participation by girls and women in educational and associational activities. This situation helps to explain the preponderance of boys in primary and secondary schools, and the general lack of women members in many of the associations and social clubs in the northern parts of Nigeria. Social clubs may thus consist solely or mainly of male members. Indeed, one of the criticisms of the Better Life Programme for Rural Women (BLP) in the northern parts of Nigeria is that it tends to question or even jolt the norm of women's seclusion in the purdah system and their expected non-participation in open associations. Also, the practice of male dominance in indigenous societies has tended to place women in contemporary post-colonial African patrilineal societies at a disadvantage in terms of open and uninhibited access to sources of economic empowerment. Thus women's relative poverty, indigenous norms, and the social structure have placed traditional constraints on their popular participation in Nigeria. Similarly, the demands of the relationship between patrons and clients, for example in Hausa and Nupe societies, tend to restrict the scope and freedom of participation by men of low and high status in different associations.

Secondly, individuals sometimes avoid the cultural demands of one sphere in the indigenous or non-indigenous organization, and switch to the other depending on anticipated benefits. For example they may indulge in corrupt enrichment when the opportunity presents itself in the civic culture of the Nigerian society, ignoring or submerging the moral demands and accompanying sanctions enjoined by the indigenous society. Hence, as Ekeh and Ashiwaju put it, Nigerians may praise or hail a situation which brings 'the receipt of benevolence from wealth acquired by an individual, even illegally, from the civic domain'. And they point out that 'it now seems that it is fully permissible and legitimate for an individual to enrich himself, possibly by stealing, from the civil cultural domain provided his primordial cultural domain benefits from such wealth'.[9]

Some of the associations, as arenas for popular participation, are hybrid in their structures and operations, while others coexist as parallel spheres of indigenous and non-indigenous participation by individuals in their communities and society.

Popular participation, the individual and the community

Participation in democratic institutions and activities is essentially by individual free choice. But the individual may participate through the medium of an association or associations. Thus the individual is both autonomous and dependent as he or she participates in the affairs of his or her community. The social sciences conceptualize community in both geographical and social terms – as a socio-spatial unit found in both rural and urban areas. It is thus a territorially bounded group of people and a social system, with generally functionally integrated sub-systems which operate with both consensual and conflictual consequences. A community may be defined scientifically as a society with its own interrelated subsystems. Communities can be indigenous and non-indigenous and some, such as indigenous enclaves in urban centres, can combine features from both types. Each type has consequences for the kinds of associations through which individuals participate in local and national affairs.

Civil society, government and the state

A community may be part of a large rural or urban settlement, which is itself part of a 'national society' such as the Nigerian civil society. In this case, the concepts of civil society, government and the state become closely related. A civil society is not merely a system of social relationships in classical social science terms, but also a social space in which different associations, unions, clubs and other groups mediate between the state and the families and individuals. Thus, by its very essence, civil society is a participatory arena.

In many respects, the needs and desires of people predispose them to form groups with other individuals and to be part of human collectivities, beginning from the family and other forms of blood relationships. With development and the accompanying social complexity, individuals form secondary groupings and associations for similar but progressively diverse purposes within the state. Although the state coexists with other formal and informal associations and organizations within a socio-spatial formation, it is distinguished by its predominance and its imposition of binding rules over all other groups.

Neither a society constituted by individuals nor the state, however, can exist without government. Although government, individuals, civil society, and the state are analytically distinct, they are closely related. Despite its many definitions, government deals with and involves ideals of the public good, social justice, consent and popular participation, amongst other things. It is both a structure involving legislative, executive and judicial spheres, with checks and balances to guide office holders as a group of people, and a process which involves governance and methods of governing. Government is often spoken of in relation to the nation or state but it is also found in subordinated bodies or associations such as churches, universities, local town and village communities and their councils. Also, government does not exhaust all the different kinds of activities of various interest groups in a society, hence associations, unions, clubs and other smaller organizations exist to promote the welfare of members and the development of their local communities. Every society has some form of government; ideally it consists of people with legitimate authority and responsibility for exercising power and maintaining social control.

Although the terms state and government are used interchangeably by some scholars, others refer to the state when they actually mean government. This is particularly the case whenever the state is defined in terms of the total society or of a sovereign authority with the monopoly of coercive power within the society and its territory. Thus people in fact refer to government when they talk about popular participation, transparency and corruption, or about the management and development of human and material resources as these affect their daily lives. Government responds to social pressures on sensitive issues and to the pluralistic demands of various sections of the society in a democratic setting. Governments are often arranged in such a way as to reach and be effective at both the centre and the grassroots. In Nigeria, for example, government is arranged in three tiers: the federal, state and local government levels. Policy decisions and various kinds of interaction generate changes in both government and the social system. It is within this setting – in cognizance of the linkages between individuals, society, government, and the state – that the case studies in this book seek to determine the nature, role and importance of popular participation in the democratization process in Nigeria.

On the basis of the above observations, it is important to attempt to find out 'the best social locations of popular participation'. According to Adedeji:

> These positions are in the state apparatus and civil society. The pervasive lack of democracy in Africa is also associated with the paralyzing weakness of civil society – mass organizations, interest and social groups, local communities and individuals. Hence, effective popular participation in Africa should involve the urgent and deliberate strengthening of civil society in order to whittle down the large relative autonomy of the African state. This centres on the institutional building up of mass organizations, trade unions, peasant associations, cooperatives, women's organizations, student unions, professional bodies, political parties, etc.[10]

Notes

1 Economic Commission for Africa (ECA), *African Charter for Popular Participation in Development* (Addis Ababa: ECA, 1990), p. 19.
2 *Ibid.*, p. 28.
3 *Ibid.*, pp. 28-9.
4 A. Imam, 'Democratization process in Africa: problems and prospects', *CODESRIA Bulletin*, 2 (1991), p. 5.
5 See P. P. Ekeh, 'Colonialism and the two publics in Africa: a theoretical statement', in *Comparative Studies in Society and History*, 17, 1 (1975).
6 See E. E. Evans-Pritchard and M. Fortes, *African Political Systems* (Oxford: Oxford University Press, 1940).
7 See I. Nzimiro, *Studies in Ibo Political Systems* (Berkeley: University of California Press, 1972).
8 See O. Otite, 'On the concept of a Nigerian society', *The Nigerian Journal of Economic and Social Studies*, 13, 3 (1971).
9 P. P. Ekeh and G. Ashiwaju (eds), *Nigeria Since Independence, The First 25 Years, Vol. II, Culture* (Ibadan: Heinemann Educational Books Ltd, 1989).
10 Adebayo Adedeji, *The African Alternative: Putting the People First* (ECA, 1990), p. 29.

II

Seven Nigerian Case Studies

4

The Case Studies in the National Context

An Introductory Note

ONIGU OTITE & SINA KAWONISE

The Nigerian setting

Nigeria, reputed to be the 'sleeping giant' of Africa, is also the most populous country in the continent. Its area would accommodate a combination of Belgium, France and the United Kingdom, or Texas, Louisiana and Mississippi. Nigeria's coastline is about 700 kilometers long while the distance from the coast to the country's northern boundary, as the crow flies, is about 1,040 kilometres. Nigeria's population (1991) has been estimated provisionally at 90 million people.

Nigeria's vegetation and ecology are varied. From the coast northwards, the vegetation changes from mangrove swamps to evergreen forests, which are succeeded by deciduous and sparse forests and savannah growth up to and beyond the Niger and Benue rivers. Desert conditions exist in the extreme northern states of Sokoto, Kano, Jigawa, Katsina, Yobe and Borno. The highest plateau, about 1,200 metres above sea level, is around Jos, which has near-temperate conditions. The eastern boundaries of the country are mountainous and cool, with the highest point rising above 2,000 metres. Located within the tropics, Nigeria has two main seasons. The dry season, from November to March, also has a cool dusty *harmattan* in December and January; while the rainy or wet season starts in April and ends in October with a dry spell in August.

In addition to substantial agricultural wealth, Nigeria is blessed with mineral resources. Since 1958, the country has derived most of its income from petroleum.[1] Nigeria is also one of the few African countries with well-trained personnel in scientific, technological, economic and other fields.

Despite its wealth, Nigeria is classified as one of the world's 30 least developed countries. Part of the explanation for this poor politico-economic performance is the mismanagement of vast human and material resources, institutionalized corruption, and, as we noted in Chapter 3, the weakness of civil society, lack of popular participation, and weak democratic institutions and processes, particularly in the rural areas where the vast majority of Nigerians live.

While Nigeria's geographical boundaries with its neighbours Cameroon, Chad, Niger and Benin may be clear, the social and cultural boundaries are blurred and artificial. This is because of the arbitrary partition by the former colonial governments – following the 1885 Berlin Conference and subsequent statutes – of certain ethnic groups and kingdoms, such as the Yoruba of Nigeria and Benin, and the Hausa and Fulani of Nigeria, Niger and northern Cameroon. Within its geographical space, Nigeria accommodates over 370 ethnic groups.[2] Each is defined by its cultural exclusiveness, with traits and norms which either facilitate or restrict popular participation, generally unevenly for men and women as noted in Chapter 3.

The geographical region of Nigeria was largely unknown to the outside world until about the fifteenth century when Europeans, such as Portuguese traders, missionaries and adventurers, came to the west coast of Africa from 1471. The Portuguese influence was replaced by that of the Dutch in the seventeenth century. In turn, the Dutch were replaced by the French and the British, who monopolized the booming trade involving slaves, spices, ivory, coral beads and their manufactured goods. The Royal Niger Company, which was a combination of George Goldie's group of companies, became dominant. It not only monopolized the trade and commercial life of the area, but also signed treaties with the indigenous rulers and politicians, thereby limiting the scope and spheres of popular participation, particularly in political, commercial and judicial matters. But its charter was terminated by the British government in 1900, and Nigeria thereafter became a British protectorate. On 1 January 1914 the northern and southern parts of the country were amalgamated, along with Lagos, to form one country: Nigeria.

There was therefore a common consciousness in the modern government and politics of the country from 1914 onwards. More importantly, several constitutional developments occurred to consolidate the oneness of Nigeria as a political entity. Constitutions were issued in 1922 (Clifford), 1946 (Richards), 1951 (Macpherson), 1954 (Lyttelton), and 1960 (Independence). Subsequently, there have been the 1963, 1979 and 1989 constitutions. These constitutional developments also gave rise to three regions of Nigeria between 1946 and 1963, four regions between 1963 and 1967, 12 states between 1967 and 1976, 19 states between 1976 and 1987, 21 states between 1987 and 1991 and 30 states between 1991 and 1996 when the number was increased to 36 by the creation of new states by the military administration of General Sani Abacha on 1 October 1996 when 183 additional local government authorities were also created.

Throughout the colonial and post-colonial periods, indigenous communities maintained their own institutions for popular participation: for example, the age grades and the town unions and local associations. During the colonial period, especially after 1916, the Native Authority System was developed on the pattern of political intervention used by the Royal Niger

Company by administering Nigerians through their own indigenous structures and organizations, with kings and kings-in-councils, or with 'chiefs' whom they chose as leaders of their people. This system, known as indirect rule, had been successfully used by Lord Lugard in the emirates of northern Nigeria. The system was followed by that of the Local Government Authority in 1951/2. In all these cases, seeds of the simultaneous existence of indigenous and non-indigenous areas of associational life were sown and cultivated.

In the 1950s three dominant political parties were formed in the three major ethnic areas of the country. These were the Action Group in the Western Region, the Northern People's Congress in the Northern Region, and the National Council of Nigeria and the Cameroons (later renamed National Council of Nigerian Citizens) in Eastern Nigeria. This development broadened the areas of popular participation, particularly through the political party arrangements, throughout the urban and rural areas of Nigeria. This tradition has been sustained since Nigeria's independence in 1960, but the scope and opportunities have been widened further with the formation of new political parties and alliances.

After Nigeria became independent in 1960, civilians ruled the country from 1 October 1960 to 14 January 1966, and from 1 October 1979 to 30 December 1983. Military regimes took control in the remaining periods with the self-imposed tasks of correcting the ills of the civilian governments, reaching the people through their traditional rulers, the kings and their chiefs, and developing a circle of functionaries to help them rule effectively and eradicate corruption. Traditionally, military administration is characterized by centralization, and military regimes normally have no structures for involving the people in their governance, politics, and development through democratic processes and popular participation.

The institutions of local government

Throughout colonial rule and after Nigeria's independence, local government, as a phenomenon of grassroots differentiation and administration, has been developed and utilized as a form of popular participation and government. According to Gboyega, four epochs marked the development of local government in Nigeria.[3] The first, as we noted earlier, was from the inception of the colonial government up to the 1950s. Local government then involved the Native Authority system which had been introduced in Northern Nigeria as from 1903, but lasted until the 1950s in the Eastern and Western Regions. The second epoch occurred from 1951 (Eastern Region) and 1952 (Western Region) under the Macpherson Constitution. The reformed local governments promoted the practical values of a representative local government system.

The military regime which followed the coup of 1966 ironically laid the foundation for a wider participatory local government in the northern states while disbanding the parodies of representative local government in southern Nigeria.[4] There was more local administration than local government in many of the states.

The third epoch, initiated in 1970, was marked by a commitment to development by means of political integration and the mobilization and utilization of resources. The fourth epoch began with local government reforms initiated in 1976. It marked a return to participatory local government. According to Section 7(1) of the 1979 Constitution:

> The system of local government by democratically elected local government councils is under this Constitution guaranteed, and accordingly the government of every state shall ensure their existence under a law which provides for the establishment, structure, composition, finance and functions of such councils.

The intentions of an essentially undemocratic military regime in creating democratic local government councils are debatable: it is even possible that the Nigerian military were democratically minded and creative in this area. Following the changes introduced in the 1970s, the number of local government areas (LGAs) has increased over time, from 301 in 1976 to 589 in 1991.

How much local participation in the LGAs?

ACDESS chose seven of these 589 (now 772) LGAs for detailed study in 1993, with special reference to the phenomenon of popular participation in the processes of democratization and development at the rural grassroots in the country. The seven LGAs provide opportunity structures for ordinary people to take part in their own government and development and, in the process, to mobilize the various indigenous and non-indigenous associations and organs for popular participation in different spheres of their lives. The extent to which people have actually utilized these local arrangements is the subject of the research and discussions in the seven case studies contained in this book.

Objectives of the study

This study has a number of important objectives. First, it attempts to identify the various local associations and indicators of popular participation in various areas of life in Nigeria. Second, it aims at providing data and analysis on the basis of which policies can be formulated and implemented to mobilize the people to develop their communities. The masses of the people have generally been excluded from vital decision making and implementation processes which affect their lives and their development, but which have always been directed by a small category of the élite, the ruling class.

Through popular participation, the people at the grassroots are expected to develop and sustain the spirit of self-reliance. The third objective of this study, therefore, is to assess the relevance and impact of grassroots organizations on the achievement of self-reliance and self-development. In doing so, the study attempts to find out how and to what extent individuals, through their local grassroots associations, already participate in the social, political, economic and other affairs and issues which affect their lives. Finally, the study aims to identify and analyse the assets and obstacles encountered in the process of popular participation and democracy in the various spheres of life at the grassroots level in Nigeria.

Methods used in obtaining data

The theme of popular grassroots participation in Nigeria's rural communities determined the methods used in data collection. At the point of research, in August 1993, Nigeria consisted provisionally of 90 million people, more than 75 per cent of whom lived in the rural areas.

The LGAs constituted the grassroots, the lowest and basic units of people's participation in their own government and politics, and in their own development. The LGAs were therefore considered the most appropriate units for studying the role and importance of popular participation in the democratization process in the rural parts of the country. The rural areas of Nigeria, as in most other countries, have often been neglected in the studies of democracy, development, and popular participation in the national scheme of things. Yet, apart from constituting the abode of the silent majority of Nigeria's population, the rural areas and their inhabitants must be seen as an important measure of the degree, tempo, and direction as well as the success or failure of development in Nigeria. Popular participation and democracy in the LGAs are also significant fields of study in their own right.

It was impossible, humanly and financially, for ACDESS at this stage to study all 589 (or 772) LGAs, and such a task would hardly have been necessary, even if feasible. Therefore, seven of the LGAs were chosen for detailed study. Although this number may appear to be small, the LGAs were chosen with care. They were the result of a purposive sampling reflecting Nigeria's vast differences in vegetation, culture, trained human and available material resources, and varying degrees of rurality (only one urbanizing area) with a spread covering the whole country. The seven LGAs also represent the three major ethnic groups in Nigeria – the Hausa/Fulani, Igbo and Yoruba – and also two of the minority groups, the Urhobo in Delta State and the Igala in Kogi State. Some particulars about the seven LGAs are contained in Table 4.1.

A combination of social research methods was used in obtaining data. These were both quantitative and qualitative. The choice of respondents in each household or in each town/village, or indeed the choice of towns and

TABLE 4.1
The Seven LGAs

No	Name of LGA	State in which located	Population Male	Female	Total
I	Afijio	Oyo	33,998	36,315	70,313
2	Dekina	Kogi	99,198	102,484	201,682
3	Ethiope East	Delta	52,173	56,530	108,703
4	Ijebu-Ode	Ogun	181,024	126,759	307,773
5	Mbaitoli	Imo	70,276	77,974	148,250
6	Ohaozara	Abia	59,467	74,501	133,968
7	Wurno	Sokoto	48,988	49,945	95,933

villages in each LGA, involved a multi-stage sampling in which the LGAs were more or less purposively sampled clusters. They were administrative units clearly defined by the National Electoral Commission (Senatorial Districts) Federal and State Constituencies Delimitation Notice 1991, effective from 23 September 1991. The towns or villages, or the individuals chosen either for study or as respondents, were held by researchers to be typical of the rest. Although the word 'typicality' may still be an elusive concept because of the questionable criteria often used, researchers were able to identify those who could answer their questions, for example teachers and local government office holders, or groups with associations which promote or hinder popular participation in the democratization process.

Documents of government, LGA and non-governmental organizations were found useful as secondary sources of data by researchers. But such documents were read against library and other documents and raw data from interviews and questionnaires. Indeed, the fundamental nature of the study compelled researchers to be physically present in almost all the settlements in each LGA. In each case, research instruments included interview schedules and questionnaires which were designed to elicit data in relation to the main concern of the study: popular participation, democracy, and development in each locality. The questionnaires were self-administered and were combined with interviews, using the local language. A standard schedule of compulsory areas covered was worked out by all the researchers in a workshop at ACDESS headquarters in Ijebu-Ode before proceeding with field work. Most interviews were conducted with males. As noted earlier, Nigerian indigenous societies are characterized by male dominance, using different norms of prevention or restriction on female empowerment and popular participation in the public domain.

The standardization of the interview schedule promoted uniformity while at the same time providing for comparative details which were found useful in our analysis and recommendation of policies. Yet, there was room for originality and resourcefulness on the part of researchers in view of the peculiarities and priorities of some LGAs. The open-endedness of some of the questions raised at interviews and in the questionnaire, as well as in face-to-face interpersonal and researcher-to-group interviews, promoted variety in the data obtained. On the whole, the quality of the data was high since the researchers were speakers of the local languages, if not indigenes, in the LGAs they studied. In addition, they were fairly well acquainted with the local government personnel and members of the local communities, and theretore needed no interpreters. This factor was of great help when interviewing the rural people who were non-literate in English. The interviewers thus easily appraised the validity and reliability of the answers they received, and were able to reduce or minimize ethical problems in their research and analysis.

One of the most important aspects of the research was uncontrolled non-participant observation. It formed a yardstick for assessing the completeness and correctness of data obtained through the other research methods. Researchers moved around their LGAs to enumerate various items, to verify ongoing and completed projects or projects that never left the policy table, to observe associations at work, to verify and explore indicators of popular participation or non-participation in various fields of life while talking freely with friends, kinsmen, old school mates, craftsmen, teachers and pupils, and well-diggers. They examined boreholes in operation or those that were inactive, talked with taxi drivers, indigenous town or village council and court elders and spectators, and sellers and buyers in daily and periodic markets, despite the hazards encountered through bad roads, grassy footpaths and the lack of vehicular transportation. The experiences gained were considerable and rewarding, particularly because they enriched the analysis of the data collected.

Notes

1 Akin Iwayemi, *Oil and the Macroeconomics Policy Issues in an Open Developing Economy: A Case Study of Nigeria, Vol. I* (Ibadan: National Centre for Economic Management).

2 O. Otite, *Ethnic Pluralism and Ethnicity in Nigeria* (Ibadan: Shanesonn C. I. Ltd, 1990.

3 Alex Gboyega, *Political Values and Local Governments in Nigeria* (Lagos: Malthouse Press, 1987), pp. 8–10.

4 O. Oyediran and E. A. Gboyega, 'Local government and administration', in O. Oyediran (ed.), *Nigerian Government and Politics Under Military Rule* (London: Macmillan, 1979), pp. 169–91.

5

Prospects for Sustainable Democracy and Accountability in Afijio, Oyo State

'KUNLE AMUWO

Studying politics, power, participation and development at the micro-analytical level – often through the prism of civil society – has become a fashionable theoretical and methodological orientation of social scientists in recent years. One rationale given for this innovation is that the state and statist conceptions of politics have not only become irrelevant, but are indeed no more than a myth.[1] This radical approach, charted since the early 1980s by the well-known French 'politist' Jean Francois Bayart, has spawned several disciples, collaborators, journal articles and a recent book.[2]

The approach seems to be influenced, if only in part, by Alain Touraine's explanation of the philosophy of contradiction and the sociology of conflicts.[3] It is also derived from Michel Foucault's illuminating argument about anti-discipline in the social sciences. His argument is that wherever there is power, there is resistance and this resistance is not external to the power.[4]

The foregoing is particularly interesting for contemporary state–civil society relations. Whereas in the early liberal, bourgeois state in Europe, according to Archie Mafeje, the state 'was seen as generally inclined to impose its will on individuals and it was thought that individuals could save themselves from the imposition by insisting on independent existence outside the state',[5] the same phenomenon can no longer hold. This is due to the fact that the state and the civil society are enmeshed with each other; neither lives outside the other. It therefore makes eminent sense to study the two categories in terms of interrelationships rather than as structures standing wholly apart from each other. Consequently, state–civil society relations ought to be conceptualized, perceived and interpreted in terms of how the strengths and weaknesses of an organization (the state) depend on its relations with wider social forces.[6] These 'wider social forces' are found in civil society, which Alfred Stephan defines as 'an arena where manifold social movements and civic organizations from all classes attempt to constitute themselves in an ensemble of arrangements so that they can express themselves and advance their interest'.[7]

In so far as the state, as exemplified in Africa, seeks a monopoly of the public (or political) space, thus denying legitimacy and liberty to non-state actors and organizations, it is up to civil society not to yield ground. P.P. Ekeh defines the challenge as follows: 'The subject matter of civil society concerns the non-monopolistic uses and management of the public realm by the state and other non-private political organizations that operate in it.'[8]

The extent to which individuals and their voluntary organizations are given free rein in a given polity is one of the salient criteria for evaluating popular participation. In the specific context of Africa, the focus, in recent years, has been on popular participation, democratization and enlargement of the public space via a more accentuated role of intermediary groups (local improvement societies, development councils, hometown associations, among many others) occasioning a shift from the developmental role of the state to that of non-state associations. There is now a sharper societal response to statist practices. For Adedeji, this nascent political culture is nothing if it does not form part of the 'development struggles' occasioned by the 'abysmal failure of the past élitist and bureaucratic approach to development policy and planning with its notorious anti-rural bias and benign neglect and marginalization of the legitimate aspirations of the majority of the population'.[9]

By the same token, popular participation is conceptualized beyond the dialectics of relations between the state and civil society. It is expressed, rather, in terms of empowerment of the people in creating structures and designing policies and programmes that serve the interests of all – that is, in terms of contribution to the development process and the equitable sharing of benefits.[10] If the central objectives of development are the basic needs and aspirations of the people – in terms of food, shelter, clothing, water, health care, education, transport[11] – to what extent have associational organizations and life in rural communities helped in attaining these objectives? How political are they in terms of links and sustained interaction with the state, typified, at their level, by local and state governments, their agencies and agents? Are these associations dominated by local power or by a political élite? Do ordinary people benefit economically or politically? The following case study attempts to probe the above questions and related ones at the level of a local community in Afijio LGA, Oyo State.

Methodology

Afijio LGA is one of the more developed LGAs in Oyo State. In terms of facilities, it can be said to be transitional, moving away from a predominantly rural (traditional) system to an urban (modernizing) system, thus possessing, in varying proportions, elements of both tradition and modernity. Afijio LGA is, *mutatis mutandis*, a fairly good representative of the local government system in its state.

The empirical indices were obtained by using several modalities. The indicators for field research which ensued from the team's methodology workshop were strictly adhered to throughout the duration of the field work. Secondly, in studying social, political and economic organizations, in terms of their internal workings and self-empowerment devices – as well as their relations with state and quasi-state agencies at the three levels of government, namely, local, state and federal – a common research procedure was adopted. Oral interviews were conducted with an officer of each organization – president, vice-president or secretary – as well as with no fewer than two floor members. For state agencies, only the officers in charge were interviewed. Such face-to-face, direct discussions were regarded as more rigorous and effective than the questionnaire method.

The main field work was carried out between 29 July 1993 and 20 August 1993, with intermittent stoppages resulting from the political crisis in the country at the time. A further two days of field work, necessitated by the review of the first draft of this paper, followed on 15 and 16 September 1993.

Afijio LGA: a profile

Afijio LGA is one of the 589 entities created by the Babangida administration (1985–93). It is located along the Ibadan–Oyo road that serves as the main link with the northern part of the country. Although it borders on Oyo town, it is principally a farming area with several communities and settlements.

Afijio LGA is bounded in the north by Oyo South LGA, in the west by Iseyin LGA, in the east by Iwo LGA and in the south by Akinyele LGA. It consists of no fewer than 350 communities. A further two large settlements are Akinmorin and Imini. The six most important 'towns' in the area are: Aawe, Fiditi, Ilora, Jobele, Iware and Oluwatedo. The name of the LGA itself is derived from a combination of the first letters of these towns.

The LGA has a long history which is tied, in several respects, to the struggles waged since the 1940s by the then *Egbe Ilu Mesan* (Association of Nine Towns), now known as the Afijio Descendants' Union. In 1957, this area was, alongside Oyo and Iseyin, carved into Oyo South local government. Following a government-sponsored enquiry in 1959, it was granted a provisional authority to become an autonomous local council in 1963. The first military coup on 15 January 1966 stopped that process and it was again merged with Oyo. Indeed, the Afijio people have had a running battle with the Oyo people.

During the Second Republic, the Unity Party of Nigeria (UPN) government in Oyo State decided, upon another enquiry in 1981, not to grant the area a separate or unique identity as demanded – not for want of persuasive argument, but due to a political desire not to 'upset political sensitivities in both Oyo North and Oyo South'.[12] The coup of 31 December 1983 again halted this experiment. The ensuing Buhari administration simply merged all local government councils irrespective of their viability. Intense lobbying by eminent sons and daughters of the area for a separate council continued, however, surreptitiously culminating, in 1989, in the creation of Afijio LGA. The headquarters are in Jobele, one of its smallest 'towns'.

The rivalry with Oyo has persisted. Out of a total of 24 councillors for the area, Oyo got 16, leaving Afijio with only eight. The area's political élite talk of cheating. The élite also resent being perceived by the Oyo and historians as a 'vassal state' of the Oyo people.

Basic demographic indicators

According to the provisional 1991 national census figures released in 1992, Afijio LGA has a population of 70,313 made up of 33,998 males and 36,315 females. Upon a petition against Oyo people on Afijio land – mainly in the Ilora area, the largest concentration in the western part of the LGA, to the National Population Commission (NPC), Oyo state zonal headquarters – the provisional population has now been put, unofficially, at 123,000.[13]

According to the NPC, data relating to the number of households as well as literacy rate by gender are still being processed. In the same vein, information on population density, the quantity of arable land and the extent of land use is still awaited from the Population Commission.

Education

By 1991, the LGA had a total of 76 primary schools, 21 junior secondary schools and 22 senior secondary schools as well as an adult education centre at Akinmorin.[14] The LGA also hosts a tertiary institution, by virtue of its location on its land at Akinmorin[15] – the Federal College of Special Education (Oyo). There is a technical college at Awe.

More male than female pupils are enrolled in both primary and secondary schools in the LGA. The ratio is said to be between 3:1 and 4:1. However, no firm data exist on enrolment ratios, although estimates range between 80 and 90 per cent. It is further claimed that child labour on farms, which is not infrequent, does not prevent children from going to school. The pupils help farmer-parents after school hours or serve as farm hands during holidays.[16]

Health

The LGA has five privately owned clinics in Fiditi (one); Ilora (three) and Aawe (one). It also has seven maternity centres in Fiditi, Ojutaye, Aawe, Akinmorin, Ilora and Iware and at Farm Settlement. There are nine dispensaries, each headed by a community health extension worker and a health assistant. They are located at Jobele, Aawe, Fiditi, Ilora, Akinmorin, Iware, Ojutaye, Imini and Ago-Oyo. There are four health outposts, an outpost being no more than a room undertaking minor treatments. Each is staffed by at least a health extension worker. They are to be found at Oluwatedo,

Ilu-Aje, Itosi, Araromi and Eleeakara market. In addition, at Akinmorin a European Union (EU)-Federal Government joint clinic has been in operation since 1991.[17]

The LGA has no fewer than 80 medical and para-medical personnel, including community health extension workers, health assistants, environmental health workers, staff nurses and midwives, pharmacy technicians, health labourers and a community health officer.

Potable water

By 1991, the LGA had nine facilities for pipe-borne water, three boreholes and 118 deep wells. Indeed, the area is well known for the latter. Each community has water, in all likelihood at least a well, within no more than one kilometre of its centre. This unusually healthy situation in a rural part of Nigeria is accounted for by recent action to provide deep wells by the state and federal governments and Global 2000, to combat the previous incidence of guinea-worm in the area. Now, even during a very dry season, the area is unlikely to experience water problems.

Energy

Electricity supply exists in the LGA's six major communities: Aawe, Fiditi, Ilora, Jobele, Iware, and Oluwatedo. Elsewhere it is non-existent.

There are four petrol stations in the area: Ladegbuwa (Jobele); Unipetrol (Eleeakara); Capital and Mark (Ilora). Kerosene can be bought mainly at the fuel stations, but small quantities exist at different points in the major communities. For instance, while Aawe curiously has no petrol station – curiously, in so far as it is the most developed community – several households sell kerosene in the town.

Jobele, the local government council headquarters, has a high concentration of fuelwood which services, though not on a large scale, the various communities in the area. Fuelwood is also available within most communities and at many roadsides.

Transport and markets

A federal road links Fiditi and Jobele (the Ibadan–Oyo–Ilorin road); while state B roads link Ilora to Aawe and Jobele to Akinmorin. There are earth roads to and within other communities. Some of these were developed communally, while others were undertaken by the DFRRI.

Most of the relevant markets are along the roadside. The famous Eleeakara market, owned by private individuals, is located by the roadside in Jobele, some two kilometres outside the boundaries of Oyo town. It is a daily market, patronized by other communities, including the Oyo people and Hausa itinerants and truck drivers. The market specializes in the staple foods of the area – such as fruit, *gari*, beans, yam, cassava and flour – but also stocks many other goods. In Fiditi, also, there is a booming fruit market by the roadside. It is in line with the tradition of the people whose customers are principally travellers.

Other markets easily accessible by road are Oja Alaawe, a five-day market which specializes in *gari,* and a big, flourishing market in Iware, a Saturday market frequented by traders from Ibadan and Abeokuta, among other places.

Economic institutions and activities

The LGA has three main shops, managed by the council and generating revenue. They are located at Aawe and Ilora (both were opened on the same day, 8 May 1993) and at Akinmorin (opened a year earlier). The latter was initiated by the community but was taken over by the council. The shops are lock-up types: 12 feet by 6 feet, or smaller.

A variety of industrial activities are found in this area. Two of these constitute the main endeavour of the people, namely agro-service and agro-based cottage industries. There are agro-service centres and an agricultural research station owned by the state government at Ilora. Agro-based cottage industries concentrate on palm oil and cassava processing. There are 72 palm oil facilities, most of which are owned by the government, scattered over at least 66 settlements in the LGA. There are local subsidiaries of multinational corporations. Worthy of note are the Bond chemical company, makers of, *inter alia*, paracetamol on a large scale; and the French Amos Sanders farms, which produce livestock feeds. Another industrial category consists of enterprises owned by indigenous entrepreneurs, including Chief D. G. Adeleke's bricks industry in Fiditi, and Folawiyo Farms, Ilora, owned by Chief Folawiyo, a national Muslim leader, farmer and industrialist, concentrating on large-scale production and poultry. There is a booming hotel industry, the oldest and the biggest of which is the International Hotel, Aawe. The Penthouse Rotekin Hotel, also in Aawe, is the newest and most modern. Aawe also houses Femkins Hotel and Baby Benz de Femkins Hotel, owned by two brothers.

It was difficult to ascertain the exact number of employees in each of the foregoing industrial sectors. For political and related reasons, several interviewees simply refused to be forthcoming. Secondary sources indicated, however, that Folawiyo Farms has between 150 and 200 employees. It is estimated that the cassava and palm oil processing industries have a similar number. The hotels have fewer hands. At the International Hotel, Aawe, there are fewer than 15 employees. The subsidiaries of foreign companies have between 20 and 30 workers each.[18] The Yanko Women Better Life factory, Erinle riverside, Ojuerugun, Fiditi, where palm kernel – rather than palm oil – is processed to make *yanko* soap (or *Adiayan*), employs about 40 hands.

There are five banks in the Afijio LGA. These are the Nigeria-Arab Bank (Fiditi, established in 1982); the African International Bank (Ilora); Union

Bank (Akinmorin) and the Community and People's Banks – both in Aawe. The Community Bank was opened by former President Babangida in 1991 and the People's Bank in 1992. At the time of the survey, the Community Bank had already awarded up to 150 loans.

Public facilities

There is only one public library in the LGA; it is situated in Aawe and was reactivated in early 1992. It seats comfortably some 20–25 people at a time. It is supplied with magazines, newspapers and books, most of which were donated by the Oyo State government library in July 1992.

There are four postal agencies in Jobele, Ilora, Fiditi and Iware; and only one post office, in Aawe. It was upgraded through communal effort and commissioned in 1992. The post office currently has about 400 boxes. There is only one public telephone, situated behind the postal agency at Fiditi. One public telephone booth is under construction in Aawe. Private telephone lines also exist in Ilora, Aawe and Fiditi. The exact number could not be obtained, but some interviewees put it at about a dozen per town.

The five motor parks in the LGA are located in five of the most developed communities – Fiditi, Aawe, Ilora, Iware and Imini. The one in Fiditi is an open space by the roadside; the one in Aawe at Orita Merin, built by the council, is under-utilized, perhaps because it is too far from the town. Others are the Oja Oke motor park in Ilora and small ones in Iware and Imini, both seemingly developing fast as they serve the large markets in the two communities.

In Aawe there are at least 20 taxis. The Rotekin Hotel has Peugeot 504 passenger station wagons that travel to Lagos. Ilora, a nerve-centre of farming in the area, has few taxis but about 10 Hi-Ace buses and about six lorries that ferry farm products from Ilora and the Farm Settlement to other communities of the LGA.

The five police stations in the LGA are located in Aawe, Fiditi, Ilora, Jobele and Akinmorin. There are about ten policemen in Aawe alone and between 25 and 30 at the Jobele headquarters, from where men are posted out.

There are five customary courts in Aawe, Ilora, Fiditi, Iware and Akinmorin. The local government also claims that since Oyo High Court is situated in Aawe it properly belongs to it, even though the court continues to use the Oyo address.

All the towns have vigilante groups. They are generally known as night guards. Part of the responsibility of the *Egbe Ibile Ilora*, in Ilora, for instance, is to oversee the security of the town through vigilante groups. For this purpose, Ilora is divided into ten areas and further broken down into quarters: Idigba, Okegege, Balogun, Jagun, Alamo, Papa-aro, Orisa, Akibio, Okediji and Okesani. This arrangement for vigilante purposes is reputed to be very effective.[19]

Mass media

The LGA has easy access to all major newspapers, radio and television stations. The area's major towns benefit from wide state and national contacts. In fact, the LGA has no TV mounting centres because people in major communities have their own TV sets. At the time of this research, daily newspapers such as the *Daily Sketch, Nigerian Tribune, Vanguard, Champion, Guardian* and *Daily Times* were especially popular in the LGA headquarters. For the three weeks that the field work lasted, these titles were seen, in different mixes, in all the departments, and were subscribed to by the council.

Magazines of a particular political or ideological bent, 'different from official news', to quote the LGA's information officer, were regularly supplied to the council. These included *Tell, Newswatch, African Concord, Viva* and, at times when the military authorities permitted it to publish, *The News*.

The LGA also has several local forms of passing messages to the various communities. Some of these forms are:

1 Town criers, which are found in every town;

2 Supervisors and councillors;

3 Schools – often when the message concerns educational matters or issues which pupils are required to remind their parents about, as in the case of mobilization for census;[20]

4 Churches and mosques – these are contacted whenever the need arises to communicate some important message (sometimes, officials of the LGA council who are members of religious persuasions are urged to pass word around on their networks); and

5 Chiefs, *Baales*, community leaders and community development associations are also used for communication.

Indicators of popular participation

Social and political organizations

Three major social and political organizations exist in the area:

1 The *Egbe Omo Ibile Aawe* and Aawe Development Corporation;

2 The *Egbe Omo Ibile Ilora* and Ilora Development Association (IDA); and,

3 The Afijio Descendants' Union.

The first organisation (*Egbe Omo Ibile Aawe*) was eliminated from this case study in order to avoid duplicating recent research by three colleagues.[21]

Instead, the Aawe Supreme Élite Club, a purely social club, was studied. But first we consider the socio-political development associations.

The Egbe Omo Ibile Ilora

The *Egbe Omo Ibile Ilora* probably dates to the second decade of the nineteenth century, as does its Aawe counterpart.[22] It is made up of the heads of all the indigenous families. No woman, however, is allowed to sit at meetings. Consequently, if the head (that is, the oldest surviving member) of a family is a woman, she is replaced automatically by the next oldest man. Membership is therefore all male and gerontocracy is the rule. The total membership is difficult to ascertain until the National Population Commission releases its data on the number of households in the LGA. Membership is limited to indigenes of the town. Elected members of Ilora Development Association (IDA) are automatic members of the *Egbe Ibile*. Membership is compulsory for each house.

The functions of the *Egbe* include the following:

1. Overseeing the overall progress, peace and stability of Ilora town;
2. Holding regular meetings with the head of the town (*Oba*), the Akibio of Ilora,[23] with a view to taking decisions on the town; and
3. Organizing the security of the town, through vigilante groups.

There are two sources of revenue generation. The first is a monthly contribution of ₦1 per house (1993 rate). The procedure emphasizes egalitarianism, and no house, however rich, can pay more than the prescribed sum. The money realized from this contribution is not much and is meant for the routine running of the *Egbe*. For development purposes, levies are imposed uniformly across the board, though here rich members know no obstacle to spending for their home town.

The *Egbe Omo Ibile Ilora* meets once a month, usually on a Saturday, as directed by the executive. Leaders are elected and members have a tradition of electing the most responsible members as leaders. The executive is normally elected for a two-year term, renewable only once. A review is being undertaken to change the initial tenure to three years. The association has only four officers, the chairman, vice-chairman, secretary and treasurer. Though no leader has ever been removed from office, the procedures for control and sanction are straightforward. The process of removing an executive from office would be initiated only after a warning, served after three consecutive absences from monthly meetings or, as the case may be, for poor performance. If a vote of no confidence were to be passed on an executive member, new elections would be held.

There is also a reward system. Committed officers are given monetary gifts, however small, usually at the end of the year, and palm wine when such officers organize ceremonies. Since the *Egbe* is a more or less exclusive preserve of family heads, the youths, those in the age bracket of 18–30 years, have no say at all in the *Egbe*. In the same vein, most of the members, being family heads, are often well advanced in age. More of them are above 60 than those between 45 and 60 years. The system takes care of the other 'age grades':[24] the IDA and the Ilora Development Youth Association take care of the interests of the middle-aged and youths.

Ilora Development Association (IDA)

As the name suggests, the IDA is a development-oriented indigenous association. Established in 1963, its emphasis is on self-reliance and popular development. The achievements of the IDA include a new palace, which has been under construction since 1974, a town hall and a post office. The latter, commenced in 1992, was due to be opened in December 1993. The IDA has also dug 15 wells, installed a public water tap, four years after the state water corporation had removed its own, and constructed five culverts.[25]

The IDA membership is open to any male or female. Although it is a voluntary association, women do not attend the meetings. As much as possible, members are given responsibilities since the association organizes itself around committees. These include education, building, social events, fund-raising and planning. There are more middle-aged people in the IDA than youths and the elderly. As in Aawe, Ilora boasts of an array of highly successful professionals and academics who frequently return home to take an active part in the running of the association.

The major source of finance is through a system of general levies. Each house is required to pay ₦500 annually (as of 1993). In addition, every male and female adult contributes ₦10 and ₦5, respectively, annually (as of 1993).

The IDA meets every last Saturday of the month, to allow indigenes outside the town and government workers to attend in large numbers. As in the *Egbe*, officers of the IDA are elected for a renewable two-year term and are ten in number. These are: president, two vice-presidents, secretary, assistant secretary, organizing secretary, public relations officer (PRO), treasurer, financial secretary and internal auditor. Its control and sanction structure is similar to that of the *Egbe Ibile*.

If there are not many young people (aged 18–35) in the IDA, it is because the body has a youth wing, the Ilora Development Youth Association (IDYA), founded in 1985 with the singular objective of mobilizing Ilora youths for popular development. It sometimes initiates projects which are then handed over to the parent body, IDA. An example is the post office project. Other characteristics of the IDA equally apply to the IDYA.

The annual Ilora Day is held on the last Saturday of November – and the whole preceding week is usually spent celebrating it. The event offers the opportunity of a regrouping or reunion of members and officers of the three interlocking associations.

Afijio Descendants' Union (ADU)

This union is the umbrella organization for all sons and daughters of the LGA. It had its humble beginnings in 1943, when its founding fathers – Reverend Oloopa (Aawe); Chief Eyitayo (Ilora) and Pa Ajao (Fiditi) and some others – met and christened the association *Egbe Ilu Mesan* (Association of Nine Towns). These towns were Ilora, Fiditi, Aawe, Akinmorin, Imini, Jobele, Ojutaye, Iware and Oluwatedo. Jobele was chosen as the meeting place and regular meetings were held at the St Peter's Primary School. Jobele is a small town and almost neutral, in that none of the founding fathers hailed from there.

The primary motive of the *Egbe*, which was renamed Afijio Descendants' Union in 1957, was to serve as a platform for asserting the uniqueness and autonomy of Afijio people *vis-à-vis* the remainder of what used to be the Oyo Divisional Council – made up of Oyo North and South. More specifically, the LGA wanted to be free from what its founding fathers saw – and their descendants continue to see – as the dominance of Oyo town and Oyo people in the area. Indeed, the ADU was meant to give the Afijio people 'one voice' to fight against 'a common enemy'.[26] The other objective is the development of the area in question.

Membership is open to all indigenes of the LGA; though females outnumber males, more males attend meetings. While there is a gradual penetration of the union by youths, it remains essentially a gerontocratic set-up. The ADU is at once voluntary and indigenous. A former secretary of the union called its membership both voluntary and compulsory in so far as all decisions taken at its meetings are binding on everybody.

There are neither monthly dues nor regular levies. Rather, people are called upon to contribute whenever urgent matters require money – and these are more often than not land cases and boundary disputes. Contributions are made through community leaders. In recent years, boundary disputes have involved Afijio LGA with Akinyele, Iwo and Oyo local governments, amongst others. Such monies are allocated on the basis of the size of the towns. Another source of finance, perhaps more regular, is the local government council. It is a historical fact that under both military and civilian regimes, the council has released money to the union just for the asking.[27]

Meetings of the ADU are infrequently held because they are irregularly called. While the Lagos branch – apparently a well-organized group and an the envy of the 'homeboys' – meets regularly, its parent body does not. Only its executive members seem to do so. Whenever serious local issues arise, however, or national policies with local consequences crop up, meetings are more likely to be called. An example of each situation is appropriate.

Early in 1993, when the LGA chairman was accused of selling land arbitrarily, if not illegally, an emergency union meeting recorded a full house, and indigenes – youth, adults and old people – were given ample time to ask questions. National issues with local consequences can also prompt calls for meetings. For example, rumours about the military junta's intention to create new local governments before its exit in August 1993 occasioned a meeting. At that time, Ilora and Aawe were seeking their own separate local government councils. They continue to do so.

In respect of election of leaders, the Afijio Descendants' Union has become very like an informal club. That has not made it moribund, however, and this is not likely to happen in the near future. This is because there is a team of committed and interested elders led by Chief Odeleye which has been steering the ship of the union since 1983. Chief Odeleye is chairman; other prominent figures in 1993 included Chief Odebunmi, the secretary, and Deacon Oyewole, a former acting vice-chairman of the local government council (1981–3), who has remained active without being an executive member.

What explains this local stability and tranquillity? Respondents talk glowingly about the political skills of the union's founding fathers. This is expressed in two main ways. The first is the separation, in as much as this is possible, between the ADU and partisan politics. This occurred during the First Republic and was expected to be repeated in the third (now aborted) phase of civilian politics. The separation thesis is encapsulated in the skill of perpetual balancing of political and community interests.

More specifically, a zoning formula has been used to allot positions in both the union and the local government council to the different towns and communities. For this purpose, the LGA is grouped into two constituencies as follows:

Constituency One:	Ilora, Akinmorin, Jobele, Imini, Oluwatedo, Onifa, Ayetoro, Farm Settlement, Temidire, Lagbe, Dijo, Abanti.
Constituency Two:	Fiditi, Aawe, Iware, Ojutaye and the various villages under them.

A degree of political brinkmanship has been exercised in the recognition historically accorded to the ADU, as the apex association to which all significant problems are referred and from which uncontested decisions flow. The local government council is, itself, routinely affected by this scenario. Several years of bargaining and dialogue and a history of common opponents have seemingly forged a political culture which emphasizes seeking solutions to problems without advertising them to the public.

It remains to say here that some control of the ADU is exercised by the people and particularly by their elders. The latter – they say in the name of the former – have been known to ratify the council budget before it is formally presented. Elders have also let incoming chairmen know the area of failure of their immediate predecessors and what the union expects of them in order to win its support.[28]

Aawe Supreme Élite Club

Founded in 1984, this is mainly a social club, organized as a youth club, but then its assigned functions go beyond social events. Its functions include seeing to the progress of the town, the 'beautification' of Aawe, and helping the town in time of need. The club is open only to males who are indigenes of the town, though women are not forbidden from attending its functions. The indigenes may be either those resident at home or those 'abroad'. It is also a voluntary club and the present membership strength is 25. Furthermore, only males aged between 20 and 35 years are admissible.

The main source of finance is annual dues of ₦200 per member (1993). This is the minimum, and members are free to pay more. Other sources are payment for entertainment (for members and their spouses), fines paid by latecomers and absentees at meetings, and voluntary gifts.

The club meets quarterly on the last Saturday of the relevant month. Officers are elected for a three-year period, renewable only once. The officers are president, vice-president, financial secretary, treasurer, auditor, PRO and chief whip. The club gives as much as a full year to an absentee member to mend his ways. He even receives minutes of the meetings during such a period of absence and will be removed only after a year's grace. Only committed officers are re-elected; they do not receive any special gift or incentive from the club.[29]

Socio-economic organizations

The communities in the rural farming area of Afijio LGA have created several farmers' associations, cooperative movements (most of which are oriented to the needs of the farmers), and credit institutions. The traditional credit institutions (*Esu* or *Olowoele*) are not very numerous; none exists in Aawe, but there is a small group in Ilora. Similarly, craft and guild organizations hardly exist, apart from some automobile mechanic and tailoring groups. They are not visible at all at Jobele, the headquarters, for example. Shopkeepers' associations are an alien concept, but the road transport workers have a relatively significant association, particularly in Ilora. Marketmen are also more visible than their female counterparts. What follows is the detailed examination of the following organizations:

1 Community Women and Development (COWAD);

2 Women in Agriculture (WIA);

3 The Eleeakara Market Men's and Women's Association;

4 National Union of Road Transport Workers (NURTW), Afijio branch;

5 Association of Automobile Engineers, Afijio, Ilora;

6 Youth Tailoring Association, Ilora;

7 Ifedawapo Contribution Society, Ilora.

Virtually all these economic organizations function as cooperative societies of some sort, apparently in line with the tradition and mores of the people and perhaps also because of the national economic crisis at the time this investigation was conducted.

COWAD

The Community Women and Development (COWAD) organization was established with the singular aim of encouraging self-help projects at the grassroots and using these as building blocks for popular development. It is the first women's organization – aside from the National Council of Women Societies (NCWS) and Women in Nigeria (WIN) – to serve as a rallying point for the Better Life Programme (BLP). At the LGA, members of COWAD used also to be members of NCWS and BLP and the meetings of the three bodies used to be held at the same time. BLP used to help COWAD, but under the civilian government in Oyo State things seemingly fell apart.

COWAD in Afijio LGA was established in 1984/5 and has since then become involved in a variety of activities: *gari* and palm oil processing, cooperative and credit facilities, crop farming (particularly citrus), and making of soap, vegetable oil and *Adire* cloth. It also organizes workshops and training sessions for interested community women. It has a cassava factory at Olorunda – chosen for it by UNICEF – as well as a nursery school in Oyo.

COWAD gives loans to market women and farmers, with due-paying members receiving double. The association gets a profit of 3 *kobo* on every ₦2 loaned out (1993 rates). Loans are repayable over 12 months and are given only to members who have regularly attended meetings for more than six months.

Membership of COWAD is open to all women in the LGA irrespective of age and creed. About 100 members meet in the chairperson's house at Jobele. Most of the members are young and middle-aged women, while only a few of them are elderly women. In 1993, the chairperson, who joined in 1986, was the headmistress of St Peter's Primary School, Jobele. Members are drawn from the local, zonal and state levels. It is a non-indigenous economic organization but several of COWAD's activities have their roots in the tradition of the people.

A major source of finance is development fees of at least ₦10 paid monthly by members as well as an additional ₦1, the proceeds of which are spent on needed materials (1993 rates). Though not everybody pays the dues, the monies so realized are used for the benefit of all. According to the chairperson, the coordinating state body of COWAD also loans money to the members in the various LGAs. The local government council has done little or nothing to help financially, after initial enthusiasm in the first six months following its take-off in the LGA. By the same token, whilst COWAD obeyed a 1990 BLP national headquarters directive that no cooperative would get assistance from it unless it was integrated within the BLP, no assistance has been forthcoming – from federal, state or local governments.

Meetings are held monthly. There are also monthly meetings at the zonal and state levels. Officers of COWAD are elected for a renewable two-year period. The officers in question are president, secretary, financial secretary, treasurer, auditor, adviser and PRO. Any officer who exhibits poor leadership qualities or absents herself from meetings is removed from office on the third occasion. Irregular members have a period of grace of three months to amend their ways. If they do not comply, they risk expulsion but are eligible to re-apply.[30]

Women in Agriculture (WIA)

This association was launched in 1982 with one or two women trying to elicit their colleagues' interest in agriculture. By 1989, WIA had become a group with about 60 members, divided into groups of ten. WIA's areas of specialization are maize and cassava cultivation. It also plants vegetables, tomatoes and okro.

WIA is also a cooperative, backed by the BLP. Based in Fiditi, an important source of fruit in the LGA and the state, it is registered as Binukonu Cooperatives. After February 1990, it was associated with the BLP and in 1991 it acquired a certificate from the state government stating the government's commitment to cater for its needs. Despite this commitment, no help has been rendered so far. The BLP's role has mainly been to organize seminars for its members.

The most ambitious project undertaken by WIA in this area is the Binukonu Fruit Juice Processing Centre located at Egbejoda, Fiditi. The fruit juice machine was purchased with the help of the Oyo State Agricultural Development Programme (OYSADEP) in late 1992. The machine cost the association about ₦70,000 out of which the local government council paid an initial deposit of ₦15,000. A lack of purified water and inadequate electricity in the area meant, however, that the machine, installed on 23 May 1993, had not functioned for a single day at the time of this case study.[31] The expenditure on this project had little or no more credit to grant loans to WIA members. Out of frustration, several illiterate members stopped attending meetings regularly.

Membership is open to all women in agriculture and is voluntary. Most of the members are middle-aged (35–50 years), with a few young and old members. Officers of WIA regard the association as indigenous to the people in so far as they are a farming population. Sources of revenue generation are the monthly dues of ₦10 per member and the ₦5 fine imposed on members who do not come to meetings (1993). WIA claims that it has never been accorded any credit or bank loan. Neither has any request been made for loans because others before them were denied credit. The association was short of money at the time of this research; it was estimated that ₦300,000 could get the fruit juice project off the ground, as well as ensuring processing, bottling or packaging, and marketing.[32]

Meetings are held every second Monday of the month. Officers are always present. Electoral guidelines exist for installing the executive, but this has not taken place. According to the guidelines, officers can be elected for a renewable three-year term. For now, the founders are still the officers – that is, president, vice-president, treasurer, and financial secretary. No control or sanction structure is yet in place, perhaps due to the dominance of the founding mothers of the association. For now, it would seem that it is the leaders who need to control the members, and not the other way round.

The Eleeakara Market Men's and Women's Association (Kajola Market)

The all-purpose, all-season Eleeakara market is only about 2 kilometres from Jobele, headquarters of the local government council. Opened in 1983, it was formed by the joint efforts of traders, market men and women and spare parts traders. The nucleus of the association was from Oyo and its environs as well as Orita-merin, Ibadan. In indigenous parlance, the three groups are called *Kajola Eledu, Onisowo* and 'spare part sellers'. Each group still has its chairman while there is an overall chairman for the entire market.

The market is thus both a private and a collective initiative and the entrepreneurs employ various categories of workers of different professional callings. Several cooperative and thrift societies thrive within the market, run by entrepreneurs and employees alike. Security guards operate for both the indigenous and the Hausa-Sabo sectors of the market. Tailors, mechanics, road transport workers and others are also there, but under the strict control of the market management.[33] The Eleeakara market is, to all appearances, an indigenous market, catering for sundry foodstuffs, particularly basic agricultural products of the people – namely, maize and cassava. It is also a voluntary association.

The membership of the market association stands at about 1,000, though not many more than 500 attend meetings regularly. Members are also to be found in Lagos and Ibadan, although they seldom attend meetings. Membership is open to men and women, and all ages work together. A major source of finance is the ₦1 per member contributed at meetings (1993 rate). When this researcher suggested that the amount was very small, the chairman replied that the association does not want to hurt its people. This was a run-of-the-mill contribution, however. For big occasions, a special levy of ₦10 was being imposed.

The association meets every other Tuesday. Officers of the association are elected by a show of hands, though there are no constitutional provisions concerning terms of office and related matters. In the beginning, representatives from Oyo, Ilora and Lagos sat on the executive. Now, the elections are a purely local affair. The last elections were held in 1987, suggesting that as long as the executive has the confidence of the assembly it could hold on to power. At Ibadan, women used to sit on the executive, but they did not go to Jobele with the men. Even though women had never had a representative on the executive, there were hardly any rumblings in their camp. The chairman of the market believed that this was due to the fact that everybody has a voice at meetings. There would probably be no protest if a woman were to be elected chairperson of the market.[34]

Stealing in the market is viewed with all seriousness and suspects are handed over to the police – who, however, cannot arrest any suspected thief without recourse to the approval of the market executives. When two members fight each other, the conflict is settled amicably since it is considered a 'trade dispute'.

National Union of Road Transport Workers (NURTW), Afijio branch

This branch of the NURTW was established in 1989, at first under the aegis of the Oyo branch, but later receiving the recognition of Afijio LGA. The branch has the primary function, as does the union elsewhere, of catering for the welfare of road transport workers as well as protecting their corporate existence and interest. It groups all road transport workers in the LGA. There are no female members. The age distribution is between 20 and 50 years.[35] The union is not indigenous but merely a response to the impact and reality of modernization and urbanization. Membership is compulsory, including attendance at meetings.

The major sources of revenue generation are the daily contribution of ₦5 for each member's vehicle and a ₦2 daily levy charged on every commercial vehicle plying Ilora town and its environs (1993 rates). The proceeds of the latter levy were divided into two equal parts for the union and the LGA, while from the union's share the chairman of Oyo local government council received a monthly stipend of 5 per cent, in recognition of his former role as benefactor. For big projects, there is continuous levying according to economic power. At the time of this research, a union office was under construction at an estimated cost of ₦500,000. Union officials complained that even with a well-publicized launching ceremony in February 1993, the local government council did not donate anything to their cause. Expressed differently, the union receives little or no aid from the LGA at Jobele. Although the union held its meetings every Thursday at Jobele, at the time of this research there were signs of disenchantment among members over alleged broken promises and near-indifference to the union's plight on the part of the council executive.[36] Leaders are elected for a renewable four-year term. The union has six executive members: chairman, vice-chairman, deputy chairman, secretary, auditor and treasurer. Though idle officers can be removed from office, there is as yet no precedent.

Association of Automobile Engineers (Mechanics), Afijio, Ilora

The mechanics' profession strongly emphasizes seniority, on the basis that the older you are, the better, the more competent (and perhaps also the merrier) you become. This attitude has implications for the internal governance pattern in the association. Youths between 25 and 35 years are more numerous than adults and elderly people, even though the latter tend to dominate by virtue of seniority and age.[37] Members number about a hundred, but not all attend meetings. One reason for this is the harsh economic climate which has forced many a craftsman to diversify into farming and other activities. Membership is voluntary. The association is indigenous, but the profession is less so.

A source of finance is the ₦1 contribution levied at every meeting, while for special occasions and projects further levies are imposed; and a ₦5 fine payable by any executive member absent from three consecutive meetings (1993 rates). Meetings are held fortnightly on Thursdays. While the association believes in electing its officers, pride of place is given to senior mechanics who have a good record. Officers are elected for a renewable two-year period. As indicated above, erring officers can be removed from office and this has happened in the past, though the vice-chairman did not want to be drawn into details.

The association was planning, at the time of this research, an internal cooperative society on the model of its Oyo parent body.

Youth Tailoring Association, Ilora

An Afijio Tailoring Association was established in 1972. Its members are concentrated in Ilora, where there are at least five smaller groups of tailors and, since the second half of the 1980s, fashion designers. Two of these groups are made up exclusively of women.

The parent body, like others, sends two representatives to the LGA meeting every last Saturday of the month. It also organizes an internal cooperative in which members can be loaned up to ₦1,000. But the association does not purchase machines for its members.

As the name suggests, all the members are young, and the chairman in 1993 was about 36 years old.[38] There were 40 members, consisting of 32 women and eight men. This female numerical superiority was not, however, translated into superior authority for the women. The adviser of the association was around 60 years old. It is an indigenous association, membership in which is considered compulsory. Indeed, at the local level, members are more loyal and committed to associational life and goals than at zonal and state levels. In any event, to practise tailoring successfully in Ilora it is imperative to join one of the five groups.

The major source of finance is the freedom ceremonies of graduating apprentices. Tailors wield significant power in this context. Money so realized goes to the association, rather than to the boss of the apprentice.

Other sources are the contribution per member on meeting days (₦1) and the ₦10 fine imposed on erring executive and other members of the association (1993 rates).

Meetings of the association are held fortnightly on Wednesdays. Election of leaders is by consensus, rather than by voting. Seven offices are usually filled: chairman, vice-chairman, secretary, treasurer, assistant-secretary, PRO and auditor. The election is for one year in the first instance, but renewable twice.

Ifedawapo Contribution Society, Ilora

This is a traditional credit institution. It was established in 1991 with a view to taking care of the deficiencies observed in the individual lending system. The society in Ilora has only six members, none of whom is female. The total membership of such societies in the LGA is not known. My respondent, the chairman, is also the oldest member of the society.[39] The association is at once indigenous and voluntary. In 1993, contributions were pegged at ₦5, payable during meetings, plus a levy of ₦100 for special occasions such as weddings, and fines were ₦5 for absence from meetings and ₦50 for absence without an excuse. Furthermore, according to the traditions and logic of the society, the contribution of the first day belongs to the collector.

The society meets every fortnight on Saturdays. The officers are the chairman, vice-chairman, secretary and treasurer.

Political empowerment

In mid-August 1993, at the time this investigation was conducted, both the Social Democratic Party (SDP) and the National Republican Convention (NRC) boasted significant membership in Afijio LGA. The local party chairman gave figures of 7,681 for the SDP and 5,182 for the NRC; if correct, this meant that total party registered membership was 12,863, or 17 per cent of the official population.[40] The greater strength of the SDP was shown by the party's dominance of the elected LGA council; it had seven councillors to the NRC's five and therefore also held the posts of LGA chairman and vice-chairman.

While women were quite significantly represented at the membership level (SDP: 45 per cent; NRC 28 per cent), their representation in the leadership was less than 5 per cent at ward level and 7 per cent (1 of 14) at LGA level. At the state election to the House of Assembly, the SDP and NRC put forward two representatives each, while the SDP won one seat. All of them were male.

As already described, the Afijio LGA manages, through its Descendants' Union, to depoliticize local issues and, by so doing, to give a semblance of popular satisfaction. Other factors work in favour of the LGA: a common history of struggle; a more or less homogeneous culture; and the faithfulness of founding fathers, elders and community leaders to formal and informal arrangements of power-sharing and patronage balancing. Consequently, unless fuelled by external interference, no local issue, however controversial or volatile, has ever developed into strike actions, demonstrations or boycotts with a clear-cut partisan political colouration.

The Afijio LGA is, moreover, a former area of the Unity Party of Nigeria (UPN). It appeared that the SDP had inherited the UPN's structure, resources, people and goodwill, while the NRC did not appear to have any 'resource persons' in the area and could not therefore lay claim to electoral malpractice by the SDP for the purpose of voiding an election in the LGA. It had never happened and its likelihood appeared extremely remote. During the nation-wide teachers' strike in 1992, however, due to non-payment of salaries, political meanings were read into it to the effect that NRC sympathizers had instigated the strike. It was no more than an allegation and the accusers soon became wiser.[41]

Economic empowerment

Access to means of production

It was generally believed that access to land in the area was relatively easy because the local government council had encouraged investors to take advantage of available land. An investor could apply to the council for land through the town planning department, or, in more rural settlements, obtain land through village heads.

Cooperative societies provided some credit, however little, to their members. The BLP in the area had helped some women to obtain credit facilities. For instance, cooperative groups such as Ifesowapo (consisting of about 70 members) and Binukonu (68 members) as well as organized BLP cooperative groups in Fiditi, Aawe and Oreofe had collected loans worth ₦5,000 loans or were about to do so.[42]

Access to inputs such as fertilizer, chemicals and seeds was difficult for all kinds of farmers. While council officials said that fertilizer could be obtained easily through OYSADEP, the reality on the ground was more frustrating. Larger-scale farmers of cassava, maize, cowpea, yam or melon, who need several tons of fertilizer per year, were getting only an insignificant percentage from the authorities. An educated large-scale farmer indicated that in 1992 he needed no fewer than 30 tons of fertilizer but actually received only two tons – and this after queuing for several days. He had to team up with colleagues to purchase the remainder from Lagos, Kwara and Ondo States. It is worth pointing out that with fertilizer a large-scale farmer can cultivate between 70 and 100 acres but, in its absence, can only be productive from between 30 and 40 acres.[43]

Chemicals, too, had become extremely expensive and therefore out of reach for poor, albeit serious farmers. While Citrazine (powder and liquid) was sold at the government price of ₦70.50 per kilogram in February 1993, by the following month the price had more than doubled to ₦155 and a scarcity had developed, forcing farmers to buy the product at more than ₦350 per kilogram. Similar price rises affected all other chemicals.[44] Farmers in the LGA had tractors but few caterpillar vehicles. The council had only one functional tractor, so most of the tractors were privately owned.[45] It is often said about, and in, Ilora that there are more tractors than taxis in the town.[46] The council hired out its sole tractor at the rate of ₦150 per acre for farmers and ₦200 per acre for private entrepreneurs.

Income distribution

Most members of the LGA are from the middle and lower classes, but there are no sharp divisions in status. Those who are very rich and affluent do not live in the area. Chief Folawiyo, for instance, does not even have a house in Ilora, his home town. Poverty is not too visible, but people feed mainly on starch, perhaps three times daily. The pathetic picture in the cities may not yet have reached Afijio LGA. Moreover, extended families live in compounds and help one another.

Gender-related obstacles

Access to land, credit, inputs and technology are denied to women, not necessarily because of gender, but perhaps more because of the relative scarcity of some of these means of production. Nevertheless, there are traditional, cultural and communal biases against women which only further education and public enlightenment can minimize.

In Afijio LGA, Christianity (specifically, the Baptist Church) has helped to reduce the rough edges of rampant polygamy. Since Christians are more numerous than Muslims,[47] some of the difficult gender-related obstacles seen elsewhere in Nigeria are absent.

The BLP has been of some help in this direction. Through it, women have improved access to land. In Fiditi, a vegetable garden is situated in a choice area of the town that is very much in demand, with the land reserved for the women.

Accountability and transparency

During this research, it was possible to identify several mechanisms for monitoring the performance of elected officials and personnel of the local government. They could be identified in the following theoretical terms:

1 The legislative arm of government was expected to formulate by-laws and keep a close watch on the executive;

2 Organized community leaders made requests based on the needs of their community;

3 The electorate decided whether elected officials from their areas were living up to expectation; and

4 The political parties could be held to their programmes and manifestoes.

Despite the semblance of accountability, however, the legislative council had been anything but effective. There was a general perception that the chairman had succeeded in subduing the legislature. One reason had to do with the calibre of its members. Perhaps another was the need to balance the demands of the SDP and NRC legislators. Nevertheless, when NRC members complained genuinely about projects or other matters, the chairman's reaction often led to accusations of crass and unprincipled partisanship on his part.[48]

Moreover, few members of the legislative council were educated, articulate or confident enough to defend constitutional responsibility. A constitutional requirement, that the executive should brief the legislature on income and expenditure on a monthly basis, was not followed. Again, political appointments by the chairman were not ratified by the house, as should have been the case. In 1993, the five supervisors (including the vice-chairman) had been serving without being sworn in.

The monitoring role of the community leaders was not followed either. They seemed more interested in seeing their own long list of requests granted – VIP toilets, roads, contracts – than in ensuring the council's accountability or transparency. As for the monitoring role of the electorate, this was restricted through lack of practice. At best, when the chairman was on familiarization tours, members of the electorate lodged complaints about dispensary or maternity officials who had been absent from their duty posts.

The political parties, meanwhile, had little control over their elected officials in the council. The major area in which the SDP had been important, for example, was the evaluation of the extent to which its free education programme at the primary school level was being faithfully implemented. In Afijio LGA, the programme was being implemented but inadequate facilities and materials – like textbooks, exercise books and pencils – had slowed things down. The military government directive that local government councils would not fund primary schools had done little to help matters. The SDP administration in Afijio LGA had been catering for the primary education of all communities, irrespective of party leanings.

The local government council had no mechanism for monitoring the performance of social/political and economic organizations, although one could have been installed when security reports so dictated.[49] No sanctions had been applied for poor accountability, perhaps because of a preference for informal ways of settling differences, disputes and crises.

Government institutions

MAMSER

MAMSER is credited with the mobilization of the people for participation in the 1991 census and with various enlightenment campaigns during elections. It is difficult, however, to assess the exact role of the directorate in the fluctuating fortunes of the electorate in the elections. When there was a reasonably high turn-out of voters, MAMSER claimed it was responsible. The directorate organized at least one workshop in each of the ten wards of the LGA to help the electorate assess the stewardship of elected officials, in order to enhance accountability.[50]

DFRRI

The DFRRI specialized in the areas of water supply and road rehabilitation.[51] At Oniwasu, it established a rural community development centre to provide vocational training in farming and the making of burnt bricks and local water pipes. It attracted General Ibrahim Babangida during his visit to Oyo State in August 1991, and also attracted visitors from outside Nigeria.[52]

The DFRRI was considered by some indigenes of Afijio LGA to be distant from the people, however, perhaps because it did not give loans to farmers and had no representative in the LGA. Some people complained that its only involvement in food was its annual agricultural exhibition during which people were trained in rarified farming practices such as snail-rearing and the management of grass-cutters.

Better Life Programme (BLP)

The BLP commenced in Afijio LGA in August 1989, coordinated by Mrs A. A. Ipadeola, with 40 members. According to its current coordinator, as of 1993 the achievements of the BLP in the area included the establishment of 15 BLP cooperative groups: four in Ilora and environs (Kajola, Ifesowapo, and Imini); three in Fiditi (and Iware); six in Aawe (and Abadapo) and one each in Jobele and Akinmorin. Some cooperatives secured bank loans through the mediation of the BLP. Projects included *gari*-processing centres (Ilu-Aje, Ilora and Abadapo), a pre-season vegetable farm (*Efo Akuo*) in Fiditi, and a new farm acquired at Ajegunle (Aawe).

A Better Life nursery school located at Akinmorin was functional until 1991 when the initial coordinator stepped aside for undisclosed reasons without handing over to the executive. A goat-rearing scheme in Jobele took off with an initial grant of ₦5,000, but the beneficiaries had not given progress reports at meetings.[53]

National Directorate of Employment (NDE)

This directorate was reputed to be of great service in the LGA. It gave both group and individual loans. For example, the Ore-Ofe Cooperative at Aawe got a loan of ₦5,000 to start a business venture, while several individuals had been loaned various amounts ranging from ₦500 to ₦1,000. Group loans attracted an interest rate of 9 per cent.

Banking

The People's Bank had granted loans to cooperative societies. For example, Binukonu Cooperative was loaned ₦5,000 in March 1993. Its interest rate was, at 15 per cent, higher than that of the NDE but much lower than that of the commercial banks. At the time of this research, the bank had granted no fewer than 150 loans. The Community Bank in the area was opened only in 1992 and it was yet to make its impact felt at the time of this research.

Conclusion

There is little doubt that the various social, economic and political organizations contribute significantly to an improvement in the standard of living of their members, in particular, and the people in the Afijio LGA in general. As indicated in various sections of this case study, virtually all professional organizations, even those without any overt economic objectives, organize one form or the other of cooperative or welfare schemes for their members. There is a crisscrossing of membership between traditional and modern institutions, as people try to cushion the deleterious effects of poverty. Most organizations see themselves more as a social and economic security system than as an agency or catalyst for political participation. Herein lies a critical problem, that of widespread political inactivity.

A factor common to the internal organization of virtually all the associations studied is their failure to follow laid-down or agreed procedures for control and sanction of leaders, as well as for regular elections. The ready-made response of members to queries on this issue is that there is no need to change a successful team. The ADU, the umbrella organization for the indigenes of the LGA is, perhaps not by sheer coincidence, a prototype of such so-called apolitism. The consequence of this disposition is that the leadership is, in general, at once oligarchic and gerontocratic. Although the right to elect and change leaders at regular intervals constitutes a building block of democracy, the membership has become lethargic and dull, while the danger is ever-present for the leadership, however responsive and responsible at first, to become complacent. The leadership is neither challenged nor resisted. The finding of Joel Barkan *et al.* seems corroborated here, to wit, 'participation is voluntary, but not equal and there is a tendency towards élite rule'.[54]

This phenomenon has a wider implication than initial appearances disclose. Citizens or members who find it difficult to ensure observance of democratic norms and values within their association or organization will, in all likelihood, find it harder still to press for the same at the level of government, whether local, state or national. Indeed, in relation to the state system, virtually all respondents expressed their helplessness in the face of the growing insensitivity and irrelevance of that system to their needs, demands and rights. This apparent culture of helplessness makes corruption a widespread phenomenon. It is all too easy to fall victim to official 'settlement' devices or simply to join an official looting clique, rather than to confront and expose it, when one feels there is no alternative to so doing.

While the people and their associations are politically inactive, they do not have a welfare mentality. Having been too disappointed by the inactivity of the state, the people do not expect any help from elsewhere and are ever eager to take their future in their own hands. The horizon of this initiative, however, is severely limited to sheer survival and short-term planning.

It remains to be determined which of the three major types of effort has served the community best: individual; communal/community; or local government/state. While our research findings point in a certain direction – that is, towards the first two – this should be regarded as merely indicative and tentative. A more detailed investigation is called for. In the interim, the point can be made that town unions, development councils and economic organizations play an important role in the affairs of their communities, especially in terms of: infrastructural development; community-social functions; traditional governance (this for them seems to represent an important form of political participation); and zoning of offices to wards and major towns – an experience much in vogue in the larger national political life.

In a sense, the professional, social, economic and traditional organizations studied here can be said to represent a means to an end – a means, in a way, of putting the people first. To that extent, the organizations appear human-centred, even though the people themselves do not seem prepared as yet to move beyond this facility to seize the initiative for political purposes. In other words, while the sphere of civil society is being extended, and the system is seemingly becoming more pluralistic, democratization and popular participation appear to be a long way off.[55]

A final point must be made about the difficulty of gathering data in rural communities. Such communities urgently need to set up or strengthen local data gathering capacity which could provide administrative records, surveys and other information sources for development planning, implementation and monitoring.

Notes

1 See Timothy Mitchell, 'The limits of the state: beyond statist approaches and their critics', *American Political Science Review*, 85, 1 (March 1991), pp. 77–96.

2 See J. F. Bayart, A. Mbembe and C. Toulabor, *La Politique par le bas en Afrique Noire*, (Paris: Ed Karthala, 1992).

3 Alain Touraine, *La Voix et le regard* (Paris: Le Seint, 1978), p. 81.
4 Michel Foucault, *La Volonté de savoir* (Paris: Gallimard, 1976), p. 125.
5 See Archie Mafeje, 'On "icon" and African perspectives on democracy: a commentary on Jibrin Ibrahim's views', *CODESRIA Bulletin*, 2 (1993), p. 19.
6 Mitchell, *op. cit.*
7 Alfred Stephan, *Rethinking Military Politics: Brazil and the Southern Cone* (Princeton, N. J.: Princeton University Press, 1988), pp. 3–4.
8 P. P. Ekeh, 'The constitution of civil society in African history and politics', in B. Caron *et al.* (eds), *Democratic Transition in Africa* (Ibadan: CREDU Documents in Social Sciences and Humanities, 1992), p. 190.
9 A. Adedeji, *The African Alternative: Putting the People First* (Arusha: United Republic of Tanzania, 1990), p. 18.
10 See *African Charter for Popular Participation in Development* (Arusha: 1990).
11 A. Adedeji, *op.cit.*
12 It is claimed by the people that both Chief Awolowo and Governor Bola Ige recognized the genuiness of their grievances – based as they are, on superior education *vis-à-vis* Oyo – but pacified them on the grounds that whereas 'Afijio people are well-educated, the Oyo people like to be kings and princes.' Interview with S. O. Ogunrombi, a former Secretary (1981–3) of the Afijio Descendants' Union, Jobele, 16 August 1993.
13 Both Chief F. O. Owolabi, chairman of the council, and Mr Ogunlade, zonal director of NPC (Ibadan), confirmed this account in separate interviews in August 1993. The dispute arose against the background of a diminishing population. According to the 1963 census, the area's population was 112,218.
14 See Federal Republic of Nigeria, *The Report of the National Inventory of Community Based Infrastructural Facilities in Afijio LG Area of Oyo State* (Lagos: The Presidency, 1991), p. 15.
15 Interview with Alani Bamgbose, information officer, Afijio local government council, 30 July 1993.
16 Interviews held 15 and 16 September 1993 with several personnel of the LGA and Education Department.
17 *Ibid.*
18 Personal information, 16 August 1993.
19 Interview with Kunle Oyekola, the vice-chairman of the local government council, 3 August 1993. He is also an executive of the Ilora Youth Development Association (IYDA), the youth wing of the Ilora Development Association (IDA).
20 Interview with Bamgbose, *op. cit.* (see note 15).
21 See Joel D. Barkan, Michael L. McNulty and M. A. O. Ayeni, '"Hometown" voluntary associations, local development and the emergence of civil society in Western Nigeria', *The Journal of Modern African Studies*, 29, 3 (1991), pp. 457–80.
22 Leading, old personalities in Ilora like Chief Odeleye, a founding father of IDA, who could have been more specific in this context could not be reached in spite of repeated visits. When Chief Odeleye was eventually at home, no interview could be granted as he was bereaved. (Ilora home of Chief Odeleye, Tuesday, 17 August and Wednesday, 18 August 1993).
23 According to Ilora mythology, Akibio was the founder of Ilora town.
24 I use the term 'age grade' somewhat suggestively, since no one uses it in the town and no one made any allusion, however timid, to it during my investigation. (I owe this point to my colleague, Dr 'Bayo Okunade, an Aawe indigene, and to some interviewees on 15 September 1993.)
25 Interview with Mr Oyekola. See note 19.

26 Interview with Mr S. O. Ogunrombi, see note 12. He also talked about another Ajao, a chief from Aawe, very rich, who contributed immensely, financially speaking, to the growth of the union. According to him, Pa Ajao from Fiditi was a great activist. More poignantly, Mr Ogunrombi as well as virtually all elders interviewed were irritated by the turn of events against Afijio *vis-à-vis* Oyo. They claimed that as far back as 1944 Afijio was supplying foodstuffs to Oyo. Today's seeming 'subsuming' under Oyo is alleged to have been made possible by various governments at Ibadan – the political, administrative and economic headquarters of the then Western Region, later Western State and now Oyo State.

27 Interview with Sanya Adeyemo, a personnel officer, Afijio LG, 16 August 1993.

28 Interviews with Messrs Oyekola and Ogunrombi.

29 Interview with Rogba Olutunde, 5 August 1993.

30 Interview with Mrs Ogundiran, chairperson of COWAD in Afijio LGA on 6 August 1993. Mrs A. Okelola and Mrs F. Sholola provided considerable assistance.

31 Interview with Mrs Adewoyin and Mrs Ogunrinola, president and vice-president respectively of WIA, 17 August 1993.

32 *Ibid.* We visited the centre, located about 300 metres from the main Fiditi–Jobele–Oyo road.

33 An attempt made by the researcher to interview officers of these professional groups was gently rebuffed by the mechanics within the market, Jobele, 9 August 1993.

34 Interview with the chairman of the Eleeakara Market, Alhaji Raimi Asipa, 10 August 1993. I thank him most sincerely for the warm reception given to me as well as the informative guided tour of the extensive market. The latter is planned in three phases and only the first one is currently in use.

35 Interview with the union's vice-chairman and auditor in company of four other members, 11 August 1993, at their Oke-Aje office.

36 *Ibid.* The council chairman, Chief Owolabi, claimed, however, that much work (for example, the construction of a small 'shopping complex', the sinking of wells, etc.) had been done in Ilora. It is perhaps judicious to add that the Ilora people, coming from the most populated part of the LGA, believed that they were responsible for the electoral victory of the chairman, an Aawe man. Interview with Chief Owolabi at Jobele, 17 August 1993.

37 The vice-chairman of the association, to whom I spoke is, himself, a representative of the 'new breed' generation of automobile mechanics in the area. Interview at Ilora, 11 August 1993.

38 Interview with a founding member of the association, Ilora, 13 August 1993.

39 Interview with the chairman, Ifedawapo Contribution Society, Ilora, 13 August 1993.

40 Interview with the two chairmen, respectively in Ilora and Aawe, on 15 and 16 August 1993.

41 *Ibid.*

42 Interview with Mrs F. Sholola, community development officer, Afijio local government council, 2 August 1993. Compare this with claims by some cooperatives that the BLP had been of little or no use to them.

43 Interview with Pa Oyekola at Ilora on 18 August 1993.

44 *Ibid.*

45 Pa Oyekola has two personal tractors, for instance.

46 Personal information, Ilora, August 1993.

47 This statement from some indigenes needs to be read with caution, at least until

the NPC publishes data with a detailed breakdown of the population.

48 I thank my various interviewees for their frankness. I cannot mention their names for obvious reasons.

49 Personal information, Jobele, August 1993.

50 Interview with different personalities in the local government headquarters, August 1993.

51 *Ibid.*

52 I undertook a guided visit to the centre on 16 August 1993, only to find the gates under lock and key around 4 p.m. The information was that office hours last till 5 p.m.

53 Interview with Mrs Sholola, Jobele, 2 August 1993

54 Joel D. Barkan, *et al.*, *op. cit.*, p. 478.

55 On the specific Nigerian example, see 'Kunle Amuwo, 'Treetop politics versus grassroots democracy in Nigeria: some theoretical and methodological queries', *Africa*, XLVII, 4 (December 1992), pp. 617–26; and 'Kunle Amuwo, 'Transition planning in Nigeria: a critique of the civil-military transiting variant', *Africa Development*, XVIII, 1 (1993), pp. 87–98.

6

Women and Empowerment in Dekina, Kogi State

SAMUEL EGWU

The legitimacy of the post-colonial state, derived from its interventionist role in the development process and the provision of social services, has waned considerably. In the specific context of structural adjustment, people are confronted by the phenomena of minimum government and the irrelevant state as a result of the enforcement of market rationality in the economic and political spheres.

In Nigeria, military dictatorship has dominated the political space for the better part of the post-colonial period, with the attendant consequence of militarizing the society. The inability of the civil society to assert itself *vis-à-vis* the state is also a direct consequence of prolonged military rule. The vast majority of the people are not only apathetic and alienated from the state; they have also been brutalized by its enormous coercive and extractive capacities.

There is clear evidence of a deepening crisis of governance and the failure to introduce democratic practices at all levels, with an adverse impact on the development process. Furthermore, the inherited model of development has not placed a premium on the involvement and mobilization of the people to ensure social transformation. Thus, the African Charter for Popular Participation in Development[1] asserts that Africa's environmental and ecological crisis cannot be solved in the absence of a process of sustainable development which commands the full support and participation of the people.

The most acute reflection of the crisis of development can be found in the rural areas, whose predominant peasant populations are located farthest from the centres of power. An examination of the economic and political dynamics of the rural areas, where the vast majority of the population live, can illuminate the possibility as well as the danger in accomplishing the twin tasks of democratization and development. The starting point is the inherent creative and organizational capacity of the people for their own survival, particularly outside of the formal governmental structure or the domain of the state.

In studying popular organizations for these purposes, some pertinent questions have to be answered. To what extent are these organizations democratic and, therefore, likely to serve as harbingers of democracy and genuine development? What is their level of autonomy from the state? To what extent do they resist excesses of the state or are they agents for the extension of the hegemony of the state? These are some of the questions posed by this case study.

Popular organizations attract members of the general public by reason of their open membership, mass-oriented goals and objectives, modes of goal attainment and distribution of the social product. These grassroots organizations inundate contemporary Nigeria – urban and rural. In the rural areas, in particular, they range from small mutual support networks and village welfare associations to resource mobilization (credit) societies and cooperatives. There are trade union organizations of local government and road transport workers, and various guild and craft bodies. All these constitute the veritable organs of civil society in the countryside and play useful roles in the process of democratization and development. The internal organizations of people-based associations are perceived as schools for democracy at the grassroots.

The concept of development provides a meeting point for popular participation and democratization. But if development is to be meaningful, it must also ensure a balanced spread of politico–economic benefits to reduce class, gender and other forms of social inequality. This case study examines these questions with reference to the Dekina LGA of Kogi State.

Basic socio-economic indicators

Dekina is one of the 16 LGAs that constitute Kogi State. It is one of the oldest local governments, created in 1969 under the then Kwara State administration, but it has remained one of the least developed with a dearth of modern facilities such as electricity, pipe-borne water and telephones. It is predominantly rural. Dekina town, the LGA headquarters, is not listed among urban areas because its rural situation and unique historical and geographical factors have militated against rapid population growth.

The 1991 provisional census figure put the population of the LGA at 201,682 – 53 per cent male and 47 per cent female – but this result is still subject to dispute. Dekina LGA is currently made up of eight districts. The major language spoken is Igala, 98 per cent of the population being Igala by ethnic origin. The LGA is also home to small numbers of people from other groups such as Bassa-Nge, Bassa Nkomo and Igbo.

Education

Over the years, modest progress has been made in the expansion of educational institutions. There are 138 primary schools with 1,420 trained teachers; 20 secondary schools; and one vocational school, Odu Technical School at Odu Ogboyaga, some 20 kilometres from the local government headquarters. There are also about 253 adult classes with 124 instructors.

Health

Government-owned medical institutions are inadequate and poorly funded. They include two general hospitals at Dekina and Iyale. A comprehensive health centre is located at Abocho. Almost every village has a clinic, manned by a dispensary attendant and at least two untrained attendants. Presently, a total of 138 such clinics are operating, with 613 health personnel attending to minor health problems and offering health education to rural dwellers. Another three fledgling hospitals are run by both Catholic and Protestant missions and there are a number of burgeoning private clinics. On the whole, there is an acute shortage of medical facilities. Access is made difficult by the concentration of these institutions in the semi-urban areas and the rising cost of medication.

Potable water

Access to potable water is poor throughout the LGA. Only three major towns, Ayangba, Dekina and Egume, have pipe-borne water. Even then, the taps are often dry. A few towns such as Abocho, Iyale and Ogane-Inigu have boreholes. In most cases, private water tankers undertake the bulk of water supply, particularly in the dry season. In the villages, people cover distances that range between two and ten kilometres to fetch water from flowing rivers, streams and ponds, depending on the season.

Energy

In terms of electricity, only Ayangba, a burgeoning commercial centre, and Egume are connected to the national grid. Dekina town is not, but it gets energy from a generator plant. Fuel supply is chaotic. The distribution of petrol, kerosene and gas is handled by seven oil distribution companies through their independent marketers concentrated in two towns, Ayangba and Dekina. Four of them are located at Ayangba and one each at Dekina, Egume and Abocho. The bulk of rural dwellers get their supplies of petrol and kerosene through retailers on the black market. Firewood is used for 80 per cent of domestic cooking.

Economic activities

Economic activities in the LGA are not well developed. For example, a survey of shops in the five major towns – Ayangba, Dekina, Iyale, Egume and Abocho – suggested that commercial activities were depressed. At the time of the survey several shops were closed, following the flight of Igbo traders to their states of origin in the wake of the political crisis that resulted from the annulment of the 12 June 1993 presidential elections. At Ayangba, 150 shops were counted. There were 40 in Dekina, 20 in Egume, 15 in Abocho and 11 at Iyale.

Industrial activity is virtually absent. The biggest industrial enterprise is the New Nigerian Timber Company at Okura-Lafia which produces high quality furniture and various sizes of planks for domestic and commercial purposes. It has a workforce of about 50 people. A *gari* processing mill is located at Odu-Igegeli. There is also Agy Limited, a small industry that handles the crushing and processing of palm kernel. Two palm oil processing mills at Ayangba and Egume-Achani ceased operation a few years before this study was undertaken.

Three commercial banks operate in the whole of the LGA. These are First Bank at Ayangba, ACB at Dekina and Union Bank at Egume. Three community banks have been established at Ayangba, Egume and Abocho.

Public facilities

Public facilities such as libraries, post offices and telephones are either in short supply or not available at all. The dearth of such public facilities shows the level of rural underdevelopment. There is only one public library, poorly stocked, located at the local government headquarters in Dekina. Dekina and Ayangba have post offices while Abocho and Egume are serviced by postal agencies. Telephones are not available throughout the LGA. Major towns such as Dekina, Ayangba, Iyale, Egume and Abocho have motor parks where vehicles can be boarded for a limited number of destinations within the LGA.

A total of nine courts of justice can be found in Dakina LGA. These include one high court, two magistrate courts and six grade II area courts.

Mass media

The general backwardness of Dekina LGA is marked by the absence of local newspapers and magazines. For a brief period, 1987–90, a local weekly paper, *Parrot*, was established to serve as propaganda organ for the LGA. Access to the national media is also poor. There are only two news stands in the LGA, at Ayangba and Dekina, and only at Ayangba can a variety of national dailies can be found.

Only a few parts of the LGA receive television broadcasts from Enugu while the absence of a booster station makes it difficult to receive NTA Lokoja, based in the state capital. But radio coverage is effective, from both Radio Nigeria and the local Kogi State radio. The latter, in particular, is a major source of information.

In the villages, town criers preponderate as the form of disseminating information. Usually on the authority of the village heads, town criers pass on vital information in the evenings.

Social and political organizations

Given the absence of state-organized welfare schemes across the country, it is not surprising that a variety of social and political organizations have emerged. The experience of Dekina LGA demonstrates the vibrancy of these forms of associational life in most rural areas. The organizations range from voluntary village welfare associations and kinship-based solidarity groups to women's and youth organizations. They are often multi-purpose in objectives and activities, which include social welfare and solidarity as well as reinforcing traditional social values and legitimizing the community social structure. In some instances, they perform economic functions. Although they are essentially non-political, they may seek to influence decision making at various levels and sometimes canvass support for candidates at elections.

Three broad types of social and political organizations can be identified. These include organizations of young people (18–35 years), women's organizations and non-governmental organizations (NGOs) such as social clubs which seek to influence public policy.

Youth/development associations

Youth organizations are largely village/community-based and are oriented towards development. Such groups have grown in size and influence since the 1980s, to the extent that every village now has its own youth/development association. Unlike the pattern that prevails in the eastern part of Nigeria, they are not organized along strict age lines. Membership is likely, however, to include most young men of between 18 and 35 years within each community. The associations mobilize the entire community in a wide range of activities – such as water management schemes, educational projects, construction (community roads, bridges and town halls) as well as cultural and social activities. In several instances, they handle petty criminal cases in the village, enforcing punishments and rewards without involving the police and the courts. In most cases, elders have come to recognize their role and have given them the freedom to operate. These associations have already supplanted the indigenous social organizations which used to handle some of the routine activities such as construction of roads and markets. Formerly, able-bodied men in the village were mobilized under the leadership of *Achokolobia* (the popularly acclaimed leader).

The organizations rely on formal and rather elaborate rules, in the form of constitutions and by-laws. The constitutions prescribe automatic membership for all the young people in the community – including the educated and uneducated – and specify the terms of office, membership fees and obligations, including punishments for fraudulent practices. It is worth observing that the survival and sustenance of this form of associational life might be better served by less formal networks.

In addition to the activities at the village level, these development associations have urban branches that are expected to identify with the programmes of improving village infrastructure and the general living standards of the community. There are also attempts by the élites to float similar organizations at the district level (examples include Biraidu Youths Association, Iyale Area Development Association and Ome Youths). These, however, are not mass-oriented and are not linked to village- or community-based youth movements.

Women's organizations

Women's organizations are the most entrenched and active social groups in the countryside. Although they existed before the Babangida administration introduced the BLP, the latter has been a profound influence. In the course of the survey, 272 women's groups were found to be registered by the LGA's Women's Development Unit. The introduction of the BLP in 1987 helped not only in encouraging women to organize but also in promoting accountability as BLP officials paid regular visits and checked their accounts. Women's organizations now exist in all the villages. Most are split along religious lines. Muslim women hold their meetings on Fridays while Christian women hold theirs on Saturdays and others on Sundays. The split is largely as a result of cultural factors such as polygamous family commitments and the kind of drinks that are preferred during meetings. Although membership is voluntary, the associations are restricted to housewives. A woman, once divorced, loses her membership. Most of the women are aged between 25 and 35 years.

The functions of these organizations include raising loans or credits for financially handicapped members and mutual assistance during burials and weddings as well as economic activities. Since the introduction of the BLP, women have been organized in weaving, *gari* processing and retail trade. As a result of the economic crisis, some women have diversified into farming to help in the maintenance of their households. Through the influence of BLP, women are now encouraged to collect certificates of occupancy for family land, although this confronts cultural inhibitions. Igala tradition does not allow women to engage in farming or allow them titles to land.

Women have started, through their organizations, to provide a number of essential social services. In Dekina town, for example, women have pressured the local government authority to take over funding of a nursery school they established. Similarly, Ameko women in Aocho have embarked on setting up a nursery school.

The organizations are funded through membership dues (in 1993 it was ₦2 paid at regular intervals). Dues may be paid every five or nine days. It would appear on the surface that the organizations are sustained by an open method of administration and democratic principles, particularly in view of the supervisory role played by the Women's Development Unit, which is responsible to the Commission for Women at the state level.

Meetings are held regularly, not less frequently than three times a month. Some organizations are governed by formal rules which prescribe the qualifications for membership, election of leaders and punishment for deviants. The most prevalent practice, however, is to endorse women who have a local reputation for honesty. Even though leadership changes are expected at the end of a two-year term, it is common to find that some women do not relinquish their leadership. Frequent cases of leaders violating the by-laws were mentioned by BLP officials in Dekina.

Women's organizations, as they exist today, are markedly different from what they were in the pre-BLP days when the organizations were financed by vote-seeking politicians during the Second Republic. They are now independent of politicians, though they are willing to support candidates that would support women's groups.

Social clubs

Clubs with a preponderantly youthful membership exist in virtually all parts of the LGA. However, many are concentrated in semi-urban areas, where they are concerned with local affairs. At the time of the survey, 25 such social clubs were identified. Membership is not only voluntary but also open to males and females between the ages of 16 and 30 years. In practice only educated members of society join these clubs.

The activities of the social clubs are financed through membership dues, fines, special levies and donations from public-spirited individuals. In some instances, they raise funds by organizing social and cultural activities such as dances and performances. The mode of governance varies from one club to another. Some hold their meetings every fortnight, others every month. Elections are used to choose leaders. The constitution of each club specifies appropriate punishments for offences such as embezzlement of club money.

The objectives of the clubs are numerous and essentially philanthropic. Apart from promoting the unity of youths in their various localities, they mobilize resources for the needy including orphanage homes. They are also concerned with the physical development of their areas and often make representations to the local government authority on behalf of the people.

Although club constitutions express their non-political and non-partisan character, they are nevertheless involved in politics. The manner and level of involvement varies. From interviews with leaders of some of the social clubs in Egume, Olowa and Dekina, it was clear that members had given block support to particular candidates of political parties.

Economic organizations

The existence of a variety of economic organizations in the LGA attests to the importance of the rural sector. Economic organizations found in the LGA include farmer's associations, production and marketing cooperatives, resource mobilization and credit schemes.

Farmers' associations and cooperatives

Farmer groups are perhaps one of the oldest forms of associational life in Dekina LGA. There are no women members as tradition excludes women from participation in farming.

Our findings suggested that farmers' associations may have existed in virtually all the villages. About 280 such organizations were thought to exist, each with a membership of between 20 and 35 farmers. Many associations were formed in the Second Republic between 1979 and 1983, largely to secure inputs such as fertilizers and insecticides and to obtain loans from the Nigerian Agricultural and Cooperative Bank (NACB). At the time of our investigation, however, it appeared that many of them had become dormant and that some of them had held no meetings for several years. Even the most viable association at Okowowolo in the Biraidu area of Dekina (which owed its existence to the land development scheme of the World Bank-backed Ayangba Agricultural Development Project), suffered the same fate. Here, in 1987, the cooperating farmers shared their assets and dissolved the society.

The leadership of farmers' associations tends to be controlled by rural élites who do not share the experience of the small landholding peasants who constitute the bulk of the rural population. The incidence of embezzlement by leaders and the bureaucratic hurdles in obtaining loans and credits from banks and the NACB frustrated the members, who now may have lost interest.

Cooperative societies

Cooperative societies are an alternative form of association in the rural areas of the LGA. They include registered and non-registered cooperatives, which may be production-oriented, market-inclined or multi-purpose. Some draw their members from a particular sex, age bracket or religion. At the time of our survey, 55 cooperative societies were found in the LGA, many of which were formed in 1988 and 1989. A major fillip for the proliferation of cooperatives was the awareness that government support for development could only be channelled through such bodies.

The need for efficiency and profit maximization tends to impose on the cooperatives a measure of formality and relative dependence on external sources of inputs and political legitimacy.[2] Most of them have by-laws and are registered with the state cooperative office through the local government authority. Their leadership is elected and they maintain bank accounts.

The aims and objectives of the cooperative societies are varied. For example, the objectives of the Abocho Women's Seamstress Cooperative Society include obtaining loans at reasonable interest, issuing shares and contracting loans, as well as arranging for sales of members' produce at the best price and providing facilities for deposits and savings for members. Etiaja Women's Multi-Purpose Society undertakes on behalf of members the marketing of produce, using capital which individual members cannot provide, and it organizes training. Most of the cooperative societies hold meetings regularly to review performance, to set new objectives and to strengthen mutual self-help. Elections are held every two or three years.

Given the relatively recent spread of these societies, it is not easy to evaluate their performance, although they have the potential to boost rural production, marketing and credits. They have contributed to an increase in economic activities, especially among women in such fields as soap making, marketing, weaving and *gari* processing. Careful and responsible supervision by the local government unit in charge of cooperatives could be of significant service.

Marketing associations

Women's and men's marketing associations are largely confined to major towns with large markets such as Ayangba, Dekina and Abocho. Six different types, organized around particular commodities, were found: *Gari* Sellers' Association; Palm Oil Sellers' Association (women only); Palm Kernel Dealers' Association; Fish Sellers' Association (women only); and Palm Produce Buyers' Association.

The *Gari* Sellers' Association in Ayangba had a membership of 90, including men and women, while its counterparts at Abocho and Dekina had 25 and 33 members respectively. The Palm Kernel Dealers' Association had 200 members in Ayangba, 150 members in Abocho and 100 members in Dekina. Membership of all the associations is voluntary. In fact, sellers of the various commodities who are not registered members of the associations are allowed to operate in the market, although they do not enjoy the protection of the associations when they encounter problems.

The main objectives of these associations is the stabilization of the prices of each commodity. Consequently, price hiking constitutes an offence which is sanctioned. The Palm Produce Buyers' Association ensures that only its members buy palm products which are in turn sold through local purchase order and other arrangements to crushers such as Lever Brothers or River Vegetable Oil Company.

Most of the associations have formal rules although informal networks appear to be the more viable mode of governance. Meetings are held regularly. Among the *gari* sellers, such meetings are held on the eve of every market. During such meetings in 1993, each member paid a due of ₦5. For the Palm Kernel Dealers' Association, meetings are held every nine days. Changes in leadership, through elections, are effected every two or three years.

Credit institutions

The proliferation of mutual credit institutions for the purpose of resource mobilization for individuals underlines the importance of the informal sector of the rural economy. The various forms of savings and credit associations existing in Dekina LGA today are traditional to the Igala-speaking people, among whom they have several names. In some areas, they are called *Egu*; others call them *Oja* or *Ateruga*. Several such institutions may be found in one village or community.

The popularity of this informal means of resource mobilization should be seen against the backdrop of the difficulty of obtaining credit from inaccessible and highly discriminatory urban-based banks and credit institutions. Traditional forms of credit have grown in popularity in the last few years as the standard of living of most rural dwellers has eroded. They assist individual members to defray social expenditures such as funding children's education and burial and marriage ceremonies. Some of the institutions are established to aid members in executing specific tasks such as building houses and opening business ventures. It is usually mandatory for members to spend money on projects that are commonly agreed upon. Some credit institutions, particularly those with women's members, use their money to purchase uniform dresses for major festivities such as Sallah and Christmas, and, through this, to enforce a strong sense of identity and solidarity.

The size and membership vary. For instance, a group of 50, 100, or 200 people can organize itself into a credit society for the purpose of contributing a fixed amount of money at regular intervals, weekly or monthly. The agreed sum is paid to the leader, who rotates the money collected among members. In cases where membership is large, they are split into two or more groups, each with a coordinator who collects money on behalf of the leader. Again, in such cases the money collected is rotated among the groups and individual members.

The institutions are highly informal and voluntary. They seldom have written rules or by-laws. Mutual trust and confidence provide the basis for these credit societies. Members who are faced with emergencies can always plead with the leader for assistance. Sometimes, depending on the situation, money meant for a member can be split between two members who are under economic and social pressures. Leaders are not elected as in formal organizations. More often than not, however, wealthy and influential members of the community who are also men of integrity emerge as leaders. In most cases it is they who initiate the idea. Their operations nevertheless remain highly open and democratic as individual members have access either to the leader or to the coordinator of the group.

In the few instances where leaders defraud the members, such leaders have to leave the community and go into voluntary self-exile. In some cases, members of the extended family of such leaders close ranks to pay the money because of the social stigma it brings the whole family. But whether the money is paid back or the leader departs, the social stigma is long-lasting. The fear of this kind of stigma plays an important role in checking fraud within traditional credit societies.

Crafts and guilds

The organization of craftsmen into unions or guilds is at a low level. The most prominent include associations for patent medicine dealers, electronic mechanics, photographers, motor mechanics and motorcycle mechanics. Although there are blacksmiths, they are not organized into a guild. Tailors are organized into a Tailoring Welfare Association.

Occupational groups

Road transport workers constitute the strongest occupational group in the LGA. They belong either to the National Union of Road Transport Workers (NURTW) or the Motorcycle Hire Union. The NURTW has a total membership of about 500 in Dekina LGA, and union membership is compulsory for all qualified and licensed drivers. The NURTW is a registered trade union whose objectives include the administration of motor parks, protection of and support for members involved in traffic-related offences, and the promotion of peace and progress among members. The union also seeks to protect the property of commuters. The revenue of the union is derived from gate takings as well as fines from drivers guilty of overloading. Fines are also imposed on members who pick up passengers from spots other than the motor parks, and there is a special motor park levy. Revenue generated from these sources is used in maintaining union offices and providing uniforms for patrol men.

The Motorcycle Hire Union has a membership of about 400. All motorcycle owners who intend to operate on a commercial basis voluntarily join the association, whose membership continues to grow as more and more people use motorcycles for commercial running as a means of cushioning the impact of the economic crisis. Members of the association hold regular meetings, at least once a week. Leadership elections are held at the end of a two-year term.

Political empowerment

At the time of this research, the two official political parties, the NRC and the SDP, were well entrenched in the LGA. It was established that party leadership in the LGA was dominated by relatively young people aged between 25 and 45 years, and that the membership was predominantly male. With the exception of two wards where women held the positions of treasurer, the executives of the two political parties at ward level were controlled by men.

Elected officials at the local government level included the chairman, the vice-chairman and the 11 members of the legislative council. The other ten members (supervisory councillors) who helped to form the executive council were not elected. Dekina had two elected members in the Kogi State House of Assembly and one elected member in the Federal House of

Representatives. None of the elected representatives in either legislature was a woman.

Both the social clubs and the village/community development associations have served as springboards for broader political activity and identification. These organizations have aligned themselves with the political parties and particular candidates at elections and made it difficult to aspire to political office without their endorsement. The NURTW has demonstrated its sympathy for the NRC government in Kogi State. Ome youths, Owa social clubs and the various women's organizations have also expressed support for preferred candidates in the series of elections since the commencement of the transition programme. In return, political parties have sought to court the favours of these organizations. They have mobilized support and even financed the election of candidates seeking office in these organizations.

In the second week of September 1993, a few weeks after the survey, the NURTW successfully mobilized its members against hoarders of petroleum products (petrol, diesel and kerosene) throughout the LGA. The high concentration of these products on the black market and the difficulty in obtaining them at the filling stations forced prices to rise significantly. The NURTW members, armed with axes and other dangerous weapons, directed their anger at owners of surface tanks and hoarders for three days. Several tanks were ripped open and some of the owners were wounded. Intervention by the Kogi State government, which claimed the lives of two NURTW members, was necessary to restore order. Another member was shot and wounded in the same confrontation at Dekina, where union members mounted a roadblock to enforce a 'no movement' order.

In a similar manner, the National Union of Local Government Employees went on a one-week strike, instructing members to stay at home from 21 August 1993. The strike was to protest at the non-payment of salaries to members for two months. The instruction to members to stay at home made scathing remarks about waste in the legislative council and the affluent life styles of the chairman and other political office holders.

Economic empowerment

Access to the means of production, such as land, credit, inputs and technology, has improved markedly with the proliferation of various social and economic organizations in Dekina LGA. Rural farmers face no problem of access to farming land, although women in the Igala cultural milieu traditionally do not enjoy title to land. They were, in fact, prohibited from engaging in meaningful agricultural activity. The establishment of the BLP in 1987 stimulated the growth of several types of women's organizations and women have been actively encouraged to acquire family land for purely agricultural purposes. Women struggled, as individuals and in groups, to secure certificates of occupancy over such land. Traditional beliefs about women's participation in agriculture are being broken down gradually.

Economic activities such as weaving, soap making, *gari* processing and petty trading have been expanding steadily and so has access to credit. With the assistance of the World Bank farmers' cooperative societies in Biraidu have been able to secure ₦150,000 loans with a 15-year repayment period. Several women's groups have also secured loans from commercial banks to expand their productive or trading activities. It is expected that with the establishment of community banks in different parts of the LGA, these organizations will take fuller advantage and obtain more credits.

The influence of the Ayangba Agricultural Development Project, which flourished in the LGA from the mid-1970s to the early 1980s, has led to greater use of modern agricultural technology by farmers. Modern inputs such as fertilizers and insecticides, and the use of tractors and harvesters, have become more widespread. Better and improved varieties of beans and cassava have also been introduced in the project era. The Kogi State Agricultural Development Project has continued to engage agricultural extension officers.

Our case study indicates that more members of disadvantaged social groups such as women are involved in income-generating activities and have improved their material well-being. The emergence of various kinds of associational life, especially among the artisans and sellers of different kinds of produce, has enhanced economic well-being, but has not improved the earnings of the majority of the rural dwellers.

Accountability and transparency

Between 1990 and 1993, there was no case of impeachment of any local government chairman or vice-chairman, though two legislative council speakers were removed for high-handedness and incompetence. The procedure of recall was not invoked.

In people-based organizations, particularly traditional ones, those guilty of embezzlement have always gone into self-exile as custom demands. The BLP office in the council supervised the activities of the women's organizations, handling most cases of fraud and embezzlement.

Government institutions

Although MAMSER had been in existence in the LGA since 1988, its effectiveness in spreading political enlightenment seemed doubtful. Its activities were hardly known outside the local government headquarters and the semi-urban areas. We could detect no impact on the rural populace, and there was no translation of the constitution and other basic documents of political education into the local language.

The activities of the DFRRI included the maintenance of existing rural roads – the 6-kilometre Dekina–Olowa road and the 20-kilometre Dekina–Abocho road – and the construction of a total of about 100 kilometres of access roads and a number of culverts and bridges.

The BLP, established in the LGA in April 1987, appeared to be the most effective of the existing government institutions. Through its programmes of mass enlightenment and education, the BLP succeeded in consolidating various women's organizations and groupings, and encouraging women to diversify their economic activities.

The NDE office in Dekina was involved in the creation of jobs and employment opportunities for youths in conjunction with the office of the directorate at the state headquarters. By the time of this research, 250 persons had benefited from the NDE in the LGA.

Conclusion

Although the history of people-based organizations in Dekina LGA is quite recent, there is evidence to suggest that their popularity will continue to grow and contribute to the expansion and viability of the rural economy. The proliferation of organizations of rural farmers (men), women and youths involved in productive, trading and mobilization activities shows, in an important sense, the inadequacy of the state.

The open and democratic nature of governance evident in most of the economic and social organizations studied suggests that a further deepening and popularization of these forms of associational life may become a fertile ground for learning and cultivating a democratic culture at the grassroots. The voluntary and spontaneous kind of support enjoyed by these organizations is a potential counterweight to the excesses of the state. There is a tendency, however, for local notables to emerge as leaders of some of these associations and end up moving them in the direction of autocracy rather than democracy. People in the LGA clearly require enlightenment about procedures for enforcing democracy and accountability in the use of public resources.

Notes

1 ECA, *African Charter for Popular Participation in Development* (Addis Ababa: ECA, 1990), p. 18.

2 I. A. Eteng, 'Popular organization in transition mobilization, some participatory models', paper presented at the National Workshop on Mobilization of Popular Organization Towards the Success of the Transition Programme, Hill Station Hotel, Jos, 20–22 July 1993.

7

Age Grades in the Civil Society of Ethiope East, Delta State

ONIGU OTITE

While social scientists and other scholars concerned with development have tended to concentrate their attention on the national level, activity at the local level can provide a more accurate barometer for gauging the degree and form of the success or failure of the development of the nation. The state of affairs at the local level is indeed a window through which we can assess national development both quantitatively and qualitatively.

While the state, through the medium of government, is expected to act as a catalyst for development, individual citizens take their own personal decisions to join or form associations through which they participate democratically in community and national development. A focus on the individual actors is logical when considering various kinds and spheres of participation in local and national development, because the individual, rather than an association or group, constitutes the unit of democratic decision taking. Group decisions of associations, based on the interaction of individuals, are viable aspects of democratic processes in many contemporary nations. The individual, the association or group, and civil society are involved in many forms of interaction occurring during popular participation in the democratization process in contemporary nation states.

It is increasingly accepted that those concerned with the development of nations at the state and local levels must lay emphasis on people's participation and must 'put the people first'. This involves the acceptance of the principle and practice of democracy, whereby the people's rights are sovereign and they expect participation in decisions and processes which affect their lives. The socio-economic and leadership profiles of the people must be known and adequate provisions must be put in place for accountability in the management of both material and human resources.

This case study examines these issues with reference to Ethiope East Local Government Area (LGA), one of 19 such areas in Delta State. We used both qualitative and quantitative methods to obtain our data with the assistance of five briefly trained research assistants covering the whole of the LGA. The field work took ten days from 30 July to 9 August 1993 and covered the headquarters, Isiokoro, and more than 90 per cent of the 85 town and village settlements that make up the LGA. Library work was done later to complement data obtained through field work.

Socio-economic profile

Demographic indicator

Figures drawn from three censuses concerning this LGA overlap somewhat with those of other areas, although the 1991 census figures reflect the composition of the LGA, which was itself created in 1991, at the same time as Delta State itself came into being. Between 1963 and 1991, the area now covered by Delta State was part of the Midwest Region/Bendel State of Nigeria. Two Urhobo polities are grouped to form the Ethiope East LGA.[1] These are Agbon and Avwraka.

In 1963, the whole of the Urhobo Division had a population of 564,886 living in 14,922 square miles with 308 persons per square mile. The census figures showed that Avwraka had a total population of 20,106 while Agbon had 62,064 people. The LGA headquarters at Isiokoro had a 1963 population of 1,009. The three most populous town settlements were Okpara Inland, with a 1963 population of 6,719, Kokori Inland (8,664) and Eku (8,162).

The breakdown and details of the 1991 census are not available. Ethiope East LGA had a total population of 108,703 people (52,173 males and 56,530 females) out of the total 1991 Delta State population of 2,570,181. The figures for the component towns and villages, and for the households in them, were not available from the census office at the time of this research.

Education

There are 57 primary schools in the LGA, providing facilities for 28,917 pupils (14,544 boys and 14,373 girls) and employing 662 teachers (305 women and 357 men). There is also a private university staff school attached to the Delta State University at Avwraka. Apart from this private school, the LGA authority pays for the services and facilities of all primary schools in the area.

There are 20 secondary/grammar schools in the LGA, with 245 classrooms for 253 classes with a total of 11,436 students (4,870 girls and 6,566 boys). The LGA employs 292 teachers, (225 men and 67 women) for the schools.

The schools are evenly spread throughout the LGA, and there is therefore no discrimination against sections of the population in terms of educational empowerment. Women are not discriminated against with regard to school admission, although fewer girls than boys actually attend and remain to complete their courses in the schools.

The only post-secondary institution in the LGA is the newly established Delta State University.

Health facilities

There are six health centres, two health clinics and one health post in Ethiope East LGA. There are also six hospitals (three in Abraka, two in Eku and one in Okpara). In the health centres and clinics, the local government employs senior nursing officers, midwifery sisters, staff and nursing midwives, community nurses/midwives, community development officers and assistants, and community health extension workers. There are also pharmacy technicians and supervisors. The total number of personnel for these local services is 61, consisting of 30 skilled and 31 unskilled or para-medical personnel. There are also two health workers/officers in the local government secretariat.

Potable water

In addition to water sources from indigenous wells and also from streams and rivers, some of which do not run in the dry season, nine towns in the LGA have pipe-borne water. These are Avrwaka, Urhuoko, Urhuovie, Eku, Orhono, Kokori, Okpara, Ovu and Oviorie. A total of 57 boreholes serve 17 LGA settlements; Eku, Avrwaka and Kokori alone account for 34 of these boreholes. Moreover, the LGA has 420 wells providing water to 34 different towns and villages. People who are not served by wells or boreholes have to walk to the nearest source, usually between 500 metres and 3 kilometres distant, to obtain their water.

Energy

The main sources of energy in the LGA are electricity, kerosene, firewood and petrol. Fourteen towns benefit from electricity supplies in the LGA. These are Avwraka, Ajalomi, Eku, Erho, Oviorie, Ovu Inland, Oria, Urhuoka, Isiokoro, Kokori, Okpara Inland, Okwakpo, Orhoakpo, and Orhono.

The five petrol stations in the LGA are located at Isiokoro, Okpara Inland, Oviorie, Eku and Avwraka, and are used by visiting car owners and taxi drivers. Kerosene is also sold at the petrol stations and by private traders in their houses or at the market. Petrol is generally available within a 5-kilometre distance, while firewood is obtained from farms and forests usually no more than three kilometres away.

Transport

The principal means of transport within the LGA are cars, buses, taxis, bicycles, motorcycles and canoes.

Roads are both tarred and untarred, and are usually waterlogged, with deep potholes, in the wet season. There are a few exceptions, such as the roads running from Sapele and Warri through Okpara Waterside and Oviorie, and passing Eku and Avwraka, to Agbor and Asaba. Within the towns there are very few good roads, such as those in Eku and Avwraka.

Most rural towns and villages are connected by road and every settlement is connected at least by footpaths.

Economic institutions

There are only four supermarkets, two at Avwraka and two at Kokori. While traders are found in every settlement, with buying and selling taking place in their houses and wherever commodities are needed, there are generally no shops in the villages and smaller settlements. Two towns, Eku and Kokori, each had between 60 and 100 retail shops in 1993. The other towns, including Avwraka which has to meet the demands of a university community, also had shops, numbering between three and 60. A large variety of commodities were stocked for sale, including beverages, plastics, laundry materials, cooking pots, food items, tailored clothes, drugs, farm implements and produce, books for primary and secondary schools, domestic animals and electrical goods.

Local industries in the LGA are essentially home-based or cottage industries, with insignificant capital investment, for soap making, construction materials and pomade manufacture. The only fairly large industry organized in a formal manner is a rubber processing industry at Okpara Waterside. There are also six medium-sized cassava and palm oil processing industries at Kokori and one at Okpara Inland.

There are many local gin manufacturing, cassava grating, and palm kernel shelling industries in various parts of the LGA. There are 91 cassava processing businesses and 117 oil processing units. In general, the capital investment of these industries is low, with only a few hands employed. The personnel are essentially household members, usually between two and ten people.

The problem of capital formation is gradually being addressed through the introduction of banking facilities. At the time of this research, there was one bank at Avwraka, which was fairly well patronized, judging from one week's observation. Two other banks were being constructed at Okpara Inland and at Isiokoro, the headquarters of the LGA.

Judicial institutions

The state government established three categories of courts in the LGA, the customary court, the magistrate's court and the high court. There are two customary courts — the district court located at Avwraka and the area court at Isiokoro. Each court consists of three judges and several supporting personnel, with appeals carried from Avwraka to Isiokoro. The high court and the magistrate's courts are located at Isiokoro. All the courts deal with various kinds of offences, and with matters of social control and conflict resolution involving local people in the LGA.

Public facilities

There are no public libraries in the LGA. There are two post offices established at Eku and Avwraka. Three postal agencies are located at Kokori, Orhoakpo, and Okpara Inland. They function irregularly in terms of their opening hours and services.

The LGA has four motor parks located at Eku, Avwraka, Oviorie and Kokori. Most of the settlements are served with resident or non-resident taxis and small buses. In Kokori and Eku taxis and buses are most numerous, with up to 50 plying the roads on Kokori market days. Each taxi carries about five passengers in addition to heavy loads, while a bus may carry about 20 people. Small lorries also convey goods, particularly food commodities such as *gari*, starch and yam, from various settlements in the LGA and beyond it to Kokori, Eku, and Avwraka markets. Around 20 taxis move between Eku and other towns in the LGA – excluding those taxis, buses and ambulances that are used to convey patients to, or corpses from, Eku Baptist Hospital, particularly on Fridays and Saturdays.

Security

There are three police stations in the LGA: the Divisional Police Headquarters at Isiokoro with a superintendent and about 80 police personnel; the divisional police headquarters at Avwraka with a chief superintendent and about 60 personnel; and a police station at Eku with about 20 personnel organized under Avwraka. The police officers carry out normal duties in their stations and the areas under their jurisdiction in the LGA. In this respect they liaise very closely with designated senior age grade leaders and agents of the town councils of elders.

Neighbourhood security operations

Each town and village settlement consists of wards or family sections from which males are selected to serve in vigilante groups. The purpose of these groups, which operate between 11 p.m. and 5.30 a.m., is to ensure the peace and safety of persons and property. Thieves and other offenders who are apprehended, usually with circumstantial evidence, are taken to the indigenous town council/courts where their cases are handled. Thereafter they may be handed over to the police.

Perhaps even more important is the vigilance which every citizen exercises as part of face-to-face relationships in the rural situation. Strangers and unsponsored or unattached visitors are easily identified, monitored, and sometimes questioned and challenged about their movements and concerns in the locality.

Mass media

There are three main types of indigenous communication used in the LGA, according to the culture of the people. The commonest and the most popular one is the 'town crier' or announcer, who rings a bell or shouts to gain the attention of people. Market days provide the largest gathering for announcers. The town crier is mandated to announce new laws and decisions reached at a town council or court. He draws attention to instructions or news meant for the town's public.

A second popular indigenous type of media is the beating of the drum or gong, to bring villagers together for a meeting in the market place or town hall. This medium is also used to assemble a designated category of workers, for example a group of vigilantes, reminding them of the time to report for duty.

Messengers, for example those sent by the head of an elders' council, may be used to communicate some information to chiefs or other functionaries with designated authority, who in turn pass on the information to heads of families within the locality. Everyone is thus kept abreast of the news, instructions or advice designed for the local population.

Although there are no telephones in the headquarters of the LGA, three people in Okpara Inland, including the traditional ruler, two in Ovu and several in Eku and Avwraka, have personal telephones. The Delta State University and the Baptist Hospital, Eku have telephones in their establishments. Countless individuals also have personal radio sets and several people have television sets in their houses in the 14 towns where electricity is available in the LGA.

There is no organized supply of newspapers in the LGA. Individuals living in urban areas such as Warri, or in semi-urban areas such as Ughelli, are requested by officials to buy newspapers when coming to work. Except at Eku and Avwraka, on the highway to Asaba, individuals make their own private arrangements to get newspapers. At the time of this research, the most favoured newspaper was the *Guardian,* followed by the *Nigerian Observer* and the *Daily Times,* but only a few people could afford the cost of these papers. The few obtained were passed from hand to hand, or read by two or three people at the same time. Magazines were not generally read. Thus the most important and readily available sources or means of mass media were the radio and the television.

Indicators on popular participation

Indigenous social and political organizations

Throughout Urhobo land, people are organized according to their ages.[2] Those who are about the same age or status move from one age grade to another, the transitions marked by rites of passage. Each age grade is a social status with defined duties and obligations in respect of the community as one totality. Women and men have separate age grade organizations.

MEN'S AGE GRADES

Men have five age grades.

(1) *Imitete:* This grade consists of males up to the age of 15 years. Their only importance is their potential; the society looks up to them as the future workforce and future leaders. Otherwise, they are ignored in many respects. The duties of the *Imitete* are essentially domestic. They run errands for their parents and relatives, involving short distances and light responsibilities. Males of this age are normally circumcised between six and eight years old. Nowadays, the *Imitete* form the school age for both primary and secondary schools. The *Imitete* and their duties have been influenced profoundly by the school system which makes it compulsory for six-year-olds and above to be at school. That is, the *Imitete* are now expected to be out of the indigenous system, at least temporarily, during school hours.

The type of school system they are initiated into at this young age is Euro-American in orientation. The *Imitete* learn to be individualistic, not community-oriented, and not inclined towards community work. They learn to be self-seeking and self-developing. Thus their devotion to duties, even at the domestic level, has been impaired. Their perception of their indigenous responsibilities as they grow up and move to the next and future grades is affected similarly at this early stage of their development. They want to become medical doctors, engineers, accountants, teachers and lawyers, but not local youths or town elders. They learn early to be involved alternately in a double set of participation: at home in local affairs, and at school in wider but rudimentary impersonal activities and clubs.

(2) *Imighele:* This grade consists of males between 15 and 20 years. They generally clean up the streets, wards, town centres and footpaths. They are also active in farm and community work. They are engaged in errands of public importance and greater responsibility. But there are generally no special ceremonies to mark the passage to or from this age grade.

Many of the *Imighele* are still students. They start school late in life, for one reason or the other, or drop in and out of school, struggling to reach the top class. The school influence is profound, both on their attitude to duties and on their relationship with those below and above them. They perform certain of their duties, however, for example town hall repairs or the clearing of streets and surroundings, particularly at festivals. They obey the local rules and laws of moral behaviour championed by the elders.

It must be added that all the settlements in the LGA are not evenly rural. There are different degrees of rurality. And while the *Imighele* perform few of their duties in such town settlements as Avwraka, Eku, Kokori, Okpara, Orhoakpo and Ovu, those in the more rural and smaller settlements are more closely associated with their traditional roles.

(3) *Otuorere:* Literally translated as the 'group of the town', this age grade consists of men between 20 and 30 years. Prior to the nineteenth century, this group provided the town's warriors and defence personnel. Members of this grade do the heavy work in the wards and towns, such as the clearing of bushes and the building of shrine houses, and are generally regarded as the junior arm of the next age grade.

For the purpose of political and economic participation, the members are selected from the wards. Such wards vary from town to town. Okpara Inland has three wards, Urhuerhi, Etorogba and Urhueregbe, and Kokori likewise has three: Urhuokpokpo, Anaka and Umiaghwa. On the other hand, Eku has five wards: Ikhidioka, Iyadjaro, Ekrerewha, Ukromokun and Urhusi. The organization of the town duties requires the delegation of authority to the ward leaders.

This arrangement ensures that no healthy male escapes town duties. High value is placed on participation, and there is a general feeling that it is a bad thing to seek to be excused, sometimes even when ill, from one's contribution to town work and development. No good person is or wants to be excused from such duties, including the payment of one's share of monetary contributions.

As a result of the school influence discussed earlier, and the improved means of quick transportation through taxis and buses, members of the *Otuorere* take individual decisions to emigrate or to move from time to time to the nearest urban areas of Warri and Sapele. A few of them move farther away to Benin, Lagos and other places to meet or live with relatives.

Many of the *Otuorere* have passed at least through the primary school and remain interested in performing their local age grade duties and obligations if they stay in the local environment. They eke out their living locally. Part of their responsibility involves vigilance, for example over the maintenance of the electricity and water supplies provided by the authorities and the community. Their leaders link the group effectively with their seniors, the *Ivwraghwa*. Together they take part in carrying out town duties as a means of ensuring their safety and unity, as well as their happiness, survival and social harmony as rural dwellers.

(4) *Ivwraghwa:* This group consists of males who are between 30 and 50–60 years. The younger members are hardly distinguishable from the older members of the preceding age grade. The *Ivwraghwa*, of course, are more experienced as keepers and practitioners of their local culture and are also more expert in traditional construction.

The *Ivwraghwa* form the largest age grade in the local population, and constitute the main workforce of the local town or village. They help to supervise members of younger age grades when carrying out specific duties relating to town and village development. Members of this age grade are skilful builders of bridges and roads. In pre-colonial times, leading warriors and captains were also drawn from the *Ivwraghwa* for defence purposes. They carried out the orders of the town council of elders.

The *Ivwraghwa* are more permanently settled rural dwellers, not concerned with the level of education of some of their members. They are committed to their age grade duties and the welfare of the town. They assist the council of elders in the organization and government of the town, particularly through their leaders and locally titled members.

(5) *Ekpako:* This group of elders, the constituent members of the town councils and the courts, head the local gerontocracy. Members are 60 years and above, usually with large families, compounds and social responsibilities. The head of the *Ekpako,* that is the oldest male in the town or village, is called *Okpako'orho* or *Okarorho*. Rites are performed to install a new *Okarorho* at the moment of succession. The elders are expected to be cultural trustees and impartial and responsible judges at local disputes involving people from within and between wards. They govern the town through tradition, using an unwritten constitution and code of laws. The elders' councils/ courts meet every market day or indigenous Sunday, called *Edewo*.

Senile elders are often ignored, however, and their misbehaviour interpreted as a result of old age. The head of the council of elders, the *Okarorho,* is often so old that he may be incapable of good reasoning. In this case the *Otota,* the town's spokesman, or, in some cases, the senior son of the *Okarorho* acts and talks on his behalf.

WOMEN'S AGE GRADES

Women also have their own separate age organization, made up of four main age grades.

(1) *Imitete:* Like their male counterparts, girls of up to 12 years old are generally called *Imitete,* or small children. They run little errands, play about and around their parents, especially their mothers, and render assistance in the domestic domain. The school system influences them just as it influences boys, as already discussed.

(2) *Emete:* This is the group of young unmarried girls, of between 12 and 20. They are circumcised, both privately and later publicly. The private one involves the cutting of the clitoris, while the public one involves ceremonies, market attendance and services and participation by the girl's fiancé. The *Emete* age grade is one which provides or includes marriageable females and potential wives.

Western-style education makes them look beyond their locality. Apart from aspirations to become future teachers, lawyers, doctors and nurses, they look forward to individual success in marrying wealthy and educated men who, preferably, live in the urban areas. They always assist their mothers and, at such critical social moments as festivals, participate in their age group's ritual dances.

(3) *Ewheya:* This grade consists of women who are aged between 20 and 50. These are normally married people, divorcees or lovers, that is *Ose* or *Obevwemikpo*. This group constitutes the largest and most powerful group of women. They are married from within and from outside the town. Whenever they have a case or petition to the town elders or community leaders, they elect an *ad hoc* president and spokeswoman to act on their behalf.

Their duties mainly concern propitiation and purification rites whenever found necessary through divination, for example to cleanse the town whenever a woman dies in childbirth. They also perform rites to induce or promote the fertility of women and crops, and help to prevent domestic animals, such as goats and pigs, from destroying crops. They may also organize protests to the town council. Improved transportation facilities promote the movement of the *Ewheya* as traders.

(4) *Ekwokweya:* This age group consists of old women of more than 50 who have passed menopause and child-bearing age. The group includes widows, divorcees, and very old women (called *Emetogbe*) who have returned to live amongst their kin. Members of the group elect their own spokeswoman, especially in a situation of crisis, to present their petitions and suggestions to the town councils of elders.

MAIN FEATURES OF AGE GRADE ORGANIZATIONS

The movement from one age grade to another is not immediate but gradual, and the movement of individuals from one grade to the next depends on personal maturity and wisdom. There is an overlapping of membership and roles at the thresholds, and members of one group do not all move automatically. Each age grade is social but it also has political implications under the headship of its leader, called *Olotu* (*Onotu*). The age grades and their functions make the structure and processes of local indigenous government diffuse. Essentially, government involves everybody.

Although children do not feature in indigenous government and politics, they have their special place and relevance in the social organization. They contribute to the economy and their parents' social status, prestige, pride and satisfaction. As a means of ensuring the survival of their society, they are apprenticed at appropriate ages in various forms of occupation such as palm produce, fishing, bush clearing and farming, and the planting and harvesting of crops. In the company of the older citizens, they watch their parents and elders legislate and judge cases in the town hall. They take part in festivals. These various experiences have the cumulative effect of preparing every citizen for participation in the social, political, economic, and governmental affairs of the locality and the LGA.

As citizens are socialized in the localities, they become gradually committed to integrative roles enjoined by the age grade system in respect of each town or settlement in the LGA. Members of each age group know one another well, their relative ages and capabilities. Their leaders belong to the upper age limit of the members of the grade and are regarded as persons whose reliability has been tested through participation in the group's affairs; they are accustomed to receiving and executing orders with despatch.

There is an emphasis on public participation in all local affairs, and on the establishment and maintenance of confidence in the provision of public works to meet public needs. A familiar code of social justice is applied and there is a high moral tone in the management of public matters and financial accounts. One is not expected to steal from or mismanage the community funds. The moral pressure surrounding this expectation is a living source of public accountability.

Within the small ward and town communities, all the people participate in the conduct of their own affairs through free discussion, and act as final arbiters in the governmental processes directed by the elders. Town elders in council always seek the opinion of their executive assistants, the age group leaders, and also make their own investigations into particular aspects of the town's government, politics, general administration and welfare. Thus the town rulers and politicians are in close contact with the various members of their community.

The current migratory movements from the various settlements within the LGA to the urban centres of Warri and Sapele, some 30 kilometres away, have resulted in a high degree of detachment from the rural age grade system. Yet the separation is largely geographical rather than social. Emigrants maintain their links with their age mates, parents and kinsmen, and visit their homes frequently. They are aware of developments in their LGA home towns and find ways to participate in home town affairs.

The age grade organization has not remained intact, of course. Reference has been made to Euro-American education and emigration. The rapid development of individualism and materialism has broken the bonds of the age grades. The emphasis now is less on one's age group than on one's home town. Members of all the age grades often come together as groups of townsmen in the rural and urban areas. Indeed citizens of one town often form their union or association in the urban area. Such associations embrace people of all ages who care to join for a variety of reasons.

While membership of the traditional age grade association is comprehensive, expected and compulsory, it is voluntary in the new associations derived from the local citizenship of a particular town. Local citizens who join their associations in the urban areas team up with rural-dwelling citizens left behind in the LGA towns to build town halls, maternity homes, roads and schools, as has happened in Okpara, Eku and Kokori, for example. The urban members also use their influence in social as well as politico-economic networks to lobby government and non-government organizations and their agents to bring development, such as electricity, to rural towns. Such achievements are not attributed to any specific age group.

The age grade organization, in its original form, operates more or less as a mass party, with features of essentially compulsory membership and participation in local community work. Its new form, as an integrated urban-rural association of home-town citizens, operates similarly on the home-grown tradition of expected participation in local affairs and development. Non-participation could lead to ridicule and exclusion from certain places such as town halls built through the contributions and labour of others. Participation of urban-based citizens of rural home towns could also be through identification with the local policy-making bodies. Taking a local chieftaincy title and carrying out assignments have become necessary to the participation of a select group of people in local policy formulation and implementation.

In the local towns, members of the top age grade – the town elders – meet in council and court every market day as well as every *Edewo*, a day of rest from farm work when farm products and other commodities are carried to the market. Market days occur every eight days in the case of Kokori, while *Edewo*-cum-market day occurs every four days in the case of Okpara and Eku. The elders' council is also attended and assisted by leaders of the lower age grades, particularly those of the *Ivwraghwa*. They help arraign offenders or disputants before the council and court, and execute their decisions and rulings. Finance for the elders' council meeting and the administration of the town comes mainly from contributions. Families constitute the units of contribution within each ward. Donations are sought and received from urban dwellers or citizens of rural home towns, and, where appropriate, contributions take the form of free labour by rural dwellers.

Finally, it should be noted that the age grade organization is still the most important single and pervasive organization in the constituent towns and villages of the LGA. Although it is indigenous, the age grade organization has also formed the basis of new or modern associations of hometown citizens who share in the aspirations of their rural kinsmen and voluntarily help to accelerate the development and welfare of these towns and rural dwellers.

Indigenous economic organizations

Indigenous economic organizations involve family or household labour in utilizing land resources on a daily basis. Economic crops and ponds are part of the resources at the disposal of those living in the LGA. People are empowered economically through their access to land. Each family has a portion of the land on which to farm; such land belongs to the descent group, and every member of the lineage has a right to land from which he can maintain his wife or wives, children and dependants. The use of farmland is managed under the authority of the eldest male of the group. Farmers in a community or ward neighbourhood arrange to assist one another in groups at farming peaks such as clearing, weeding and harvesting. This is done in turns and, in the process, neighbours reduce boredom in rural life and share their common goodwill.

Rural economic organization also involves oil palm processing and rubber tapping. Ripe oil palm nuts are processed with labour supplied by the man, the wife/wives, their children and invited or hired male assistants. Women render help to men, while the latter engage in energetic activities. Women are given the kernel as their share of the produce while the men arrange to sell the palm oil, leaving some for domestic consumption. Rubber tapping is done nowadays by both women and men.

People in the LGA engage in trade in a market ring. In the past, only fish, cassava products, processed salt and domestic animals such as chickens, goats and ducks were sold. Nowadays what is sold includes beverages, books, clothes, maize, yam and various other commodities. Households accumulate small amounts of capital from their economic activities. Such capital is often used to set up a small shop, to increase the stock of an existing one, to finance the education of children, or to buy clothes, household appliances and furniture.

There are no formal associations to promote these indigenous economic activities, only *ad hoc* arrangements which are an integral part of household-based economic organization and activities. Rural people are further assisted by capital formation through economic organizations in the non-indigenous sector.

Non-indigenous economic organizations

There are about 40 prominent economic associations in the LGA, according to information obtained in the field and from the Directorate of Commerce and Industry at Isiokoro. Twenty of them are multi-purpose cooperative societies, 11 are farmers' multi-purpose cooperative societies, five are credit and thrift cooperative societies, one is a workers' cooperative society and one a traders' multi-purpose society. Some cooperatives were also members of the BLP at the time of this research.

The functions of the various societies and organizations are to promote members' interests in the production of their commodities such as crops, poultry products, soap, weaving, dyeing and fish. Where appropriate, as in farm crops, they are organized to ensure access to fertilizers. They also raise funds for social engagements such as attending burial ceremonies connected with their members.

The associations buy shares and pay subscriptions as a means of generating capital for investment. The subscriptions vary from ₦10 to ₦50 monthly or per meeting (1993 rates). They also seek loans as registered societies in order to obtain capital beyond what they contribute, routing their applications through the chairman of the local government authority to the state government. For example, the People's Bank of Nigeria (outside the LGA) in 1992/3 granted loans of ₦20,000 through the BLP to cooperative societies in each LGA, and two of the societies in the LGA – one from Okpara Waterside, the other from Ekrebuo-Isiokoro – were awarded such loans.

The average number of members of a society is 15; they are drawn from the locality, irrespective of sex. Meetings are held irregularly. The main problems they face include finance and management. Membership is voluntary and officers are elected democratically.

The associations or societies registered have virtually displaced the indigenous financial and capital accumulating organizations such as the *Esusu*. The latter are now rare and, where found, are restricted to trusted friends and kinsmen living in the neighbourhood. There is also a gradual shift from the individual-centred collection of the lots due to members in rotation to developmental concerns which involve the community.

The main aims and objectives of the multi-purpose cooperative societies are to benefit individual members. It is only through informal connections that occasionally they can become politicized. Although membership is not compulsory, the cooperatives and the associations promote a sense of general public participation through members' attendance at marriage, burial and other ceremonies involving the relatives or friends of members. Eligibility for loans from accumulated capital is another inducement to new members.

Cooperative societies and economic associations also function as social insurance devices. Many of them include in their activities voluntary donations to help members who have incurred misfortune, been robbed, or lost a breadwinner. Members also look forward to local festivals or national holidays such as Christmas, when they have the opportunity to share in group dances and displays.

There are also new and all-embracing town progress unions and associations of local and urban-based indigenes in the main town units of Okpara, Kokori, Eku, Orhoakpo, Igun and Ovu, with home and urban branches. Although, as their names and constitutions imply, these are generally concerned with the development of their respective towns – through the construction of roads, bridges and town halls – the political crisis in the country at the time of this study made it impossible to obtain reliable information and adequate details about them.

Political organizations and empowerment

It became obvious throughout the field work that people were very active in and sensitive about party politics in the LGA. Opportunities were provided for people to participate and to express their political opinions in a democratic way. During the 12 June 1993 presidential election it was noted that about 49 per cent of the eligible voters exercised their right to vote. Executive members of each party and leading supporters of presidential candidates had earlier brought their campaigns even to remote parts of the LGA.

Political tactics had not involved strikes, demonstrations or boycotts in the LGA by the time this research was conducted. The LGA had two representatives in the state's House of Assembly and one of them was chosen as a commissioner in the state government. Both the state and local governments were controlled by the SDP.

It was observed at the time of this research that political party membership was a critical factor in employment opportunities at the local and state government levels. The political factions and conflicts in the LGA derived from competition and rivalry at initial moments of election campaigns and from activities connected with political succession.

Accountability and transparency

Economic and political life in indigenous society in the LGA is hedged about by a moral code. It would amount to moral depravity if a member of an indigenous organization were to misappropriate his or her community's, town's or union's funds. It is also considered irresponsible to fail to do one's share of the community work. Sanctions might involve shaming mechanisms, ostracism, fines, or exclusion from places or gatherings. The word of a town council of elders is paramount and may not be challenged.

At the level of the local government, we were informed that the legislators (councillors) received statements from time to time from the chairman, who was also the chief executive. Internal auditors cross-checked this statement while the external auditors were sent from time to time from Asaba, the Delta State capital. Goods or items purchased had to be seen by the external auditors before they were used. It was assumed that the internal auditors did not connive with the external auditors and the purchasers of the goods to defraud the local government or the people.

Elected members of the local government council were expected to report and explain their activities to their constituencies. The legislators were often reminded about bringing 'political goods' home to their constituencies. Good roads, water or school furniture were seen as part of the gains of political participation through their elected representatives. There had been no impeachment, dismissal or recall of elected members of the council.

Conclusion

Popular participation is both an old and a new phenomenon in Ethiope East LGA. Rural people in the LGA are in a situation of implicitly rather than explicitly compulsory membership of indigenous social, political and economic organizations, which they depend on as a means of local identification and of validating local citizenship. Participation is compulsory as a means of coping with problems of survival in economic and political contexts defined by scarcity of resources.

It is from this local and cultural background that the people in the LGA proceed to engage in new forms of participation on a voluntary basis, implying free choice according to one's needs and aspirations. Here the same rural grassroots people participate not only in town but also in local government and in the new state-based associations. People in the LGA alternate between the indigenous and the modern sphere without necessarily integrating them. The future character of popular participation based on this ongoing socio-cultural and politico-economic interaction is not yet clear.

It is recommended that the local authorities provide more physical infrastructure, evenly distributed, for accelerated development, communication and democratic activities. It is also recommended that the local government should improve its policy on education by including such subjects as social and cultural studies, moral education and citizenship education in the school curriculum. This will not only help promote transparency and accountability in public matters, but will also help people to get involved more effectively in democratic arrangements and to develop harmonized personalities as they engage in popular participation while alternating between the coexisting indigenous and modern spheres of local rural life.

Notes

1 For more details on the Urhobo, see M. P. Okumagba, *A Short History of the Urhobo* (1982) and O. Otite (ed.), *The Urhobo People* (1982).

2 For more information on Urhobo age grade organization, see O. Otite, 'Continuance and change in an Urhobo age grade organization in Nigeria', *Cahiers D'Etude Africaines* , 12 (1971), pp. 302–15.

8

Civil Society in a Mixed Urban and Rural Area: Ijebu-Ode, Ogun State

SINA KAWONISE

The idea of the developmental state is now greeted with widespread scepticism (if not cynicism) not only by students of African political economy but also by those, within Africa and outside it, who make policies for the continent.[1] While the justification for this scepticism remains controversial, what is incontrovertible is the fact that the majority of the states in Africa are in retreat in terms of development.[2]

The corollary of this negative perception of African states is the shift of research focus from the state as the main catalyst of development to organizations within the vast tracts of civil society. The new research attempts to determine not only how individuals and groups survive and live within the context of macro-economic decline and perceived state failure but, more importantly, what those organizations contribute and can contribute to the development of their social formations.

The growing pressure for democratization of the essentially praetorian and authoritarian African state throws up a conflict between strong desire and weak actualizing power. While there is no doubting the existence of strong pressure for democratization on the continent, questions are raised about the current feasibility of democracy in Africa.[3] Conventional institutions, agencies and mechanisms are few and inadequate, while states in Africa are well versed in the pre-emptive channelling of democratic initiatives, in conditional surrender to open politics and pluralism, and in sustained vacillation between reform and reaction.[4]

Since the state is not greatly disposed to opening up its institutions and channels to democratization and popular participation, attention is again shifted from it to the civil society for popular initiatives and actions. The African Charter for Popular Participation in Development constitutes the background to this chapter, which proceeds from the Charter's definition of popular participation as the empowerment of the people to 'involve themselves in creating the structures and in designing policies and programmes that serve the interests of all', to contribute to the development process, and to share equitably in its benefits.[5] This emphasis on popular participation does not neglect, however, the direct or indirect contributions of the state to the process of development through empowerment.

Although the definition of popular participation assumes that the initiative for participation must come from the people themselves, the actualization must lie, at least in certain crucial instances, within the purview of the institutions and structures of the state. The objective here is thus to delineate 'the many interchanges between the state and society' such that 'it might be possible to attain a better understanding of the rhythm of unfolding processes' between the two.[6] Rather than seeing the state and civil society as separate entities, or as the entities depicted in Rene Lemarchand's metaphor of 'a potentially predatory species' pitted against 'a defenceless and fully domesticated pigeon',[7] this study thus adopts the position that the state and society are engaged in a continuous process of engagement and disengagement, depending on the circumstances and the issues at stake.[8] From this basic premise, civil society may be regarded as 'those intermediary and autonomous organizations which function and sometimes flourish in the space that exists between the state and the household'.[9]

The questions this study seeks to answer include the following: What is the nature of the organizations of civil society? How pervasive are they? What roles do they play in the democratization process? Do they exert any impact on the development process generally? What indeed is their relationship with the post-colonial state? To obtain empirically informed answers to these questions, Ijebu-Ode Local Government Area (LGA) in Ogun State is used as a case study. Although its headquarters is in an urban district, the LGA covers a wide area of semi-urban and rural settlements. It was chosen with a view to understanding the dynamics of the relationships between a medium-sized urban centre and numerous surrounding rural settlements, and their implications for development.

Method and procedure

Following indicators for field research designed in the ACDESS methodology workshop held before the commencement of this case study, the basic socio-economic profile of the Ijebu-Ode LGA was obtained from its secretariat in Ijebu Ode. Preliminary enquiries were made about the type, number and location of social organizations in the council area.

For the actual study of the social organizations and their relationships with the three tiers of government, two interview schedules were prepared. The first schedule, designed for leaders and members of socio-economic organizations, solicited information on: the functions, constitution and internal mechanisms and processes of the organizations; the degree of their participation in community affairs; and the level of economic enhancement which members derive from the organizations. The second interview schedule, designed for coordinating officers of government and quasi-government agencies overseeing socio-economic organizations, solicited information on their functional relationships with socio-economic organizations within their purview.

Using the interview schedules as a guide, oral interviews were used to get not only first-hand and direct responses, but also the nuances and tenor of such responses. The president or secretary and at least two ordinary members of each of the selected organizations were interviewed. The idea was to juxtapose the views of the leadership and members of each organization in order to come to a balanced conclusion about it. For the coordinating government agencies, the officers heading them were interviewed.

The setting

Basic demographic indicators

The Ijebu-Ode LGA is one of the 15 local governments in Ogun State, which is one of the 30 states of the Federal Republic of Nigeria. The original Ijebu-Ode LGA was established at the same time as Ogun State in 1976. The new state merged two provinces, Abeokuta and Ijebu, from the former Western State. Ijebu-Ode, which hosts the administrative headquarters of the LGA, served as the headquarters of Ijebu province from colonial times to the date of the creation of the state and the LGA. The area is inhabited mainly by Ijebu-speaking people, who are a sub-group of the Yoruba ethnic group. The original Ijebu-Ode LGA had a land area of 82,986 hectares. As of 1990, the estimated population of the LGA was 630,000, with 287,510 (45.64 per cent) in the urban centres and the remaining 342,490 (54.36 per cent) in the rural areas.[10] The published results of the national census of 1991 gave the population of the newly defined Ijebu-Ode LGA (created in 1992) as no more than 307,773 people, of whom 181,024 were males and 126,759 were females – without giving a breakdown of the respective rural and urban populations. The new Ijebu-Ode LGA is bounded in the west by Odogbolu LGA, in the south by Lagos State, and in north by Ijebu North LGA.

The main economic activities of the people of the area are trading and farming. With an annual rainfall of between 1,500 mm and 2,000 mm, and an average temperature of 84°F, the area is especially conducive to farming.

Education

Ijebu-Ode LGA boasts 10 pre-primary, 119 primary and 37 secondary schools. In any one year, approximately 47,000 children are enrolled in the primary schools and approximately 20,000 at the secondary level. Numbers of boys and girls are evenly matched. There are four post-secondary institutions in the LGA: a college of education at Ijagun; a technical college in Ijebu-Ode; a school of nursing/midwifery in Ijebu-Ode; and a school of health technology at Ilese.

The LGA has one central public library within the local government secretariat complex and small libraries in three of its five area offices.

Health

The LGA has one state hospital, 15 private hospitals, 20 private maternity centres, 24 dispensaries, 10 leprosy clinics, and one community mental health centre. Apart from the health personnel in the state hospital under the ownership and control of the Ogun State government, and the qualified doctors and other health workers in charge of the private hospitals and private maternity centres, the LGA has one doctor in its health department, 32 pharmacy technicians, 34 nurses, 53 midwives, 50 traditional birth attendants, 26 environmental officers, and 87 primary health workers.[11]

Potable water

The towns of Ijebu-Ode, Isoyin/Erunwon, Isiwo, Itamapako and Ilese are relatively well serviced with potable water, distributed through pipe networks from the two main water schemes in Ikangba and Yemoji. There is also a small water scheme in Ilugun/Alaro. About 32 villages which surround these major towns get their water supply from the 54 deep wells and six boreholes provided jointly by the communities themselves, the local government authority and the DFRRI. In addition, privately owned water tankers hawk and sell water to households at a price ranging between ₦5 and ₦7 per 200-litre barrel (1993 prices). Except when there are major breakdowns in the operation of the main waterworks, in which case water becomes scarce in the towns, people generally do not have to move further than 200 metres to obtain potable water.

Energy

All the major towns, but only eight of the autonomous communities, have electricity supplied by the National Electric Power Authority. For fuel, Ijebu-Ode serves as the central point of supply to other main towns and villages. From the 20 fuel stations in and around Ijebu-Ode, people in the settlements purchase petrol, diesel, engine oil and kerosene for domestic and commercial uses. For kerosene, which is used widely for domestic cooking and lighting, fuel tankers from independent marketers supply most of the villages through retailers, who usually have tanks to the capacity of between 2,000 and 4,000 litres. As a result, few households have to walk more than 200 metres to purchase kerosene. In some of the villages, kerosene is hawked in 75 cl bottles in the evenings. Firewood is also widely used for cooking, especially in the villages, and is readily available.

Transportation

As in the case of fuel, Ijebu-Ode township serves as the fulcrum around which the transportation system of the LGA revolves. Apart from serving as the gateway between the eastern and western parts of the country through the Sagamu–Benin Expressway,[12] the road networks in Ijebu-Ode constitute the main access routes to other towns and villages in the LGA area from other parts of Ogun State. Many villages are linked with each other by feeder roads throughout the LGA. It is often possible to travel from one village to the other in commercial vehicles that travel to and from Ijebu-Ode. Within Ijebu-Ode town, taxi cabs ply the major roads and motorcycles both the major roads and the inner streets. Fares by both modes are largely affordable to the people. Overall, there are about 20 motor parks in the LGA from which commuters travel within and outside the area.

Economic institutions and activities

Apart from two large markets in Ijebu-Ode (Bisi Onabanjo market complex and Oke-Aje market) there are many smaller markets within Ijebu-Ode and in each of the other towns and villages. In Ijebu-Ode alone, there are eight smaller markets and one evening market (popularly known as *Ita-Ale*). All the markets, both in Ijebu Ode and in adjoining villages, are easily accessible in accordance with the prevailing Yorubaland principle that markets must be in the centre of settlements.[13]

Most of the manufacturing concerns in the LGA are located within or close to Ijebu-Ode. Prominent among these are Odutola Group of Companies (manufacturing tyres, food and alcoholic beverages, and crown products), Bisrod Furniture and Gateway Pharmaceuticals. There are numerous sawmill firms and many small and medium-sized agricultural ventures like poultries and piggeries.

Shops of various sizes, stocking different goods and rendering different services, are common in both the main towns and the villages. While most modern artefacts, ranging from brand-new automobiles and electronic gadgets to pharmaceutical products, can be bought in Ijebu-Ode, shops in other towns and villages of the LGA stock mainly petty goods such as canned food items and household utensils. There are also ten branches of commercial banks, two mortgage bank branches, one branch of the People's Bank, three operational community banks and ten insurance company offices in the LGA. Three of the commercial bank branches and two of the community banks are outside Ijebu-Ode township.

There are 17 federal establishments in the area, of which 15 are located in Ijebu-Ode.[14] The LGA has virtually all the infrastructural facilities of modern development (except an airport and rail link), although their distribution is skewed to the disadvantage of the villages.

Security, law and order

There are two policing divisions in the LGA, each with its own divisional headquarters. The eastern part of the LGA is overseen by the Igbeba main police station, the western part by the Obalende police station. There are eight other police posts in the LGA, three of which are in Ijebu-Ode. Other state institutions include a high court, a magistrate's court (both in Ijebu-

Ode), and five customary courts (one in Ijebu-Ode). There is also a medium-security prison in Ijebu-Ode.

To augment the security provided by the police, vigilante groups are formed in towns and villages to ensure the safety of lives and property at night. The vigilante groups are organized on a neighbourhood basis and it is compulsory for all able-bodied men (usually between 18 and 40 years) living in the neighbourhood to participate on a rotational basis. In addition to this, main entrances to the villages are usually manned by vigilante personnel to prevent vehicles moving into or out of the villages between 11 p.m. and 6 a.m. The same effect is achieved by erecting single-bar gates at the entrances, which are locked for the same periods. A few streets in Ijebu-Ode also adopt the method of the single-bar gate to prevent vehicles from moving into or out of the streets during the specified times, usually inscribed on a notice-board. Households in some Ijebu-Ode neighbourhoods contribute money to employ between two and five nightwatchmen to patrol and provide security for the neighbourhoods at night.

Public facilities

The LGA is served by a central post office in Ijebu-Ode and one postal agency in each of the other towns. These postal agencies service the adjoining villages. Mail is distributed through private post office boxes or mail bags, or directly to residential addresses by postal personnel. There are also telephone services in the main towns of the LGA. There is a public telephone exchange in Ijebu-Ode at which local and international calls can be made round the clock every day. Coin-operated telephone booths at strategic locations in Ijebu-Ode and other towns were at the time of this study all out of order. The Nigerian Telecommunications (NITEL) exchange services are augmented, albeit illegally, by private telephone line owners who make their facilities open to interested users on a commercial basis. In addition to telephone services, telex and fax messages can also be sent through the NITEL exchange in Ijebu-Ode.

Mass media

The LGA can receive local, state, national and international news on many radio channels from medium-wave, short-wave and FM stations. At least three state television channels can also be received. Most national newspapers and magazines are available daily in Ijebu-Ode and other towns. Readers in the villages obtain their supply by commissioning commercial drivers in their villages to buy for them. Besides the national dailies and weeklies, there are two monthly publications – *Ijebu News* and *Obanta News* – which focus mainly on the LGA and its environs. With these means of mass communication, people of the LGA are usually very well informed about local, state and national issues. For specific issues and events in particular towns, public notices are broadcast on the two radio channels of the Ogun State Broadcasting Corporation. The villages, however, still use village criers to pass important village-wide information.

Socio-economic organizations

Ijebu-Ode LGA has a vast array of socio-economic organizations which may be characterized as 'associative groups' whose orientation of social action rests on a rationally motivated agreement beyond the scope of blood and kinship ties.[15] Such is the richness of associational life that a vast majority of people belong to one social or economic organization or the other.

The various organizations in the LGA include those which perform essentially social functions for their members; those which serve mainly economic and occupational ends for their members; those which combine both social and economic functions, mainly to members and indirectly to their communities; and those whose essence is the infrastructural and economic development of their communities. In the case of the last category, individual members of the organizations benefit from the results of the activities of the organizations only incidentally, as members of the community.

The organizations in the LGA also vary according to the nature of the relationships they have with (and the assistance they receive from) state agencies at the local, state and federal levels. While some of these organizations (such as purely economic and occupational ones) have few dealings with state agencies, others have intense interactions with these agencies. The overriding pattern is that the more interaction an organization has with state agencies, the more overtly political the organization becomes. This will become evident in the following description and analysis of the purposes, nature, organizational pattern and orientation of each body covered by this case study.

The socio-economic organizations selected for examination are cooperative associations and traditional credit institutions, market associations, craft and guild associations, the Road Transport Workers' Union, social clubs and age grade associations, town development associations, BLP associations and community development councils. State-inspired and fully or partly funded institutions such as the People's Bank, the community banks, the DFRRI, the NDE and the BLP are also studied in their specific interactions with socio-economic organizations in the LGA. For the purpose of orderly presentation, the organizations are divided into traditional and modern groups.

Traditional organizations

TRADITIONAL THRIFT AND CREDIT INSTITUTIONS

There are two kinds of traditional thrift and credit institutions in the LGA, *Ajo* and *Esusu*.

Ajo: This is a non-organizational savings practice operated by individuals. A collector goes round visiting people, either at their workplaces or at home, and collects fixed amounts for saving on daily, market day, weekly or monthly bases. The collector, known as the *Alajo,* is usually someone known and trusted by his/her clients. Those who patronize the *Alajo* are usually small artisans, petty traders, daily-paid workers and other small-income earners who are not very literate. The purpose is the saving of specified amounts of money by low-income earners who do not patronize a modern bank. Individuals who have been contributing consistently with a particular collector can demand an overdraft or a loan in times of need.

The system operates by individual enrolment with the collector. If, for instance, the contribution is daily, a card listing the 12 months of the year and the days of each month is issued to the contributor by the collector. With a minimum of ₦1 daily, the contributor specifies the amount he/she will deposit daily, and the agreed amount is entered in the column specifying the daily rate. On the basis of this agreement, the collector visits the contributor every day to collect the specified amount which he signs on the contribution card until the end of the month. The collector enters the contributions simultaneously in his own ledger, with a column for every contributor.

The contributor has the option either to collect his/her contribution for the month at the end of that month or to leave it to accumulate with the collector. The contributor also has the freedom to recall his/her contribution at any time, with notice of two working days. Rather than paying interest on the deposits, the collector actually receives an interest of two daily contributions out of the total made in each month. This interest of two daily contributions is invariable, irrespective of the number of days defaulted in the daily contribution within the month. In fact, the first two days' contribution are regarded as belonging to the collector. A contributor is thus free to default in the daily contributions, so long as the first two contributions have been made.

Subject to the trust and confidence of the collector in the contributor, the latter may be granted an overdraft or loan of not more than his/her total savings at the time of the demand. The loan is usually repaid through the daily contribution or by an agreed-upon phased repayment schedule. Cases of collectors' inability to pay back contributions by their clients occur only very rarely. When they do, social pressures are usually mounted on the collector to pay back, if he/she has not absconded from the town. Police and the law courts are seldom involved in such cases of default.

This thrift and credit practice is very widespread and involves a wide spectrum of non-literate and modestly literate low income earners in the LGA. Its mode of operation and benefits are voluntary and individual.

Esusu: The *Esusu* thrift and credit system assumes both informal and organizational forms. At the informal level, a few individuals, 'perhaps six', come together and agree to contribute a specified sum weekly or monthly (usually the latter). An equal contribution is made by each of the six individuals. The total contribution so made monthly is given in turn to each member until the cycle is completed. The turn at which the members collect is determined either by ballot or according to need. In the case of the latter, someone who has a pressing responsibility or financial commitment, and who receives the sympathetic understanding of other members, may be given priority to collect early. This form is prevalent mostly among salaried workers in both private and public concerns and, to a lesser extent, among petty traders and artisans. The purpose is individual economic survival without any community or political intent.

The organizational form of *Esusu* operates among age grade associations and some of the modern social clubs. As part of their service to members, these bodies provide a context for operating the *Esusu* system, using their monthly meetings to collect contributions and give to the person whose turn it is to collect. Many of the surviving age grade associations and a few of the social clubs in the LGA engage in this practice.

Esusu provides individuals with an opportunity to make compulsory savings (once voluntarily started) towards a lump sum of money to effect some tangible project which may otherwise be impossible. Default is rare because of the personal nature of the system.

Apart from rare cases of default, the major disadvantage of the system is that in a situation of high inflation it is inequitable. The contributor who collects first enjoys higher purchasing power than all those who collect after him/her. This disadvantage is making *Esusu* less attractive to those who have used it in the past.

MARKET ASSOCIATIONS

From time immemorial market women have organized themselves into powerful economic and political pressure groups within the different communities of Yorubaland. Although the associations are now composed of both sexes (unlike the traditional all-women's association), women still constitute the overwhelming majority of the membership. There is no age limit. The purpose of the organizations is to work for the improvement of the market environment, to maintain order and discipline in the markets, to constitute a bulwark against the exploitation of members by government authorities (through unjustified levies and charges), and to unify and mobilize market traders for the development of their host communities. The market women's and men's associations are based at the Olabisi Onabanjo Market Complex in Ijebu-Ode, with branches in all the other markets.

The sources of funding of the central association and its branches are statutory membership contributions, special levies, fines and voluntary donations. Its leaders are selected through elections, which come up every two years, but officers can be re-elected for as many terms as the congress pleases. At the time of this research the leadership had been unchanged for three years. The executive council of the association meets fortnightly, and those of the branches meet with the same frequency. The general assembly meets only when summoned by the executive council; this usually occurs in times of emergency or when it is necessary to mobilize members for a particular cause.

The main disciplinary problems among members which the association confronts are: failure to pay statutory dues promptly; failure to take turns in sanitary maintenance of the market environment; and disputes among members (usually over space encroachment and complaints of snatching another seller's customers). Such problems are usually reported to the president of the association or any other officer(s) present and the judgement of the case is binding on the parties in dispute. At times, the officers use personnel of the War Against Indiscipline (WAI) brigade in the employ of the local government to enforce their decisions. For their part, ordinary members can in theory fine, suspend or remove from office any officer whose conduct is undesirable, although this has never happened.

The association is involved in numerous developmental projects in the LGA. Its leaders are usually invited to the launching of community development projects (building schools, providing water, building Obas' palaces, executing health programmes such as the Expanded Programme of Immunization). For these, the association often levies its members token amounts (sometimes graduated according to kinds of stalls and shops) which, due to the size of its membership, amount to substantial sums. The association thus maintains a lively interaction with both the traditional and the modern authorities. It also holds periodic meetings with elected representatives from the LGA in all tiers of government.

There is a policy of sponsoring and promoting candidates for election to public office. Among the sponsored and promoted candidates are a few of its members and prominent sons and daughters of the market men and women whom the association considers positively disposed to its interests. At the time of this research, the candidates supported were all from the SDP, in which the vast majority of its members were active. Association officials claimed that no candidate it had supported had ever failed at an election, and that candidates from the SDP who did not win elections were those they did not endorse.

The association engages in demonstrations and market boycotts to protest against government policies which affect it and its host community negatively. In particular, the association claims it spearheaded the many protests that drove commercial water tankers off the streets and led to the repair and upgrading of the water network in Ijebu-Ode. It also protested, in the week of this interview, against the doubling of the squatters' levy to ₦1 daily. As a result of that protest, the Oke-Aje market was closed for a week by the local government.

The association declares market-free days to honour important political figures (who are in support of their interests) whenever they visit the LGA for important political events such as campaign rallies. In 1993, the association thus honoured both Governor Olusegun Osoba of Ogun State and the SDP presidential candidate in the 12 June election, Bashorun M. K. O.

Abiola. Twice in the month following the annulment of the June 1993 election, the association embarked on protest rallies and market boycotts. At the same time, the association was planning further protests against the local government chairman, whom it accused of serving his selfish interests to the neglect of those of the community in general and the association in particular.

Association officials could not say precisely, nor guess, what might be the minimum and maximum incomes of members. Even ordinary members were not forthcoming on this subject. The association does not operate a package of financial assistance to its members, although it does link its members with the People's Bank for credit facilities and many members have benefited from these facilities. Association officials praised the concept, establishment and operations of the People's Bank.

AGE GRADE ASSOCIATIONS

As the name suggests, these associations are formed by people (of both sexes) who fall within a particular age bracket (with an age interval of between three and six years) within a community. An association, which usually takes on a name with the prefix *Oba* or with *Oba* as part of its name composition, does not automatically take in all those who fall within its age bracket. Usually, only age mates who are friends or acquaintances form associations of this kind. With such names as *Obafowora, Obayori* and *Bobagunwa*, these associations take the community's traditional authority as their source of legitimacy and the head of the community (*Oba* or *Baale*) as the focal authority. In fact, the *Oba* or *Baale* provides or endorses the name of any age grade association found in his domain. The association bears the name so given until it becomes moribund, usually due to the aging or death of members. The name can then be recycled and given to a new age group.

These associations are pervasive in the towns and villages of the LGA. Typically, those who belong are indigenous people (sons and daughters of the soil) of particular communities. Their members either live and work within the communities for the greater part of the year or come home frequently. They may not be very educated in the formal sense, but they have a particular attachment to their communities of origin. Although these associations continue to exist in both towns and villages of the LGA, they are more active in the latter. In Ijebu-Ode town, in particular, most exist in a condition of relative dormancy, eclipsed by the social clubs which many of their members have joined.

The purpose of age grade associations is to serve as a unifying platform for age mates; to assist members and to rally round in the event of personal social celebrations (weddings, house warmings, burials), to assist each other economically (usually through the *Esusu* system and individual personal lending); to participate as groups in communal festivals and celebrations; to contribute to community development; and to preserve the customs and traditions of their communities. Out of the five age grade associations studied, only two practise the *Esusu* thrift and credit system, but all claim to be rendering financial assistance to members in need. Overall, their dominant activity is in the social realm, where celebrations and festivals stand prominent.

Membership contributions, fines, levies and donations are the main sources of funding for age grade associations. Although the mode of leadership selection is by election, the leaders are rarely changed, except in the event of prolonged illness or death. Both their executive council and congress meetings are held monthly – usually on a fixed Sunday of every month. Common disciplinary problems are lateness and absence from meetings, defaults on the payment of dues and levies, and rowdiness during meetings. These are handled by the officers, who impose fines, suspension or, in the worst cases, expulsion. The leaders, too, are called to order through criticisms and fines. Suspension or impeachment of officers is rare.

Age grade associations participate in the traditional authorities of their areas. They play prominent roles in appointing traditional chiefs and rulers. Many of them are represented on the traditional ruling councils of their communities. Beyond this they are not influential in terms of modern politics. None said they had interacted with the local government authorities and none sponsor candidates for election. Although three of those studied said some of their members had benefited from the People's Bank credit facilities, none had an organizational relationship with it.

Modern organizations

COOPERATIVE SOCIETIES AND UNIONS

Cooperative societies in the LGA are of three different types: (1) cooperative thrift and credit societies (CTCSs), (2) cooperative consumers' societies, (CCSs) and (3) cooperative multi-purpose societies (CMSs). Each of these different societies is composed of between 25 and 50 members of both sexes who join on a voluntary basis. Each society is affiliated to a central union of its kind. Thus, all CTCSs are affiliated to a cooperative thrift and credit union (CTCU). All the CTCSs in the Ilugun Alaro area of the LGA, for example, are affiliated to Ifesowapo Idona Ilugun Alaro Ijebu CTCU, with its head office in Idona. Likewise, all CMSs are affiliated to a cooperative multi-purpose union (CMU).

Thrift and credit societies: The purpose of these societies is to save specified but varying amounts of money contributed by members for subsequent borrowing by them. A society operates by asking each member to specify the amount which he/she can contribute monthly. With a minimum of ₦10, each member can undertake to contribute any amount monthly depending on his/her capability. After continuous contributions by a member for a minimum of months, the contributor can apply on a form (sold for between ₦2 and ₦10, depending on the society) for a loan of twice the amount he/she has contributed. Although a contributor is qualified for the loan after the minimum period, the availability of the loan is determined on a first-come, first-served basis. The interest payable on loans at the time of this research was 1.5 per cent per month. There is no collateral, except a guarantee by two other members of the society who have no outstanding borrowing at the time of the proposed loan. For the first loan by a contributor, the repayment period is a maximum of six months. When a loan has been liquidated, another one can be obtained the following month, if funds are available. The second loan is repayable over a maximum of nine months, while the third and subsequent loans are repayable over a maximum of 12 months. Default on repayments is rare and, when it occurs, payment is enforced through peer pressure, with the assistance of the Bureau for Commerce and Industry which supervises the societies and unions, or, in extreme cases, through the sale of the property of the debtor to the amount he/she owes. None of the societies reported having taken the latter measure.

Membership in a CTCS is voluntary. Any indigene of the LGA with gainful employment who has been recommended as trustworthy by at least two members of the society is eligible to join. Entrance fees range between ₦ 20 and ₦ 50, depending on the strength and reputation of the society concerned. Total membership in each society ranges between 25 and 50. Societies are funded mainly through the savings of members and the interests charged on loans. Other sources may be fines imposed on offending members, donations or levies (usually for specific social and organizational purposes).

Each CTCS has an elected executive committee. The tenure of its members is one or two years, but they can be re-elected as long as the congress is satisfied with their performance. The key executive posts are president, home secretary, treasurer and chief whip or welfare secretary. Both the executive committee and congress each meet monthly, except in an emergency when meetings can be called at any time by the president. The congress meeting is usually preceded by an executive committee meeting. Decisions are usually taken, after due debate, by majority vote through a show of hands. The leadership of the society is obliged to abide by and implement whatever decision is arrived at through this process, with the help of provisions specifying their removal from office if they fail to please the membership. No society reported to have at any time suspended or removed any of its officers. On the contrary, the societies reported that they were pleased with the performance of their leaders. Problems of latecoming and absence from meetings are handled by the chief whip or welfare officer through fines or suspension. The former is the more common, while the latter is rarely employed.

The average CTCS does not participate in community affairs in any significant sense. None reported helping to provide any community facility or service, or influencing the politics of the local community. Members who participate in community affairs do so strictly as individuals. The main reason given for the societies' non-contribution to developmental projects is that their organizations are too poor to contribute meaningfully.

None of the societies could assess precisely the pattern of income distribution among its members. The rough estimate which came from our investigation is that ₦400 per month is the least income of any member and ₦ 3,000 per month the maximum. This income differential of members does not influence their standing within the organization, however, beyond its implication for their monthly contribution and the size of loans that can be secured by each member. Overall, members believe strongly that the societies enhance their economic well-being.

Cooperative thrift and credit unions: CTCU membership is corporate rather than individual. CTCSs contribute and borrow money, with each society specifying a fixed amount which it thinks it can contribute every month without default. The mode of lending is as in the societies. Money borrowed by a society goes to its loanable fund for its members.

Each union has an administrative secretary or administrative manager employed full-time and paid by the union. The unions' internal processes are similar to those of the societies. Their sources of funds are the same, with additional sources from possible loans and dividends from the Cooperative Bank, in which the unions have shares and where they keep their accounts. The unions can also borrow to the tune of five times their savings with the Ogun State Cooperative Financing Agency, to which all cooperative unions are compulsorily affiliated.

The unions adopt democratic procedures in their internal processes, and are essentially egalitarian. They are also strictly apolitical and do not make significant contributions to community affairs.

Cooperative consumers' societies: The purpose of a CCS is to buy consumable items (such as foodstuffs and household utensils) in bulk and retail this stock, mainly to members at relatively cheap prices. Membership in it is voluntary, with a membership strength in the range of between 15 and 40 in each society. Its funding comes mainly from unit shares bought by members. The number of shares owned by each member depends on his/her capability. The shares are usually in units of 50 *koba* to ₦ 1. The society is also funded by trading profits ploughed back into business, fines and special levies. The benefits are the reduced price of goods and the dividends at the end of each trading year.

The organizational processes of a society are the same as those of a CTCS. Its dispositions to community affairs and politics are also the same. Unlike the CTCS, the CCS is not affiliated to any central union. It is not as pervasive, either, and we discovered the existence of only six societies.

Cooperative multi-purpose societies: A CMS combines the functions of both the CTCS and the CCS. It operates in the same way as a CTCS, while its consumer function is broader in scope than that of the CCS. A CMS buys a broader range of goods (food items, household utensils, building materials) and sells both to members at concessionary prices and to the general public.

Profits accruing from trading are partly ploughed back into the consumer business, and partly used to augment the loanable funds, with the remainder going as dividends to members at the end of each financial year. There are 124 CMSs in the LGA.

Cooperative multi-purpose unions: The CMU is the umbrella organization of the CMS. Its membership is corporate, its operational mode the same as the CTCU's and its organizational dispositions to community affairs and politics identical with those of the CTCU. There are three unions of this sort in the LGA.

OCCUPATIONAL ORGANIZATIONS

Road Transport Workers' Union: This organization caters for the interests of commercial vehicle drivers and their conductors in the LGA. Named the Alare Road Transport Employee Association, the organization protects its members from police harassment, provides litigation services to members in cases arising from the lawful pursuit of their jobs, shields members from excessive taxation by the local government authorities, and sees to the proper maintenance of motor parks and roads in disrepair within the LGA. Since only men operate commercial vehicles in the LGA, membership of the association is all male. The minimum age for registration with the union is 21 years. Although membership is voluntary, virtually all licensed drivers and motor park operators in the LGA enrol with the association.

The main source of funding of the association is the daily levy of ₦1 (1993 price) charged on every commercial vehicle operating in the motor parks of the LGA. Both the executive council and general assembly of the association meet once every month, but emergency meetings can be called at any time. Leaders of the association are selected through elections held at the annual general meeting of the association. The tenure of each office is one year, renewable through re-election.

The main disciplinary problems among the membership are passenger overloading, reckless driving and physical combat among motor park operators. These problems are handled by the leaders through the imposition of fines, suspension from driving or operating in the motor parks for a maximum period of one week, or, in the worst cases, advising commercial vehicle owners not to employ the services of the culprit. For their part, while the ordinary members interviewed appeared satisfied with the performance and conduct of their leaders, they reported nevertheless that their leaders sometimes claim excessive privileges and sometimes misuse the resources of the association. They reported that on two occasions in the past they had removed some of their leaders for abuse of office.

The association is affiliated to the Ogun State chapter of the Road Transport Employee Association, to which it makes monthly contributions for the running of union activities. The main contribution of the association to the development of its host community is the routine repair of roads, usually by filling up potholes. The association recently contributed money to the building of the Awujale's palace, still under construction.

The association usually interacts with the local government authorities on issues of the daily levy which their members are charged in the motor parks, on the maintenance of roads and motor parks, and on the problem of police harassment which the association believes is incessant. The association also occasionally meets with the police authorities in the LGA. While the association believes that these meetings sometimes yield results, on occasion they have had to withdraw their services and boycott the motor parks to protest at what they considered excessive demands by the local government and the police. The association believes that public officials can be made responsible and accountable by such protests.

Although the association makes contacts with elected officials from the LGA in local, state and federal institutions, it does not have a policy of sponsoring candidates for election or supporting a particular party at organizational level. Those of its members who participate actively in the politics of the community do so strictly as individuals. None of its members have ever been elected to any state office.

The income of association members ranged between ₦400 and ₦4,000 monthly at the time of this research. About 60 per cent of its members were in the low-income category, while the remaining 40 per cent had high incomes. Beyond the assistance the association gives to members in getting vehicles for them to drive, it does not give them any financial assistance.

Motor Mechanics and Technicians' Association: The purpose of this is to improve the working environment and working conditions for automobile mechanics and technicians in the LGA. Membership is compulsory for all graduated and practising mechanics and technicians. It has about 1,000 members, over 95 per cent of whom are male. There is no age limit for membership. Its funding comes from compulsory contributions, special levies, voluntary donations, fines and, recently, grants from the state government. The Ogun State Government in late 1992 made a donation of ₦200,000 each to the two mechanics' villages in the LGA to support their efforts to fence round, and instal lighting in, their work sites.

The association has an executive council, whose members are elected every two years. The last change of leadership was two years before this research. Both the executive council and the general assembly meet every fortnight. The major problems the association faces are quarrels among members in their workplaces and reports by clients of shoddy jobs and non-delivery of paid-for services by mechanics and technicians. These two problems are handled by the peace and disciplinary committee of the association which operates through monitoring groups set up in the two mechanics' villages. While in principle the general assembly could fine, suspend or remove from office any officer found guilty of some offence, none of the officers have ever been so punished in the life of the association. The ordinary members interviewed expressed satisfaction with the performance of their leaders.

Apart from embarking on projects to fence round their work sites and provide lighting, the association made a donation to the Awujale's palace and bought shares in the Iwade Community Bank which was preparing to start operations. The association interacts quite frequently with the local government authorities to solicit assistance for the improvement of the working environment of its members.

The association does not have a policy of sponsoring particular candidates for election to public office, although it encourages candidates of any party it finds capable of catering to members' interests. As this report was being written, the association was on a three-day boycott of work to protest at the annulment of the election of M. K. O. Abiola by the Babangida military administration. None of its members have ever been elected to public office, with the exception of the appointment of one of its members in 1992 as the chairman of the SDP caretaker committee in the LGA. That appointment lasted for about six months, after which new executive councils of the two parties were elected.

Association of Tailors and Fashion Designers: This is a compulsory association for all tailors and fashion designers in the LGA. It is composed of both sexes and has no age limit. Its purpose is to provide a platform for members to fix minimum charges on their various designs and products, to advise members on matters relating to their craft, to settle disputes among them, and to buy inputs in bulk for retail to members. The association has five zonal branches in the LGA, with each comprising about 250 members. Each zonal branch has its officers elected at the annual general meeting for a term of one year, renewable for as many times as the congress pleases. These zonal executives constitute the central body of the association, again for a term of one year renewable for a maximum of three terms.

The executives of the zonal branches meet weekly, while the general assembly of the zones meets fortnightly. Representatives of the central body and its executives meet monthly. Sources of funding include membership contributions, special levies, registration fees, fines, donations and profits from its sales of inputs to members. A large part of the resources goes into purchasing sewing inputs such as thread, buttons and machine needles for onward sale to members. Because supply always falls short of demand, sales are often rationed to ensure that the inputs get around as much as possible.

The association takes action against members for lateness and absence from meetings, and for charging below the minimum rates. Reports are investigated by the zonal executives and appropriate punishments are effected where anyone is found guilty. The punishments include fines, suspension from the association or seizure of work implements. For an officer found wanting in his/her duty, similar sanctions are imposed, in addition to a possible suspension or impeachment. Some officers have been impeached in the past.

The association is strictly apolitical. It does not participate in and has not contributed to any community project and does not interact with either the traditional or the local government authorities in the area. The association has never of its own volition engaged in any political rally, boycott or protest.

Some members have (as individuals) benefited from the credit facilities of the People's Bank. The estimated lowest income within the association was ₦400 per month, while the maximum was around ₦5,000. During festival periods in the LGA, earnings could be much higher. On the whole, it does not normally take more than six months after graduation from apprenticeship for a new tailor to be able to set up on his/her own.

SOCIAL CLUBS AND TOWN DEVELOPMENT ASSOCIATIONS

Social clubs: These are association of friends and acquaintances mainly from the same community or from the same area. Social clubs are in many respects similar to age grade associations although they are not as oriented towards traditional political authorities as the latter. A typical club is composed of friends of similar age or educational achievement.

Membership in social clubs is voluntary and open to both sexes. The majority of social clubs in the LGA were formed by young indigenes who live and work outside their communities but nevertheless visit home periodically. Their sources of funds are statutory monthly contributions, admission fees, special levies, fines and donations. Their leaders are selected through annual elections and tenure is usually between one and two years. Individual officers in particular posts usually do not go beyond two terms. Both the executive council and the general assembly hold meetings, usually monthly on a fixed Saturday or Sunday. Other internal processes are the same as in age grade associations.

Social clubs take an active part in communal festivals and also give strong support to their members in any social celebration. Virtually all social clubs in a community are affiliated to the development association of that community, although many of the clubs reported that they had not contributed much to community projects.

Social clubs are an important platform for the social solidarity of indigenes living at home and 'abroad'. There are about 350 social clubs in the LGA, with 148 and 41 of these in Ijebu-Ode and Isoyin, respectively.

Town development associations: Since 1985, when the Ijebu-Ode Development Association (IDA) was founded, this type of umbrella grouping has been developing in other towns of the LGA. For this study, two of these associations – IDA and the Isoyin Community Development Association (ICDA) – were studied. Both associations consist of all the registered social clubs in their towns. The IDA is composed of 148 social clubs, while the ICDA has 41. Both exist to integrate and unite the social clubs for the development of their respective areas, to advance the welfare of their members, to serve as social rallying points for the sons and daughters of their areas at home and 'abroad', and to revive, protect and promote the traditions and cultural values of the Ijebus.

Membership in the associations is of two types: corporate and associate. Corporate members are social clubs of at least ten members, while associate members are individuals who are not associated to any social clubs but identify with the purpose of the associations. The difference between the two forms of membership is that the former has a voting right, where the latter has observer status. At the time of this research, both types contributed an annual due of ₦ 500. The two types are voluntary, open to both sexes, and have no age limits. The associations are funded with membership contributions, special levies, fines and donations.

The executive council of the IDA is elected for a single non-renewable term every two years; that of the ICDA every year for a one-year term, renewable as many times as the annual general meeting pleases. The executive council of the IDA meets once a month, while the general assembly meets quarterly. The executive council of the ICDA meets quarterly (and monthly only in times of emergency), while its general assembly meets anually. Decisions in both associations are reached by voting and on the principle of simple majority.

Any officer found wanting can be disciplined by the members through fines, suspension or removal, but no officer in the two associations has been so punished. Apart from the widespread complaint by the smaller social clubs (especially those composed of young people) that the associations are dominated by the rich, professionally senior and elderly members from the big old clubs, the memberships appeared to be relatively satisfied with their leaders.

The associations are involved in conceiving, designing and executing community projects. Both have contributed variously in equipping schools and hospitals, building roads, tidying up their towns, and awarding scholarships to students from their areas in tertiary educational institutions around the country. The ICDA, for example, has helped in building a high school and a primary health care centre, in providing boreholes and electricity, and in extending telephone lines from Ijebu-Ode to the Isoyin community. Both IDA and ICDA are major shareholders in the Obanta Community Bank and Isoyin Community Bank, respectively. These banks provide modern thrift and credit facilities at concessionary rates to members of their associations and to their communities at large.

The two associations interact closely with both the traditional authorities in their respective areas and the local government authorities. They also maintain links with the state government for the purpose of realizing their organizational goals. Both reported that the local and state governments have been responsive to their needs, although they expected them to do more.

The two associations claimed that the majority of all elected public officials in the three tiers of government from the LGA were members of their associations, although they had not sponsored them. If the associations were political at all, it was in the context of the meetings they had held with elected and appointed public officials to lobby for government assistance in their development projects. Neither of the two associations could shed light on the income distribution pattern of its members. While acknowledging that the current economic squeeze might be impacting negatively on many of their members in 1993, they admitted that their associations were doing better than in the previous year.

COMMUNITY DEVELOPMENT ORGANIZATIONS

Development councils (DCs): These are community development organizations composed of indigenes and local notables of a particular community. The council usually has between 12 and 20 members, at least two of whom must be women, with two others being the resident councillor and state House of Assembly legislator as nominated members. The traditional head of the community or his nominee is usually the chairman of a council. Membership in a council is through election at a community-wide general meeting summoned by the head of the community. As much as possible, a council is representative of all the sections and quarters in the community. Officers of a council, excluding the chairman, are elected among the members themselves. All the villages and towns in the LGA have different DCs. In a big town like Ijebu-Ode, DCs are organized on the basis of quarters making up the town.

The purpose of a DC is to conceive, design, execute and maintain community development projects on a self-help basis. It attempts to channel people's energy towards participating in and spearheading the development of their communities. A DC is funded with voluntary contributions and special levies by members of the community; proceeds from the community's economic projects and landed property sold or on lease; and grants-in-aid from private donors, the local and state governments. Meetings of the executive committee of the council are held monthly and general meetings of the entire community are called by the executive committee at any time the latter deems necessary. In both contexts, decisions are reached on the basis of majority votes. Both meetings are usually attended by an observer who is an official of the local government's Community Development Department (CDD).

A DC identifies projects that may be beneficial to the welfare of the community – a fish pond, a poultry farm, a *gari*-processing unit, a school, a health centre – something not too capital intensive, and also easily understood and maintained by people in the community. Once approved by the community and endorsed by the CDD, the project is funded and executed through a tripartite arrangement in which the community contributes both money and labour to the tune of about 50 per cent of total project cost, while both the local and state governments contribute the remainder over a period of time. The two tiers of government usually share their contribution equally; if on completion the project requires recurrent expenditure and capital maintenance which it cannot generate itself, either the local or the state government may take it over.

For coordination purposes, all the DCs are divided into four development areas (DAs), which are affiliated to the zonal area, which in turn reports to Ogun State's Association of Community Development Councils (OGACDC). The four DAs are: Atan DA, Isoyin DA, Itamapako DA and Ijebu-Ode DA.

Elections to higher levels of the DC are made from the bottom up. Since this structure was evolved, five years before our study, many community development projects (usually food processing and water projects) have been executed – despite long delays on the part of government in paying its share of the funds for executing approved projects. The DCs put this down to the failure of elected public officers to fulfil pledges made during election periods. In interviews, the DCs proposed that in future they would only endorse candidates who had been active members of DCs or DAs for at least two years before standing for election to any level of government. An implication of this is that DCs may in future field their own members as candidates for elections.

Better Life Association: This is the organizational form of the BLP. Membership in the societies is open only to women. Market women, farmers, artisans and craftswomen living and producing in particular communities are encouraged to become members. There are usually three executive posts in the societies – president, secretary and treasurer – each elected from among the members. The sources of funding are membership contributions, fines, grants-in-aid, donations and proceeds from economic ventures.

The purpose of the associations is to improve the economic well-being of women as a specially disadvantaged social category; to enhance their productivity; to make them independent through economic empowerment; and to strengthen their participation in community affairs. The philosophy and mode of operation of the associations are similar to those of the DCs.

Operating from the premise of self-help, self-employed women in a community organize themselves into a society, which conceives and designs a project. The project is then proposed to the Better Life Association, with offices at the local government headquarters under the headship of the wife of the chairman. If the project is approved by the association, the society is advised to look for resources to execute the initial phase of the project, with a promise by the association to complete the remaining part of it. For instance, a society desirous of having a mechanized *gari*-processing centre may be advised to secure a piece of land for it and construct the shed under which the necessary machines will be sheltered.

Apart from interaction with local government officials and periodic meetings with elected public officers from different areas, the societies have a policy of supporting and promoting electoral candidates who appear to be positively disposed to their interests. None of their own members have been so sponsored or promoted, however, and none were occupying elective posts at the time of the study. Societies at various times have declared work-free days for their members and mobilized themselves to attend campaign rallies of politicians they support.

While all the societies interviewed had a positive view of the programme and the majority of them believed they had benefited from it, all of them complained that the central association did not fulfil its promises to them in good time, if at all. Some societies had been told to build sheds for *gari*-processing machines, which they did, but they were still waiting, two years later, for the association to supply the machines. The societies also alleged favouritism on the part of the leaders (especially the chairperson) of the association. Many of them also accused the association leadership of wasting scarce resources on showy events such as celebrations and receptions for visiting officials to the LGA.

Community banks (CBs): A CB is intended to provide services to grassroots socio-economic organizations and individuals who may otherwise find the conventional banks and their requirements too remote and difficult for their economic purposes. In particular, a CB is intended to provide credit facilities to its customers at concessionary interest rates and without stringent collateral requirements.

At the time of this research, there were three operational CBs in the LGA: These are Obanta Community Bank (OCB) in Ijebu-Ode, Isoyin Community Bank and Ilese Community Bank. Plans were afoot to establish five others in the LGA in the not too distant future. To use the example of the OCB, the bank started operation in late 1992 (the first in the LGA) with a share capital of ₦ 7 million contributed mainly by IDA and the Oyingbo Motor Park Taxi Owners Association. Its depositors were social clubs, petty traders and artisans. To qualify for a loan or an overdraft, the applicant must have maintained a deposit account for at least three months. With an interest rate of between 20 and 28 per cent per annum (depending on the duration of the loan), the maximum available overdraft is ₦20,000, and the maximum loan ₦90,000. Interest on deposits is 14 per cent per annum on savings accounts and 30 per cent per annum on fixed deposit accounts.

As well as three months' continuous deposit, obtaining a loan from the OCB requires a personal knowledge of the customer by the bank's staff, a positive view of the running of the customer's deposit account, a knowledge of the customer's line of business or vocation, and an assessment of the viability of the venture for which the loan is sought. The bank's credit and marketing officers are required to visit customers in their different places of business or vocation at least every fortnight. Apart from the assessment function of those visits, the officers use the opportunity to advise customers on business and accounting procedures.

The OCB reported that its customers had been quite credible, responsive and appreciative of its services. Deposits rates were encouraging but the federal government had not paid its statutory share capital of ₦ 500,000, which the bank said it needed to augment its credit facilities.

STATE AGENCIES

Bureau for Commerce and Industry: This Ogun State government agency oversees the operations of both the cooperative societies and the unions. The bureau advises and guides them in administrative procedures and bookkeeping, and arranges periodic seminars, lectures and training courses for members of the organizations. It also checks their account books and authenticates them at least quarterly. On rare occasions the bureau helps the societies recover debts from members.

The bureau's officials commonly advise the cooperatives not to get involved in the politics of the area. Their reason for this is their belief that organizational involvement in politics invariably divides the members and ultimately damages, if it does not kill, the organization concerned.

Community Development Department: This Ijebu-Ode local government department coordinates and supervises the activities of socio-economic organizations and state agencies for the purpose of community development. Under the purview of the department are community development councils (CDCs), community development associations (such as IDA and the Isoyin Community Development Association), the BLP, the DFRRI and MAMSER. The functions of the department are: helping in the organization of community development efforts; monitoring the conduct and internal processes of community development organizations; advising and educating them on how to achieve effectiveness and efficiency in their operations; and closely interacting with community-based organizations in order to know, at first hand, the felt needs of the communities and how they intend to go about satisfying those needs. The passwords of the department are: 'self-help' and 'government helps those who help themselves'.

In specific terms, officials of the department attend the meetings of the CDCs, monitor their activities, participate in designing and implementing self-help projects, and periodically check their account books. In fact, a community development officer in charge of an area is statutorily a signatory to the accounts of each of the CDCs in the area of his/her supervision. All expenditures must also receive his/her endorsement. In addition, the officer represents government interests in and presents its perspective to the CDCs. The department claims that the organizations under its purview influence its decision making and implementation processes. Avenues for doing this are the interactions its officials have with the organizations and their representation on the department's project evaluation committee. The department encourages the organizations' interest and participation in the politics of their area in the belief that involvement in politics is a good means of keeping elected public officials responsive and accountable.

The department has an inadequate number of qualified personnel trained in community development and grossly inadequate working facilities (such as transportation). It suffers from the inability of the government (at state and local levels) to deliver on promises of financial support. These problems detract, not insignificantly, from its effectiveness. The department reports, however, that the organizations are friendly and appreciative of its efforts.

The People's Bank: Established by the federal military government in 1989, the People's Bank lends money to its clients at a very low interest rate (5 per cent per annum in 1993) on a guarantee by two persons considered as creditworthy and responsible. Usually, the loan granted is in multiples of the bank balance of the applicant. In 1993, loans ranged between ₦ 500 and ₦ 25,000. The local government has just one branch of the People's Bank. The bank believes that the people it serves are quite responsible, reliable and trustworthy, citing a repayment rate of loans of over 80 per cent, even when the economic decline in the country adversely affects the petty businesses and vocations the bank's clients engage in. The problems it acknowledges are the difficulty of serving a large area and its limited loanable funds.

The Directorate of Food, Roads and Rural Infrastructures (DFRRI): In Ijebu-Ode LGA, the DFRRI has constructed deep wells in 22 villages. Three villages have benefited from the rural electrification programme and the DFRRI has also established information centres in three villages where radio and television sets are provided for the use of the communities. The DFRRI has also constructed feeder roads in the remote parts of the LGA, although this study could not establish the extent of these.

Overall, the presence of the DFRRI was not felt strongly in the LGA, a fact supported by the acknowledgement of its activities by only one community organization (ICDA) in the LGA. Even in the few areas visited for verification of the DFRRI's claims, its activities were not acknowledged.

The National Directorate of Employment (NDE): Although it is a federal government agency, the NDE's activities in the LGA are coordinated from an office in the local government secretariat in Ijebu-Ode. In theory, the NDE may obtain farmland from the local government which is then allocated to unemployed persons who have enrolled with it. Loans may then be provided at very low interest rates to assist them in buying inputs and meeting the operational costs of their farms. School certificates may be taken by the NDE as collateral. The NDE may also train school leavers in different crafts, using a vehicle which spends some weeks in an LGA. Trainees who distinguish themselves during this period may be registered and put under the apprenticeship of established craftsmen and women of different trades in the LGA.

A major problem faced by the NDE is that people often use its loans for other ventures and the repayment rate is very poor. As a result, the NDE normally recommends those it considers in need of loans to the People's Bank.

This case study could not establish the number of people who have benefited from the NDE's programme in the LGA. The official of the NDE we interviewed could not tell how much it spends annually on its programmes and how many have obtained loans from it. Significantly, none of the socio-economic organizations studied reported that any of their members have benefited either from the NDE training programme or from its loan facilities.

Economic empowerment

People's access to means of production in the LGA varies considerably, depending on what they aim to produce. Farmers, for example, whose major means of production is land, generally find it possible to secure enough for both subsistence and commercial farming. The vast majority of farmers in the LGA live and work in the villages of which they are indigenes. In the villages, every household has some portion of land (usually relatively large, given the sparse population density of the villages) on which any member of the household can farm. Even settlers in the villages have access to land for farming purposes, either through the hospitality of some indigenes they are friendly with or on the payment of a token rent, usually amounting to no more than between 5 and 8 per cent of the total yield of the farm at market price.

For virtually all the productive ventures undertaken in the LGA, access to modern technology is restricted. The technology available is usually rudimentary. Farmers still work mainly with hoes and cutlasses, mechanics with spanners and chisels, tailors mainly with hand-driven or treadle-powered sewing machines. While those implements may have certain advantages such as ease of maintenance, the fact remains that they are outdated.

For credit, producers in the LGA rely mostly on the cooperative societies to which many of them belong, on friends and relations, or on borrowing from the People's Bank. Many individuals acknowledged the help which the People' s Bank has provided. The point that must be stressed, however, is that a majority of those who have access to one form of credit facility or the other manage to secure only a fraction of the resources they actually need to be optimally (even moderately) productive.

Self-employment is commonest in the areas of farming, craft and petty trading. For formal employment, the local government and other state agencies, together with private concerns such as the few factories in the LGA, petrol stations and shops, provide some openings in Ijebu-Ode. The number of people involved in formal employment in the LGA can hardly be more than 5,000. The proximity of the LGA to such big cities and state capitals as Lagos, Ibadan and Abeokuta, however, provides considerable advantages to job seekers. Indeed, many indigenes of the LGA earn their livings in those cities.

Following the general pattern in Nigeria, there is a small affluent minority, with a few people who are moderately comfortable, while the mass of people are impoverished or below the poverty line. No precise figures are available to validate empirically a pattern that is visible even to a first-time visitor to the LGA.

Women have equal access to means of production in almost all economic endeavours in the LGA. Except in commercial vehicle driving and the motor mechanic's trade, women are represented in all occupations and can perform as well as men in terms of economic empowerment.

Political empowerment

Political participation takes four main forms: voting; political party membership and activism; community activism; and protest activity.[16] Voting patterns in Ijebu-Ode LGA during the two-party period introduced by the Babangida military government showed a strong preference for the SDP. Of 17 local government councillors, 15 were from the SDP. The two local representatives to the Ogun State House of Assembly were both from the SDP and so was the one local representative to the national House of Assembly. Out of a total of 144,930 registered voters[17] in the original LGA (including Ijebu-Ode and Odogbolu) there were 16,900 registered party members (10,144 in the SDP and 6,756 in the NRC). Thus 11.7 per cent of registered voters were party members, 7 per cent in the SDP and 4.7 per cent in the NRC . Although we could not obtain a breakdown in the figures for registered voters and party membership in terms of sex, it would appear (given the fact that all elected officials in the LGA are male) that women were active only in voting.

A careful reading of the section on socio-economic organizations would suggest that only a few of them are political in the sense of community activism and preparedness to support protest activity. In significant ways, only those organizations which have some relationship with the state, and those whose purpose is to develop their different communities, have engaged in political protests like boycotts or demonstrations, or have attended political campaign rallies. It is clear, however, that many people of the LGA, both within and outside the organizations, have and maintain a keen awareness and interest in local, state and national politics. Pro-democracy protests, such as the two peaceful mass rallies in July 1993 and the two three-day stay-at-home protests ordered by the Campaign for Democracy (CD), took place in the LGA.

Accountability and transparency

Among the majority of socio-economic organizations, the leadership is accountable to its members, who on the whole believe that their affairs and the business of the organizations are run honestly and transparently. This positive tendency which runs through all the organizations studied is not replicated, however, in either perceptions of or relationships with state agencies and personnel. The general perception of most people is that state officials are corrupt and that elected public officers aggrandize themselves in office.

The overriding response to questions on what the organizations thought they could do to hold federal, state or local government officials accountable was that they could do absolutely nothing, beyond withdrawing their support from already elected officials in any future election. Although most people knew that there were constitutional mechanisms by which elected public officers could be removed from office, they doubted the effectiveness of those mechanisms since those who might use them were themselves state officials who were very much part of the corruption network. This lack of accountability and transparency in federal, state and local government affairs, and the feeling of helplessness among the people and their organizations, attest to the low level of political empowerment and democracy in the LGA.

Conclusion

This case study reveals that associational life is rich and pervasive in Ijebu-Ode LGA. People organize themselves in various associations and make persistent efforts mainly for individual economic survival, sometimes for the upliftment and development of their various communities, and only secondarily for the purpose of political participation.

All the cooperative societies and unions and virtually all the craft and guild associations studied exist essentially for the purpose of enhancing the economic well-being and professional survival of their members. Few of these organizations participate directly in community development or in the politics of their areas. In the case of the Motor Mechanics and Technicians' Association, there is interaction with the state in the form of donations secured from the state government and the land rents paid to the local government, while in the case of the Road Transport Workers' Union this interaction is in the form of the daily dues paid to the local government and contacts with the police. The political disposition of these two associations is also shared, in a more profound manner, by the Market Women's and Men's Association. Here, again, the fact of the ownership and control of the markets by the state, and the rents and levies paid to it, dispose the association to politics. This relationship with the state, and the reality that markets provide the venue where the majority of economically productive women and their dependants can be reached and mobilized for political purposes, accentuate the political significance of the association. Because politicians and the state recognize the political potency of the association, attempts are made to court and appease it. Such attempts in turn further imbue the association with a sense of its political significance and indispensability. In spite of this, however, the association has not exploited its power significantly (by sponsoring a number of its members for key elective state offices, say).

The only organizations which recognize the political importance of sponsoring their members for election are the development councils. This is because the realization of the goals of the DCs depends largely on the support they can get from the state, which makes the favour and understanding of elected officials very crucial. In addition, the very essence of the DCs (community development through collective initiatives and efforts) predisposes them – along with town development associations – to politics. The theoretical inference that can be drawn from the foregoing is that the greater the interaction a non-state socio-economic organization has with the state, and the higher the content of collective (rather than individual) enhancement in its purpose, the more outwardly political the organization becomes.

Another significant finding of this study is that, except for the Community Development Department of the local government, all other state agencies which serve, oversee or interact with socio-economic organizations are essentially patronizing in their relationships with them. The agencies assume an all-knowing posture and adopt a top-down approach in their dealings with local organizations, ignoring the advantages to be gained from involving them in policy making.

In terms of the internal processes of the socio-economic organizations, it would appear that they are essentially democratic. The principle of leadership selection through election is universal among the organizations, leaders are changed periodically even if infrequently, and meetings are held regularly (except the Market Women's and Men's Association whose general assembly meets only in times of emergency). More significantly, leaders of the organizations enjoy widespread legitimacy and command respect among their followers. The incidence of widespread absenteeism among members at meetings and the infrequency of leadership changes in the organizations, however, would seem to suggest an oligarchic tendency within most of them. Yet, ordinary members are broadly satisfied with the performance of their leaders, despite occasional charges of undue privilege or dominance.

It is evident that the task of paving a way for popular participation in governance and in democratic processes belongs squarely with the people themselves and their organizations. Yet few organizations see the need to participate in politics and influence decision making at the state level (by whatever means), let alone to develop means and capabilities for doing so. Few organizations realize that the burden of socio-economic survival and development (at both individual and community levels), which they valiantly attempt to achieve at the micro level, would be greatly lessened and relieved if, and only if, they had significant influence within the structures and institutions of the state, and they succeeded in making the state responsive and responsible. It is a recommendation of this study that non-state community resource and mobilization centres should be established, with the goal of working out and implementing the modalities of positive engagement between socio-economic organizations and the state, at every level.

Notes

1 For more on this, see A. D. Yahaya, 'The developmental state in the process of transformation: the implication for the political science discipline', first annual lecture of the Nigerian Political Science Association (NPSA), Ibadan, 1989.
2 See Claude Ake, 'The limit of pluralism in Nigeria', *Nigerian Journal of Critical Social Science*, 1, 1 (January 1988).
3 For an interesting articulation of this reservation, see Claude Ake, 'The feasibility of democracy in Africa', CREDU Occasional Publication, No. 1 (Ibadan: 1992) and Wale Olaitan, 'Democracy and democratization in Atrica: not yet the glorious dawn', in B. Caron, A. Gboyega and E. Osaghae, (eds), *Democratic Transition in Africa* (Ibadan: CREDU, 1992), pp. 429–34.
4 Peter Anyang Nyong'o, 'Democratization processes in Africa', *CODESRIA Bulletin*, 2 (1991), p. 4.
5 ECA, *African Charter for Popular Participation in Development* (Addis Ababa: ECA, 1990), p. 19.
6 Naomi Chazan, 'Patterns of state–society incorporation and disengagement in Africa', in Donald Rothchild and Naomi Chazan (eds), *The Precarious Balance. State and Society in Africa* (Boulder: Westview Press, 1988), p. 122.
7 Rene Lemarchand, 'Uncivil states and civil societies: how illusion became reality', *The Journal of Modern African Studies*, 30, 2 (1992), p. 177.
8 For an explication of this, see Michael Bratton, 'Beyond the state: civil society and associational life in Africa', *World Politics*, XLI, 3 (April 1989), pp. 407–30; and P. P. Ekeh, 'The constitution of civil society in African history and politics', in B. Caron, *et al.*, *op. cit.*, pp. 193–6.
9 Joel D. Barkan, M. McNulty, L. Michael and M. A. O. Ayeni, '"Hometown" voluntary associations, local development, and the emergence of civil society in Western Nigeria', *The Journal of Modern African Studies*, 29, 3 (1991), p. 457.
10 Much of the background information about the LGA presented here was gleaned from the *Ijebu-Ode Local Government Official Hand Book* of February 1991. Most of the figures contained therein, however, would have been altered by the excision of much of the western part of the local government area to form part of the Odogbolu LGA, which was created in 1992. In the absence of up-to-date information on what is left of the old LGA we used the available figures for the purpose of this research.
11 Our verification exercise revealed that about 75 per cent of these health-related facilities are located in Ijebu-Ode township, which hosts the headquarters of the LGA.
12 Bamidele Badejo, *Ijebu-Ode in Perspectives* (Ijebu-Ode, Fairweather Books, 1992), p. 33.
13 See O. O. Odugbemi, 'Nigerian culture and space utilization with special reference to Yorubaland', in O. Y. Oyeneye and M. O. Shoremi (eds), *Nigerian Life and Culture* (Ago-Iwoye: Ogun State University, 1985), p. 177.
14 Bamidele Badejo, *op. cit.*, p. 75.
15 Max Weber, *Theory of Social and Economic Organization* (New York: Oxford University Press, 1947), pp. 136–7.
16 See Lester W. Milbraith and M. L. Goel, *Political Participation: How and Why Do People Get Involved?* (New York: University Press of America, 1977), pp. 10–24.
17 This sizeable figure of registered voters must be seen in the context of state compulsion of citizens to register during the last voters' registration exercise. Both the state and local governments threatened to make the possession of voters' cards a

precondition for the enjoyment of state facilities and services such as school registration, hospital attendance, etc. Although the threat was never actualized, it succeeded in persuading reluctant voters to register.

9

Survival and Renewal in the Grassroots Organizations of Mbaitoli, Imo State

NNAMDI C. OFONDU

Past and present development policies and strategies to effect genuine development in Third World countries since the 1960s have all but failed. Part of the reason for this failure is the phenomenon of élite rule which over the years has tended to alienate the vast majority of the people in the rural areas from the democratization and development processes of these countries. As a result, state power has tended to be concentrated in the hands of a small group of people.

In Nigeria, the tendency has been to focus on the federal and state governments and the privileged groups which revolve around those centres of power. The creation of local governments and the series of reforms undertaken since 1976 have not resolved the problem of popular alienation from politics and the development process as a whole. If anything, the dynamics of élite power and their negative consequences have tended to trickle down to the third tier of government.

Relevant to an explanation of this pattern is the nature of the process of élite formation and consolidation. Lacking the necessary economic base to consolidate social and political power, the élites seize the machinery of the state in order to realize their accumulation objectives.[1] The consequent primitive capital accumulation results, quite significantly, in the outflow of resources from the rural areas to the urban centres where most of the economic interests of the élites are located.[2]

Apart from the fact that the received formal structures of government have failed to integrate the local people and their traditional institutions, the over-centralization of power and concentration of resources have tended to emasculate traditional political, social and economic organizations in the rural areas. The weakness of these organizations has been exacerbated by political oppression resulting from the abuse of power, corruption on a wide scale, and the violation of the fundamental rights of the local people. There has been, therefore, a pattern of progressive decline in local initiative to seize available opportunities for self-generated development. This situation is particularly important in explaining the plight of women as social minorities in the rural enclaves of the national economy.

The task of this case study is to refocus on these problems as they are manifest in concrete forms in the locality being surveyed. On the basis of the analysis, it recommends practical guidelines for designing policies for people's empowerment towards more effective participation in the democratization and development process.

Mbaitoli LGA was chosen for this case study. It is located 15 kilometres north-east of Owerri, the Imo State capital. We surveyed 101 village settlements and designed questionnaire items to measure and evaluate indicators of popular participation in the democratization and development process in the locality.[3] Each set of questionnaire items was administered to inhabitants of village settlements, with responses from community leaders residing in the village to corroborate the responses by residents selected by random sampling. The responses were further corroborated by field visits to identify community projects, organizations and facilities.

The LGA is made up of nine town groups. Each town is made up of a number of villages, each of which is divided into kindreds. The field visits covered all the villages and kindreds. The nine sets of questionnaires for the nine town groups were collated to obtain a single set of questionnaires for the LGA. Additional data were collated from the responses of elected officials and personnel of the local government and political parties.

Basic socio-economic indicators

The Mbaitoli LGA is located approximately at the centre of Imo State. It has a population, based on the 1991 census figures, of 148,250. The breakdown shows that there are 70,276 males (47.4 per cent) and 77,974 females (52.6 per cent).[4]

The village is the predominant mode of settlement in the area. Each village is divided into kindreds, which are the smallest units within which members are held together by kinship ties that do not allow intermarriage within the unit. A constellation of villages make up an autonomous community or town. In all, there are 101 villages and about 262 kindreds. The nine close-knit communities are connected by an elaborate network of laterite roads and footpaths.

Education

There are 76 primary schools, 20 secondary schools and 18 vocational institutions in the LGA. There is also a special school for the deaf at Ofekata-Orodo.

Total primary school enrolment in Mbaitoli LGA in 1992 was 34,772 (18,253, or 52.5 per cent, were boys; 16,519, or 47.5 per cent, were girls) in about 960 streams/classes. The staff strength stood at 894 (321 men and 573 women teachers). These figures reflect the high level of appreciation of formal education in the LGA. Facilities in most of the primary schools visited were in a very poor condition and were grossly inadequate for effective learning. At the time of the survey (August 1993) primary school teachers were owed two months' arrears of salary and those who had retired a year before had not been paid their retirement benefit. Most of the schools were built by community self-help efforts and were also mainly maintained by them.

Pupil enrolment in secondary schools in 1992 was 11,316 (6,139 or 54.3 per cent were boys; 5,177 or 45.7 per cent were girls). The staff strength was 630 (339 men, 291 women teachers). Most of the secondary schools in the LGA were also built by community self-help effort. The teacher–pupil ratios in the LGA were 1:39 for primary schools and 1:18 for secondary schools. These figures indicate a poor staffing situation. The local government was nevertheless finding it difficult to foot the primary school teachers' monthly salary bill.[5]

Health

Medical and paramedical facilities in Mbaitoli LGA include two general hospitals. One of these, located at Ogwa, was established initially by community effort, before the state government took over and expanded the facilities and scale of operation; a part of the complex has now been upgraded to a psychiatric hospital. The Mbieri hospital, commissioned in 1993 by the state government, was also started by community effort.

Much of the community effort in the establishment of health facilities focuses on health centres/clinics and dispensaries, as well as maternity homes. There are 17 private hospitals and 25 maternity homes in the area. Most maternity homes also serve as dispensaries and health centres. Several villages are without health facilities and the operational efficiency of the facilities available is hampered by poor roads, an erratic electricity supply and an inadequate water supply.

Potable water

Ninety-three out of the 101 villages surveyed have no pipe-borne water. The main source of water supply is tankers from Owerri, about 15 kilometres away from the LGA headquarters and further from other villages. A drum of water was sold at an average of ₦15 in 1993. Rain water, pond water, wells and stream water from Okitankwo and Njaba streams supplement the water purchased from the tankers. A number of villages in Mbieri, Ubomiri and Ogbaku are supplied through the Owerri-Orji capital territory water scheme. Other outlying villages in Orodo, Umunnola and Ogwa are partly supplied from boreholes sunk by various community self-help projects and government water schemes.

Energy

The major source of energy in the locality is firewood. Of the 101 villages, only 19 are fully electrified; 19 are partially electrified; and 63 are not electrified at all. A number of electricity projects in the LGA are being executed by community self-effort. That large sections of the LGA are yet to be electrified indicates that the various levels of government have not responded actively to these local initiatives in terms of providing adequate resources to complement community efforts. There are several incomplete and abandoned electricity projects scattered across the LGA. The high cost of materials and the widespread poverty among local people, due to increasing economic difficulties, have slowed down the pace of community effort in this direction.

Transport

Most roads within the locality are laterite or bush paths, while the major market centre (Owerri) is connected by tarred road. The most available means of transport are bicycles and motorcycles. Motor vehicles ply between market centres scattered across the LGA. Beyond the market centres, motorcycles are used to connect inner settlements. Few roads are motorable and some villages have been cut off from neighbouring ones.[6] A number of tarred roads have been washed away by gully erosion. The road maintenance schedule has not been satisfactory.

Economic institutions

There are about 158 provision stores and eight supermarkets located in the market centres and along major road links in the LGA. There is a modern market for building materials located in Umuonyeali, Mbieri, and daily markets at Orodo. Other market centres in the locality are not fully developed.

There are two community banks in the LGA, one at Orodo and the other at Ogwa. The only commercial bank is located in Nworie-Ubi.

The survey noted 261 small-scale industries in the LGA. Prominent among them are all-purpose grinding machines, cabinet works, cottage oil mills, blacksmith works and a few bakeries. Altogether, these ventures employ about 841 persons.

Judicial and security institutions

There are two customary courts – one located at Nworie-Ubi and the other at Eziama-Obiato. The only magistrate's court is located at Nworie-Ubi. Apart from these, people of the various communities usually have recourse to traditional institutions for the settlement of disputes. Once a case has been decided by any of these institutions, the verdicts are binding upon the parties and recognized by the community. Parties not satisfied with the decisions of the traditional institutions may seek further redress at either the customary court or the magistrate's court at Nworie-Ubi.

There are three police stations and 75 police personnel. There are also about 75 neighbourhood traditional security organizations spread over the 101 villages.

Public facilities

These include a public library under construction by community effort at Umuahiami; eight post offices/postal agencies; and six motor parks located near the major market centres.

Mass media

In 1993, the *Statesman*, published in Owerri, had a circulation of 100–150 in the LGA, as did the *Sunray*, published in Port Harcourt. The *Horn*, published in Owerri by the local government chairman in 1993, Chief Oni Egbunine, had a circulation of 80–100. Newspaper readers often collected their papers at Owerri if they were working in the state capital.

In the case of national newspapers, The *Champion*, published in Lagos by Chief Emmanuel Iwuanyanwu from Imo State, had a circulation of 25–30, while the *National Concord* sold between 20 and 30. The *Daily Times* had a circulation of 15–30 while the *Guardian* had 10–15. Magazines were not sold in the LGA.

The majority of households in the area have at least one radio set. Very few have television sets since most communities have no electricity.

Local forms of communication include the use of town criers, the distribution of circulars and announcements in churches and at meetings. Once in a while, radio/television announcements are used to publish the obituaries of prominent personalities.

Indicators of popular participation

The kinds of social and popular organizations that exist in Mbaitoli LGA are: town/community union 'governments'; village unions; kindred meetings; women's wings of the town unions, village unions and kindred meetings; daughters' wings of the unions; age grade organizations; *Mmanya-Orie* market meetings;[7] and social clubs.

These organizations perform the traditional functions of government but with a strong bias in favour of social functions and cultural development. The various 'home' and 'abroad' branches of the organizations are development-oriented; more importantly, they are socio-cultural organizations with a number of social welfare schemes especially for financial members. They generally serve to meet the social and cultural needs of members while projecting the identity of the homeland. There are elaborate social security schemes for registered members, particularly at the 'abroad' branches, covering such eventualities as burials, naming ceremonies, wedding and accident insurance. They also project the culture and tradition of the homeland. The cultural function is more important in the case of 'abroad' branches in other parts of the country, since members regard themselves as strangers in many of the cities around Nigeria. In addition, they serve as agents of socialization for younger people as well as agents of informal and traditional education.

The social and political organizations also have economic functions, including organizing public works, raising funds for development activities, raising loanable funds for operating loan and investment schemes, and participating in community banking, market development, post offices, schools, town halls and the provision of social and recreational facilities. They serve as bases for conducting relationships with government agencies involved in development activities and also with other groups in the various communities.

In the case of traditional social and political organizations membership tends to be compulsory. As a result, all adult males or females from 18 years of age, living in the communities, are members. The men hold their meetings separately from the women. In the 'abroad' branches of the organization daughters may register and attend the meetings of male-dominant organizations. Married women hold their meetings separately. Membership is exclusively male in *Mmanya-Orie* and age grade organizations, since women are not organized into age grades. Age grade associations group men into age groups between three and five years apart. Social clubs at the town level have between 500 and 1,000 members and those at the village level between 200 and 500. These clubs have a gender bias and are often male-dominated.

The most important indigenous social and political organizations are kindred meetings and village unions organized around the *Umunna* (persons with kinship ties). These meetings, attended by every adult male, take important decisions about the organization and the government of the various communities, execute those decisions and settle disputes among members. The *Mmanya-Orie* meetings perform complementary roles. Membership is compulsory for all adult males. Age grade organizations function like pressure groups and membership is compulsory for those who fall within the age group. The non-indigenous organizations include social clubs and political parties: their membership tends to be voluntary and male-exclusive.

The tendency, therefore, is for indigenous social and political organizations to demand compulsory membership. Membership provides an opportunity for initiation into the traditional society and for political socialization. Membership is also a symbol of identity and belonging. Because of this, the idea of voluntary membership suggests alienation rather than choice.

Sources of finance for the social and political organizations are membership dues, fines, proceeds from the sale of confiscated property not redeemed, voluntary donations, loans, levies, charges and rents from the sale or lease of community property such as the town hall, land, economic trees and food crops harvested from communal farmlands.

Meetings of the social and political organizations are usually held once or twice a month and during the Christmas and Easter vacations at the home base. Elected officers can hold office for between two and five years. A range of sanctions is stipulated for a number of offences by members. Failure to pay membership dues for upwards of three years may lead to loss of membership rights and benefits in the event of death – but without loss of nominal membership in the case of indigenous social and political organizations, given that membership is usually compulsory. It is unusual to impose such sanctions, as expulsion symbolically amounts to expulsion from existence.

A failure to perform official duties may attract sanctions such as fines and dismissal from office in extreme cases. Embezzlement is very rare because of the social stigma it attracts. When this occurs, however, the culprit is made to refund the money and may also be fined or surcharged, or property may be confiscated and sold to recover the funds. Failure to attend meetings or lateness attracts a fine or reprimand. Social isolation or ostracization is recognized as a significant sanction for offences which violate a number of taboos, but they are not often applied in view of their severity.

Economic organizations

There are two kinds of cooperative societies, one for men and another for women, at the town and village level. Few of these are active in view of pressing economic difficulties, lack of support by various levels of government, and a reduction in the availability of agricultural inputs. There are numerous artisans' and craft guilds in the locality. These exist for wine tappers, shoemakers, timber men, witchdoctors, transport workers (motorcyclists), masons, daily paid labourers, mechanics and teachers. Most of these craft and artisan groups are organized at town levels and at LGA levels. There are also trading associations for the sellers of goods such as *gari*, vegetables, yams, meat and fish. *Esusu* (traditional credit) contribution groups abound in the locality, operating at the family, kindred and village levels in the LGA.

Membership of the cooperative societies ranges between 50 at the village level and 200 at the town level, where they are better organized. One gender is usually dominant and they are open to persons of all ages involved in the economic activities covered by the cooperative. Membership of craft, professional and artisan guilds is open to persons of all ages practising the trade. Most of these guilds are exclusively male since women rarely engage in the more established crafts. Trading associations allow as many members as are engaged in a particular commodity trade. There is usually no age restriction and membership is of mixed gender. Some trading lines (like vegetable sellers), however, may be dominated by females, while meat vendors, for example, are usually males. Membership of *Esusu* groups varies between five and ten at extended family level and between 20 and 50 at kindred and village levels. Usually, they are dominated by one gender, with only adult members eligible to join any particular group. Some *Esusu* groups restrict membership to a particular age grade association or to cultural groups (such as the *Owu* masquerade groups often organized at kindred levels in localities such as Orodo, Ifakala and Umunnoha). *Esusu* contributions linked with the *Owu* festival are aimed at meeting expenses to be incurred during the festival.[8]

Generally speaking, few age restrictions apply to the membership of indigenous economic organizations and membership tends to be voluntary. All members of the family are expected to join hands in the various productive activities for sustaining the community. Farming is widespread among the people in the various communities and is carried out by households, given the subsistence nature of agricultural production in the area. Individuals engage in trading and services in order to boost their incomes.

The sources of finance of economic organizations include membership dues, fines and levies, periodic contributions, donations and grants from government agencies, fund-raising activities and returns on investments.

Meetings of economic organizations are held much more regularly than those of social and political organizations. Elected officials serve for between three and four years. Sanctions are stipulated for specified offences.

In non-indigenous economic organizations such as banks and cooperative societies, severe sanctions – such as dismissal, expulsion, and suspension from duty – may be imposed if necessary. An offender's pay or promotion may be withheld or delayed when embezzlement or misappropriation of funds are committed. Kinship tie considerations tend to be played down since these organizations serve a wide range of customers from near and distant communities.

Case studies of economic organizations

MBAITOLI BRANCH OF IMO STATE FARMERS' CLUBS

The Mbaitoli branch, like its mother organization, was formed in 1978, during the political stirrings connected with the Second Republic. It is a political association formed by the élite and aimed at capturing political power. Very little farming activity is carried out by members, except the procurement of fertilizers and other agricultural inputs. As soon as the Nigerian People's Party (NPP) was voted into power in the state the farmers' club withered away, having achieved the aims of the élite group that sponsored it. On the formation of the two political parties (NRC and SDP), the club resurfaced and reorganized to mobilize members and the community toward providing political support for the SDP in the LGA and the state as a whole.

NATIONAL UNION OF ROAD TRANSPORT WORKERS (NURTW)
This is a prominent economic organization in the LGA, drawing its membership from commercial transport workers (mainly taxi drivers and motor park touts). It operates in the six motor parks in the LGA, regulating the activities of members to ensure compliance to decisions about transport fares and routes. Its main concern is to protect members from police harassment and undue increases in charges and rates imposed by the local authorities for the use of the motor park facilities. The union is very well organized and effective in executing its programmes. Its members rarely get involved as a group in political activities.

THE ORODO AND OGWA COMMUNITY BANKS
The community bank in Orodo was established in 1990 while that in Ogwa was commissioned in June 1993. The banks were established by members of the communities where they are located. The community bank at Orodo has been giving out credit to members of the community to finance small-scale trading and services as well as farming. Recipients are usually guaranteed by their kindred and/or village leaders, and collateral is not usually demanded. Some other community banks in the LGA were preparing to set up their own community bank in 1993. The banks enjoy a very high rate of patronage by members of the community, especially small-time traders. The rate of default among customers has been very low.

Political empowerment

The researcher could not obtain information on the numbers of registered members of the two political parties. It was also impossible to obtain information on the numbers of delegates in the various wards of the LGA. Information was available, however, on the level of women's empowerment. For the SDP, there was one elected woman out of the 12-member working committee of the party in the LGA. Out of the 172 party delegates for the LGA, 32 were women. There were also nine women among the 54 elected to the party state congress from the LGA, but no woman was elected LGA delegate to the party's national convention. There was no elected woman councillor. In the case of the NRC, there was only one woman among the 12-member working committee of the party in the LGA. Out of the 120 ward officials of the party, ten were women. Similarly, only ten women were among the 170 elected delegates from the LGA to the party's state congress. Lastly, only one woman was elected supervisory councillor out of 20 elected councillors from ten wards. The two elected members from the LGA at the state House of Assembly were men and the one member of the LGA elected into the House of Representatives was also a man.

Most of the persons interviewed confirmed that support for both the SDP and the NRC was generally high in the LGA. They claimed that almost every person supported either the SDP or the NRC. There was evidence, however, that the politicization of social and economic organizations had been used to coerce the populace to turn out in large numbers to cast their votes during elections. There was little to show as benefits to the people in return for their support. Rather, the people generally complained that elected officials tended to distance themselves from them once elected and did not fulfil their electoral promises. There was no evidence that people and their organizations in the LGA had embarked on any form of political protest.

Economic empowerment

Besides subsistence farming and petty trading, there are very few opportunities for paid employment in the LGA. This is because there are no significant manufacturing concerns and no state agency other than the local government itself, which employs only a few workers.

As most of the people are peasants and subsistence producers who supplement farm income with petty trading and services, it can be said that 90 per cent of the people of the LGA are low-income earners. There are a few who depend on wage income as public servants in both the local and state governments. Fewer still earn their living from private sector establishments in Owerri. Many of the elderly depend on transfer payments from their wards in the villages and in the cities outside the LGA. Overall, there is an impression of generalized poverty in Mbaitoli.

The survey identified a number of gender-related obstacles to economic empowerment. These include the fact that most local women earn low incomes, or have no regular income. They therefore tend to depend on men for much of their livelihood. There is a generalized land shortage in the LGA and women, in particular, do not have ready access to land required for farming. Since they cannot inherit land, they can only farm on their husband's land. They take advantage of the mixed cropping practice dominant in the area by planting 'women's traditional crops', such as cassava, vegetables and maize, alongside the 'men's traditional crop', which is yam. Since they require separate land to plant cocoyam, the backyard of the family building is used for this purpose and is passed from mother-in-law to daughter-in-law. This is the only piece of land that a married woman may directly inherit. The size of the backyard farm determines to some extent the size of the cocoyam barn and hence the economic status of the woman.

People in the area do not have ready access to credit, principally because the local people do not have the necessary collateral. This is more critical for women who, as noted above, usually do not directly own land. The situation is aggravated by the fact that the traditional society is male-dominated; most important decisions about the allocation and distribution of resources are taken by men, even when women may have contributed much in generating the resources. Women generally accept this skewed economic order because they do not think that there is any other alternative or reality.

Accountability and transparency

There are some laid-down mechanisms for the effective monitoring of the performance of officials of the local government, but most of these exist only in theory. While the state government is supposed to send supervisors from time to time to the local government, for example, it often fails to do so. Even on the few occasions when state officials come on supervisory tours, the local people are never able to take advantage of the visit since they are far removed from the activities of government.

Community leaders are expected to have easy access to the local government authorities to discuss the problems of the area. Evidence from the survey shows that this is not always the case. Responses from persons interviewed reveal that the local people exercise little, if any, influence on councillors once elected. The survey also shows that local government personnel are unwilling to discuss anything with visitors because they fear that they may be agents of the political opponents of their bosses; the same personnel have a tendency to express sympathy for the political party in government, mainly to avoid being victimized.

Although judicial enquiries may be demanded by the people to monitor the activities of the local authority, they have no control over the mechanisms for bringing about the inquiry. There are also means by which political office holders and local government personnel can be brought under the scrutiny of the Code of Conduct Bureau. Most local people and their leaders seem to be unaware, however, of the existence of any such mechanism for ensuring public accountability among officials. In theory the state legislature can also be employed by the people and their leaders to monitor the performance of officials. They may petition the legislature for an inquiry into certain actions of the local authorities. But the survey did not find any community members or leaders who had taken these measures or were contemplating doing so. There are no apparent means (such as through the press, for example) of expressing some of the criticisms of government policies and activities made to this researcher, thus bringing the weight of public opinion to bear on erring officials. Local people are mostly unaware that they have the right to attend the sittings of the legislative arm of the council for debates on public policies. This lack of awareness has reduced the effectiveness of the available devices for monitoring the performance of public officials.

In sharp contrast to the above, there are various means by which the performance of officials of social, political and economic organizations are monitored by the members of their organizations. Generally speaking, leaders are accessible to their followers. The people often ask questions on the progress of community projects whenever and wherever they encounter the officials. The people may also visit the sites of such projects within the area. Kinship ties provide another avenue for expressing views on the activities of elected officials. The prevalence of informal means of sanctions against amoral conduct generally makes officials of the organizations honest and responsible in their dealings. Thus the leaderships of these organizations are essentially accountable to their followers.

Conclusion

The foregoing analysis paints a picture of a people struggling for development. It is a struggle in which people's initiatives are dampened by a severe lack of basic social amenities and infrastructure – clear evidence that, over the years, government agencies have not been very responsive to or supportive of community-led development efforts. Government's initiatives in the selection and execution of projects lack a sense of direction.

There has been insufficient coordination of the activities of popular organizations involved in development projects. It is not only that the 'abroad' wings of these organizations, which are in the forefront of these endeavours, are far removed from the centres of power, but also that government agencies do not fully appreciate the mobilization values of the different popular organizations.

The fact that the local government depends mainly on statutory allocations from the federal government, which fall far below the level needed for an appreciable performance, makes it imperative that the local authority find means of coordinating and integrating community self-help projects and development activities into its own schemes. There is a need to involve community leaders in planning, designing and executing developmental projects.

Given the various problems enumerated above, the following policy measures, aimed at greater development of the rural areas and a higher level of participation of the people in the development process, are suggested.

1 The state and federal governments, as a matter of urgency, should take over the responsibility for infrastructural development in the rural areas. The focus should be on roads, electricity, water and means of communication. At the same time the statutory allocation to the local governments should be increased to 25 per cent of the federation account.

2 The federal government should ensure that at least one cottage industry is located in each of the LGAs of the federation. Such economic development agencies as the National Economic Reconstruction Fund (NERFUND) and the Ministry of Commerce and Industries should see to the realization of this goal.

3 State and federal authorities should strengthen the various mechanisms for monitoring the performance of elected officials and personnel of local government by establishing a statutory body charged solely with this responsibility.

4 Local governments should appoint project development and co-ordination officers for each of the communities in their areas and an annual statutory grant should be allocated to them to provide matching grants for executing self-help development projects.

5 The various levels of government should help increase the potential for self-generated income by encouraging rural dwellers (especially rural women) to go into self-employment and by providing accessible credit facilities.

6 Local governments should expand the scope for internally generated revenue to enhance resources available for development, by entering into partnership with private business and by investing in capital projects with commercial values.

7 The various levels of government should provide conditions in the rural areas conducive to the establishment of manufacturing and business concerns by private investors.

8 More financial institutions should be encouraged to set up in the rural areas by reducing the bureaucratic obstacles in the registration processes.

9 The scale of production of peasant agricultural producers should be expanded by increasing the supply of agricultural inputs to them.

10 Adult education facilities should be expanded.

It is our belief that these measures could make for a greater level of economic empowerment of the rural populace and increase their political empowerment, both of which are necessary for effective participation in the democratization and development process.

Notes

1 See William Graf, 'African élite theories and Nigerian élite consolidation: a political economic analysis,' in Yolamu Baroungo (ed.), *Political Science in Africa: a Critical Review* (London: Zed Press, 1983), pp. 193–4.

2 See Claude Ake, *Political Economy of Africa* (Ibadan: Longman Group Ltd., 1981), p. 64.

3 These indicators were initially identified and classified during a workshop on popular participation in rural communities in Nigeria held under the auspices of ACDESS on 27 July 1993. Also see indicators specified for investigation and evaluation of popular participation in Africa in ECA, *African Charter for Popular Participation in Development* (Addis Ababa: ECA, 1990), pp. 31–2.

4 The age distribution of the population was not reflected in the available data at the Census Bureau since analysis was in progress at the time of this survey. The same applies to the data on households. The population density could not be determined, either: no data were available on the area in square kilometres of the

LGA since it was carved out from Mbaitoli/Ikeduru LGA in 1989. But the survey confirmed from the responses that the villages suffer from a severe land shortage.

5 From discussion with chairman and chief executive of the Mbaitoli LGA, Chief Oni Egbunine.

6 For example, Umuomun has been cut off from the rest of Mbieri because the Umuomumu–Orie–Mbieri road has been submerged by gully erosion. This also applies to parts of Eziome bordering Ubomiri.

7 The *Mmanya-Orie* meeting is a socio-cultural and political meeting held in most Igbo communities on the specific *Orie* market day of a particular community with the celebration of palm wine as the major focus. The meeting is light-hearted but important decisions may be taken there and disputes among members of the community may be settled at the meeting.

8 The *Owu* festival is a new yam festival celebrated with several masquerades organized by young people. It acts as a pressure group, helping to enforce decisions on the community.

10

Building on Indigenous Organizations in Ohaozara, Abia State

AJA OKORIE

The crisis in African development in the last three decades seems to have reached a climax in the 1990s. It is multi-dimensional, encompassing the economic, human, legal, political and social spheres. The central issue in the crisis has been identified as the over-centralization of power, which in turn has created impediments to the participation of the vast majority of people in social, political and economic development.[1] Most of the marginalized members of the society are found in the rural areas.

There is a growing research and policy focus, at both national and international levels, on how best to decentralize the decision-making process, thereby involving all people (urban and rural) in all aspects of the decision-making, planning, execution and monitoring processes of projects that concern their development. Such decentralization is variously referred to as grassroots democratization or empowerment. It is hoped that an environment may be created that will enable the people to unleash their energies and creativity towards improving their well-being.[2] Such socio-economic and political empowerment of the people results in what has come to be referred to as popular participation.

Our operational definition of popular participation is a process which empowers the people to involve themselves effectively in creating structures and designing policies and programmes that serve the interests of all, as well as contributing effectively to the development process and sharing equitably in its benefits. Thus, popular participation ensures that people have freedom to associate, engage in enterprises of their choice, choose their leader(s), and vote or be voted for irrespective of gender, ethnicity, religion or political affiliation. It further presupposes the existence of freedom of the press and media, as well as the protection of the judicial environment.

Structurally, popular participation involves a tripartite symbiotic relationship between the people, civil/community organizations and the state. This structural relationship implies that the people through their organizations are central to the achievement of popular participation in any society.[3] Nonetheless, the people and organizations do not operate in a vacuum but within the confines of a state, which underlines the importance of the state in popular participation as well.

The current upsurge in interest in popular participation seems to suggest that the conventional or top-down approach to development has failed, and that an analytical approach that concentrates on the state or national level as a means of finding solutions to over-centralization of power has been shown to be defective. It is our thesis that we may find the answers to the African developmental crisis by going back to the grassroots in general and to our roots in particular – the structure and governance practices of our people in the rural communities, the indigenous organizations and systems – and by examining their relationship with the agencies of the modern state.

The Igbo of south-eastern Nigeria are known to be republican in their governmental relations. Before the advent of the colonialists, they had the reputation of resolving contentious matters, formulating and implementing developmental projects, selecting their leaders and successfully prosecuting wars through what could be described as popular participation in the current social science parlance.[4] In order to help analyse the Nigerian developmental crisis in the context of indigenous organizations, as well as the extent of popular participation in the democratization process, the rural communities of Ohaozara LGA of Abia State were selected for a case study.

Methodology

Ohaozara LGA of Abia State typifies a rural community in transition where the indigenous and alien systems seem to be blending into intermediate systems. It also provides all the rudiments and ingredients of Igbo community development initiatives, socio-economic and political institutions and organizations found elsewhere. During the initial methodology workshop organized by ACDESS, indicators for the field research were developed for use as a guide by the researchers. In addition to the list of indicators, a check list was developed and used for the interview process. Oral interviews were used, to enable us to assess the authenticity of the responses, as well as to interject some probing questions where necessary.

Data for this case study were collected between 28 July and 13 August 1993. Secondary data were collected from both the local government headquarters at Obiozara and some state ministries at Umuahia. For the primary data, elected local government officials, political party officers (at LGA and ward levels), community leaders, officers and members of community organizations/associations were interviewed to obtain facts and opinions.

The background

Ohaozara LGA is one of the 17 LGAs that make up Abia State. It is made up of five autonomous communities, namely Akaeze, Ishiagu, Okposi, Uburu and Ugwulangwu. These communities are subdivided into ten political wards for electoral purposes.

The present Ohaozara LGA was carved out of the former Ohaozara LGA (which included current Onicha LGA) in 1987, while the old Ohaozara was created out of the former Afikpo Divisional Council in 1976 during the country-wide local government reform.

The LGA is rural. It is bounded in the north by Onicha and Awgu LGAs in Abia and Enugu states respectively. In the south, it is bounded by Afikpo South LGA; in the east by Afikpo North LGA; and in the west by Isurkwuato LGA, all in Abia State. It has an area of roughly 650 square kilometres, which is 8.5 per cent of the state's land area (7,627 square kilometres).[5]

Ohaozara is essentially an agrarian locality and is regarded as the food basket of Abia State, producing various food crops such as rice, yam, cassava and vegetables in commercial quantities. It also contains various mineral resources, including limestone, gypsum, lead and zinc, as well as salt deposits.

Ohaozara people are very religious and exhibit, in abundance, traditional Igbo hospitality. They are industrious, politically conscious and essentially republican. They like their communities and are therefore prepared to contribute towards their socio-economic development.

Socio-economic profile

Demography

By the 1991 census provisional estimates, Ohaozara LGA has a total population of 133,968 (59,467 or 44.6 per cent are men; 74,501 or 55 6 per cent are women).[6] The LGA accounts for 5.8 per cent of the Abia State's population though it has 8.5 per cent of the land area, which shows that the population pressure on Ohaozara resources is low relative to the other LGAs in the state. The gender population distribution in the LGA, in which the female population is greater than the male population, has implications for both economic and political empowerment, discussed later in this chapter.

Education

Ohaozara has 44 primary schools of which 27 are located in Ishiagu and Okposi. There are eight secondary schools. There are no functional tertiary institutions in the LGA, although a school of nursing is under construction in one of the autonomous communities (Uburu) and there is a proposal to move the Federal College of Agriculture at Umudike to the LGA (to be located at Ishiagu).

More accurate indicators of the availability of education facilities in the area, such as the children of school age per available school at different levels, could not be computed because of lack of disaggregation of the 1991 census figures. The existence of 11 vocational institutions, all privately owned, demonstrates a commitment by Ohaozara indigenes to educational ventures. Maintenance of schools is carried out largely by community efforts, another indication of a self-help spirit.

Health

The LGA is poorly endowed with health facilities. There is one hospital, located at Uburu, and three community health centres. In addition, there are six doctors' clinics, which the owner/doctors run on a part-time basis. There are a total of 13 doctors in the LGA health system, one each in Akaeze and Ishiagu, four in Okposi (one of whom is a homoeopathetic doctor), six in Uburu and none in Ugwulangu. There are 26 trained nurses, 13 of them at the hospital and five others at the LGA headquarters health clinic. On the average, there are five trained nurses per community. The ratio of persons to available doctors and nurses is 10,305 persons per doctor and 5,153 persons per trained nurse. The actual distribution of doctors and nurses among the communities is highly skewed, with Uburu and Okposi having the greatest number while Ugwulangwu has the least.

Ohaozara is a guinea-worm endemic area and accounts for about 25 per cent of the guinea-worm cases recorded in former Imo State. The disease adversely affects the socio-economic lives of the people, interfering with the education of children and with the farming and other economic activities of the adults, thereby reducing their economic empowerment capabilities.

In response to the guinea-worm menace, the LGA has established a chapter of the Nigerian Guinea-worm Eradication Programme (NIGEP), which organizes workshops and seminars aimed at the eradication of guinea-worm. The NIGEP campaign seems to be yielding some positive results, as shown by the falling number of recorded cases, from 7,552 in 1990/1 to 1,271 in 1992 (January–December), to only 270 cases for 1993 (January–July). Victims of guinea-worm disease are treated free of charge while cloth filters are distributed free of charge in highly endemic villages under NIGEP.

Guinea-worm is a water-borne disease and its occurrence is closely related to the type of water supply in the communities. Its endemic nature in Ohaozara is therefore the consequence of an inadequate supply of potable water.

Potable water

Ohaozara has no pipe-borne water. Before 1982, most of the population relied on water supplies from rivers, muddy streams and ponds. A few have access to spring water which, invariably, is salty. Currently, a considerable proportion of Ohaozara's population has access to borehole water supply. As a result of rural water projects sponsored by UNICEF and the DFRRI, which sank 152 shallow water boreholes in Ohaozara between 1982 and 1993, most people live within 1.4 kilometres of a water source (August 1993). Of these boreholes, 104 are functional, which implies that each services an average of 6.5 square kilometres or 1,288 persons within the LGA.

Energy

The major energy sources required for socio-economic and industrial development of a rural society like Ohaozara include electricity, fuel, kerosene and fuelwood. Four of the five communities comprising Ohaozara LGA do not have any form of electricity supply. Only Ishiagu has a few kilometres of supply, provided by the rock-crushing industries in the town. At the time of this research the Ishiagu electrification project (phase II), with 15.6 kilometres of high tension lines and one sub-station, built by the joint efforts of the DFRRI and the community, was expected to be commissioned in the near future. The Abia State government had surveyed Akaeze, Uburu and Ugwulangwu communities and awarded a contract for rural electrification of these communities. Okposi community had a rural electrification project sponsored by the European Development Fund, nearing completion. The local government administration in 1992 had donated a transformer and four drums of high tension wire each to the five communities at a cost of ₦5.2 million. The LGA headquarters also had two generators (130 KVA and 250 KVA) which served sections of the Uburu community.

In the absence of electricity, most inhabitants rely on kerosene and fuelwood for their energy supplies. On the average, kerosene supply is localized at village level with accessibility of 1–2 kilometres' walking radius. Because of the limited availability of kerosene, in terms of ability to purchase required quantities, most households retire to bed early, usually between 8 and 10 p.m. Kerosene and other types of fuel are found in the six filling stations in the LGA. There are considerable disparities in the accessibility of fuel supply points among the communities and the average walking distance to a filling station in the LGA is 5.9 kilometres.

Lack of electricity supply in most communities forces the people to depend largely on fuelwood for cooking. Fuelwood is available on a household basis, often at less than one kilometre's walking radius. Wood is brought to the compounds by most farm families on their way back from farms. A lot of the time and energy which could be used in other economic, political and social ventures are spent on obtaining fuelwood.

Road infrastructure, transport and markets

The road infrastructure in the LGA is very poor. Only two federal roads pass through it, with a total length of about 60 kilometres. The first passes through Okposi to Ukawu from Onicha[7] community and measures about 25 kilometres. The second passes the LGA tangentially from Uturu (Isurkwuato LGA), through Ishiagu and Akaeze to Oso-Edda (Afikpo South LGA) and measures about 35 kilometres. The total length of state roads in Ohaozara is 115 kilometres, while the local government roads are estimated at 144 kilometres.

All the federal roads were tarred over ten years ago and, from a lack of maintenance, have developed many potholes, which make them death traps for motorists. Only 16.5 per cent of the state roads (Amasiri–Okposi–Obiozara) are tarred and the rest are dirt roads. All the LGA roads are of laterite. While some are described as 'DFRRI rural feeder roads', many of them existed before the setting up of the DFRRI.

Most state and local government roads are in a deplorable state and muddy during the rainy season. The state of the roads makes communication difficult and slows down economic, social and political activities in the area. In particular, the supply of farm inputs and manufactured goods to the inhabitants, as well as the transportation of farm products to the urban areas, are impaired, with negative consequences for the economic empowerment of Ohaozara people.

All the major markets in the LGA are alongside federal or state roads, at less than two metres from the road. These include: Nkwo Achara and Eke markets in Okposi, Ogidi market in Akaeze, Orie market in Uburu, Nkwo market in Ugwulangwu and Eke market in Ishiagu. Only Eke market at Okposi is further (about one kilometre) from the state road (Amasiri–Okposi–Obiozara). The markets are therefore easily accessible to farmers and traders, as they are located at the centre of the community in each case. These major markets are held on the basis of the Igbo week.[8]

Rural infrastructure is critical to the success of other government efforts aimed at rural development and grassroots socio-economic and political empowerment. For example, rural people suffering from debilitating, infectious and parasitic diseases, such as guinea-worm, are unable to provide intensive labour in the production system, which relies for over 95 per cent of its energy requirements on human muscle. Rural infrastructure could help in diversifying income-generating capacities and gainful employment opportunities in the rural areas.

Economic institutions and activities

There are only two commercial bank branches in the LGA: the African Continental Bank (ACB) located at Okposi and the Union Bank of Nigeria (UBN), located at Uburu. One community bank (CB) has just commenced operation at Ishiagu. There is no People's Bank of Nigeria (PBN) in Ohaozara. The CB and PBN are being introduced to address the inaccessibility of commercial and development banks to the rural and urban poor. There are numerous shops scattered all over the communities in the LGA. The shops tend to be located at the roadside opposite the major markets, and at the centre of the communities, where population densities are high. The majority of the shops are multi-purpose village retail shops, with little specialization. However, specialized shops for building materials (such as cement and reinforcing rods), beer and liquor are found mainly at Okposi, which is the commercial nerve centre of the LGA. There are also ten local supermarkets in the LGA with four of them located at Okposi.

The operational medium-sized local industries are for rock crushing and mining. Eight of these are situated at Ishiagu community. Some of the companies mine lead, while others crush rocks for building and road construction. Salt production from salt ponds and streams exists at household levels at Okposi and Uburu communities,[9] while Ishiagu community is known for its pottery on a household basis. The small-scale industries in the area include owner-operated rice mills (totalling about 12) and cassava grating/milling machines (numbering 60 to 80). There are five hotels in the LGA; two each are located at Okposi and Akaeze and one at Ishiagu.

It is noteworthy that all the economic institutions in the LGA were privately owned as at the time of our study, except the newly opened BLP mini-supermarket at Obiozara (the LGA headquarters). This depicts the general lack of a state and federal government presence.

There is one post office at Okposi, and four postal agencies, one in each of the other communities. Mail is distributed through private boxes and mail bags; schools and churches also serve as points of mail distribution/collection. The post office is quite small with only four workers. There is no telephone facility in the LGA. The telephone service nearest to the LGA is located in Afikpo LGA, about 25 kilometres away. There is also no public library in the entire LGA.

Four motor parks are located and functional in the LGA at Okposi, Akaeze, Uburu and Ishiagu. The busiest is the Okposi park, which loads 50 to 80 cars per day at an average of seven passengers per car. Next in importance of traffic density is that of Akaeze. Uburu park loads five to 15 cars a day. The only railway station in the LGA is located at Ishiagu and the line passes tangentially to Awgu LGA in Enugu state.

It is evident that the paucity of intra- and inter-community communications (transport, telephone, postage) in the LGA hinders the full realization of the economic, social and political potentials of Ohaozararians, and thereby constitutes an obstacle to popular participation.

Security and judicial institutions

The LGA has one police station. Situated at Obiozara, it is headed by a divisional police officer with the rank of chief superintendent, assisted by a divisional crime officer with the rank of deputy superintendent. Other officers at the station are patrol and ground inspectors, and other ranks. In addition, there are four police outposts, each headed by an inspector.

To complement the security provided by the police, villages and neighbourhoods (*Onokoro*) have their traditional or local security arrangements. Inhabitants form themselves into vigilante groups and guard their environs at night in rotation, usually between 10 p.m. and 6 a.m. The groups are not based on 'age grade associations' because of the erosion of the age grade system by migration to the urban areas by the youths as well as the formation of social clubs, which cut across age grade associations. In general, the crime rate in Ohaozara is much lower than that obtaining in the urban areas of Abia State and other states of the federation.

To administer justice, the state government has established two judicial institutions in the LGA. These are one magistrate's court and one customary court, both located at Okposi. In addition, there is the traditional judicial system, which involves several organizations such as the town union, the village council of elders (*Ndi Uke*), kindred associations, women's groups and associations of different title owners. These organizations participate in the administration of justice, especially on civil matters. Except for the traditional governmental organizations such as *Ndi Uke* and town unions, which have wide powers of adjudication, other indigenous associations deal only with cases in which their members are involved.

Mass media

Information availability and technology are not well developed in Ohaozara LGA. There is no local newspaper or magazine, but the LGA has access to some newspapers. The *National Ambassador*, owned by Abia State, circulates fewer than 200 copies in Okposi and Obiozara per week. Occasionally, a few copies of the privately owned daily newspapers, the *Champion* (based in Lagos), and the *Sunray* (based in Port Harcourt) are made available to customers. Other than these three, no other newspaper or magazine is available. There is only one newspaper vendor serving the entire LGA and he is based in Okposi.

In contrast, the LGA has access to the national and international electronic media through radio and television. It receives, on a regular basis, news from many radio channels on short-wave, medium-wave and FM stations. International news is obtained from the BBC and Voice of America radio networks late in the evening and early in the morning (5 a.m. to 7 a.m.). Most families own transistor radio sets. A few privileged households own television sets.

Traditional town criers are used to deliver messages to villagers. The town crier or announcer derives his authority from either the chief, the village committee or the council of elders. He is required to make announcements at the market square when the market is in session and/or within the village early in the morning between 5 a.m. and 6 a.m., or late in the evenings between 9 p.m. and 10 p.m. A male town crier summons or gives messages to the entire village or community (male/ female) while the female town crier is limited to summoning or delivering messages to women about their own affairs. She uses a metal gong (*Ogene*) or a bell to draw the attention of the womenfolk. Also, she is restricted to delivering messages within the village and not at the market square, unlike her male counterpart.

Another traditional method of communication is the interpersonal approach through messages emanating from any of the local authorities. Messages are passed from person to person in a hierarchical order, from the authorities to those at the base. Where information is meant for a few people, interpersonal oral communication is more appropriate. Churches and schools are often used as channels of information dissemination. Such information may be on educational, religious, economic, social and (at times) political issues. Information pertaining to politics is often passed on in a subtle manner in churches .

Indicators of popular participation

The major indicators of popular participation are the socio-political organizations, economic organizations and the mass media. These organizations may be sub divided into indigenous and non-indigenous categories. For the socio-political organizations, a hybrid of the two categories can be identified.

Indigenous socio-political organizations

The major indigenous socio-political organizations found in the area include:

1 Age grade associations, *Nzuko Eburu;*

2 Kindred/kinship associations, *Nzuko Ikwu, Nzuko Umunna, Nzuko Umuada;*

3 Councils of elders, *Ndi Uke;*

4 Titled men's and women's associations, *nzuko ndi chiri echiechi.*

AGE GRADE ASSOCIATIONS

The age grade association or *Nzuko Eburu* is pervasive in Igboland and is organized along gender lines. Age grade organization is voluntary and made up of men or women born in a space of three to five years, united by their common will to protect and preserve the traditions of the community and to promote its development. The age grade has been described as having a counterbalancing force to the potentially disruptive centrifugal force of extended family and kinship ties in village life.[10]

While men and women have their separate age grade meetings, their main features are similar within the LGA. Each age grade is formed by people who must belong to the same gender and village. Each age grade takes a name of its choice, which reflects its peculiarity and is also its motto: *Igwe Bu Ike*, for example, which means 'unity is strength'. Age grade meetings are only for those who have come of age, that is those from the age of 18 years and above in the case of men, and those who are married in the case of women.[11] Membership of an age grade meeting is compulsory for all adults in each village.

In most parts of Igboland, age grade associations are recognized as agents of community development. The age grade associations are village-based, and constitute units of social and economic development. In the colonial and pre-colonial times, the age grades used to be focal points in community development efforts. Age grades, in healthy competition, used to undertake the building of wooden/bamboo bailey bridges, culverts and new roads, or the grading of old ones. They also undertook tasks such as building village halls and squares. They were instruments of maintaining peace and enforcing laws and social norms, as well as a context in which to display strength, skills and courage. Wrestling was usually on an age group basis. Among members, age grades provided social insurance as they condoled and assisted bereaved members, and celebrated with members on occasions of marriage, birth and other blessings.

In post-colonial times, however, the number, strength and relevance of the associations have been on the decline. With the increasing migration of youths from the rural areas to the urban cities, it has become difficult to find sufficient members of the same age grade at home for the close ties and daily interactions of the past. Consequently, their community development and social roles seem to have been taken over by the hybrid associations of village/town/development unions and social clubs respectively.

Age grade associations in most villages in Ohaozara seem to be dwindling in both number and relevance. The few that exist function in the manner of other village organizations. The sources of finance include members' monthly contributions, fines, levies and sometimes donations. Leaders are selected by general consensus based on a track record of honesty, trustworthiness, active participation in group activities and ability to stand firm on vital issues. In the pure form of age grade organization, the leaders were never changed except in case of death or disability occasioned by prolonged illness. Now changes in leadership may be more frequent, though not on fixed terms of say three to four years. Suspension or impeachment of officers is rare; rather, they are rewarded for good work by extension of tenure or indefinite tenure of office. Meetings are on a monthly basis, fixed on a particular Igbo market day (e.g. Sunday *Eke* or Sunday *Nkwo*).[12] There are no written constitutions and by-laws. Members are expected to conduct themselves with dignity. Breach of the unwritten laws and constitution attracts sanctions such as fines and suspension, but rarely expulsion.

Age grade associations take part in local governance through their leaders (and, at times, other members), who may become members of the village committee by virtue of their position in the age grade. Beyond that, age grade associations do not take an active part in modern politics. They do not sponsor members to elective or non-elective political offices. They are principally concerned with village development and governance.

KINDRED/KINSHIP ASSOCIATIONS

These are associations of kindred men or women. All members have a blood relationship. These associations are usually for all male or female adults of the same lineage and membership is compulsory. Meetings are either monthly or bi-monthly. Because members are regarded as one family, there are usually no constitutions or by-laws. Members are expected to be punctual at meetings and to carry out any duties assigned to them. Suspension and expulsion rarely occur, as the latter implies ostracization. Fines are imposed for misconduct, but not as often as in the age grade.

There are three types of these associations, namely: *Ikwu*, a term for men, women and children of the same lineage; *Umunna*, which means 'brothers' or 'father's male children'; and *Umuada*, which means 'the sisters'. Three officers – chairperson, secretary and treasurer – usually run the association's affairs. The officers of *Nzuko Ikwu* or *Umunna* or *Umuada* are selected by consensus. They are rarely changed except in the event of disability or death or migration to far away cities.

The *Ikwu*, *Umunna* and *Umuada* associations are solely for the purpose of promoting the welfare of the members. They settle disputes among the members, assist members financially when in need, plan and execute burials and participate in marriage, birth and naming ceremonies. Some assist in the education of members' children, by giving grants, loans or full scholarships. In some cases, it is the first port of call in terms of seeking a mandate and support for elective political office. The blessings of *Ikwu* or *Umunna/Umuada* are usually sought by a prospective candidate.

THE COUNCIL OF ELDERS – *NDI UKE*

Members of *Uke* are respected elderly men or women, selected by consensus, who settle disputes, make rules and regulations and enforce discipline in the communities or villages. They are selected on a representative basis from the members of the village or community. Their age range is 55 to 70 years. A male council of elders is referred to as *Ndi Uke* while a women's council is called *Ndi Uke Umunwanyi*. *Ndi Uke* operates within the tradition, subject to unwritten rules and regulations. It is headed by *Isi Uke*, the leader. Meetings of *Ndi Uke* are held at *Isi Uke*'s compound or at a secluded village square, presided over by *Isi Uke*. Most deliberations are oral and unwritten, though in some cases a Secretary to *Ndi Uke* is appointed. To assist *Ndi Uke* in the enforcement of decisions and judgements, some traditional law enforcement agents, *Ndi Ogba Gidi*, are selected by the village or community. They are usually of younger ages than *Ndi Uke*. *Ndi Uke* are insulated from modern politics. From the pre-colonial times to date, the *Ndi Uke* institution remains critical in village/community governance.

TITLED MEN'S AND WOMEN'S ASSOCIATIONS

Nzuko Ndi Chiri Echichi, as the association of titled men or women is known, has important social-cultural functions. As the name implies, membership is exclusive to those who have attained certain socio-economic heights in the society and performed the appropriate ritual to be honoured with the relevant title. Because of the structure of Igbo society, women and men have separate hierarchies of titles; they are never admitted to the same titles and would therefore not belong to the same title associations. The highest title for men in Ohaozara is *Onyibe*, which one acquires after completing *Ozu* title ceremonies. For the women, it is *Okenaji* title. Membership cut across all ages, though most members are aged more than 50. Membership boosts a member's ego and attracts respect and reverence from other members of the society. Members help each other in times of need, and celebrate the birth of new children and other blessings.

Leadership is based solely on seniority of title, irrespective of age. Meetings are held on a monthly or bi-monthly basis, on rotation at members' homes. As men and women of honour and distinction, they have codes of conduct which members are expected to adhere to strictly. Sources of funds are membership fees, contributions and levies. As a group, members are not involved in partisan politics.

Hybrid socio-political organizations

These organizations are in transition between indigenous and non-indigenous categories. Some examples of these are: (1) *Eze* and *Eze*'s council of chiefs; (2) village/town development unions; and (3) social clubs.

EZE AND EZE'S COUNCIL OF CHIEFS

Eze is the traditional ruler and head of an autonomous community in Igboland. Only a man can be installed as an *Eze*. In Ohaozara, the *Eze* has a council of chiefs composed of chiefs of constituent villages of the community, chosen by the villages themselves. In some other Igbo communities (outside Ohaozara) the *Eze* appoints chiefs who assist him in the administration of the community. Chieftainship is the highest honour available in normally democratic and republican Igboland, where such titles are open to every 'freeman' equally. Nevertheless, only a few were able to enter the most exalted orders in the old days. The practice of appointment of chiefs by the *Eze* has resulted in abuse which Basden has aptly described: 'In modern times, the dignity of the chieftainship has been degraded and the tendency is to bring the whole system into disrepute, owing to the wholesale and indiscriminate sale of titles to any youth who can produce the stipulated fees.'[13] This is another example of the disintegration and transition of traditional values and institutions. By reason of his elevated position, the *Eze* is non-partisan. Statutorily, the federal and state governments bar *Ndi Eze* from participation in partisan politics.

The Igbo people in general are republican and did not have the institution of traditional rulers until the colonial masters imposed warrant chiefs on Igbo communities. The institution of *Eze* has further developed a higher socio-political status with the enhancement of traditional institutions in Nigeria since the 1970s.

VILLAGE/TOWN DEVELOPMENT UNIONS

Village development committees (VDCs) and town development unions

(TDUs) are found in every village and community (town) respectively in Ohaozara LGA. These organizations are a post-independence phenomenon and emerged to reduce the frequency of village or community people's congresses (VPCs, and CPCs), which are similar to the proverbial Greek democracy. With greater modernization, people have become more time-conscious and have devised more efficient approaches to the same activities; this has been the case with the transition from VPCs and CPCs to VDCs and TDUs respectively.

The development unions have five main functions. These are: infrastructural development of the village or community; settlement of individual and inter-village disputes; promotion of community and government relations, as well as intra- and inter-community relations; maintenance of community socio-cultural functions, such as selection and burial of the community's *Eze*; and overall local governance of the community, including the making and execution of policies and laws. Town unions have been known to build and equip secondary schools, build bridges and culverts, market stalls and town halls, and award secondary and university scholarships.

Membership is restricted to men, and based on village representation in the case of the village committee. Members are selected by their villages and sent to the centre. The tenure of the representatives is rarely specified, but each village or kinship group reserves the right to recall any representative who performs below expectations. Age distribution of members on the average is as follows: 18–30 years = 5 per cent; 31–44 years = 60 per cent; and 45–60 years = 35 per cent.

The town union officers are elected by members through an open ballot system during the inaugural meeting. The officers consist of chairman/president, vice-chairman/president, secretary, assistant secretary, treasurer, financial secretary, public relations officer and three auditors. Four patrons are appointed from the eminent sons of the community. The tenure of officers is three to four years. Meetings are held once a year, except in the case of emergencies. The union is ruled by constitution and by-laws, used for control and sanctions. Funds are raised through levies on villages and kindred groupings.

Some variations exist in the structure and operations of town unions. One such variant is one in which all adult male members of the community are members of the union. In this case it is closer to the community congress. The union then has home headquarter officers, called national officers, and branch officers for branches established in all major cities in Nigeria, where many of the sons of a community live. Delegates from branches attend meetings at home headquarters at least once a year. There may be one or two general meetings annually.

The involvement of town unions in partisan politics is limited and varies from community to community. In most communities, the union limits itself to zoning of elective political offices to political wards or villages within a ward, as a means of minimizing political rancour. Zoning may be based on seniority or previous representation, but whatever criterion is used, equity and fairplay are paramount. Zoning at community and local government levels helped to usher in political tolerance and understanding during the second and third republics.

Non-indigenous socio-political organizations

Non-indigenous socio-political organizations in Ohaozara are not numerous and consisted at the time of this research of: (1) social clubs, (2) school committees, and (3) the two government-registered political parties.

SOCIAL CLUBS

These are a post-civil war phenomenon in Igboland. The nucleus of a social club is often a group of friends and acquaintances from the same village, community or area. Social clubs focus essentially on members' welfare and secondarily on community development. They can be considered as 'modified and modernized' age-grade associations. Social clubs are more sophisticated than *Isusu* and kindred associations, and are required to register with the state governments through the social welfare offices in the local government.[14] Membership is voluntary, and may be open to both sexes. Entry is by application and there is rigorous screening by the club executives. Membership may be restricted to people from the same village, community or local government, some of whom may be resident outside their communities but visit home periodically.

It is estimated that there are about 50 such clubs in Ohaozara LGA, with an average membership size of 200. Less than 5 per cent of the members are female. Okposi communities have over 30 per cent of the social clubs . Age distribution of members, on the average, is 18–30 years = 10 per cent; 31–45 years = 60 per cent, and 46–60 years = 30 per cent.

The clubs have conventional officers: president, vice-president, secretary, assistant secretary, treasurer, financial secretary, publicity secretary/ public relations officer, auditors, and provosts. Officers are elected for nominal terms of three to four years. In practice, well-performing officers are re-elected without restriction as to number of terms, and this is seen as a reward for good performance. Social clubs have constitutions and by-laws for control and sanctions. Breach of the constitution or by-laws can be punished by fines, suspension or dismissal, depending on the gravity of offences.

Clubs have home headquarters and branches in major cities in the country where sizeable number of members live. National meetings are held two to three times a year at the home base. All members from all branches are required to attend the national meetings. Emergency national meetings may be summoned as the need arises. The sources of funds for the clubs are admission fees, statutory contributions, special levies and donations. Other internal governance procedures are similar to those of age grades in some respects and to the TDUs in others.

Social clubs provide social security to members. Dependants of members are given moral and material assistance (in the form of financial donations and arranging members' burial ceremonies) in case of death. Living members are also given financial assistance in times of need (accidents, financial distress, death of kin). Clubs celebrate with members in time of marriages and births, as well as taking active part in communal festivities such as New Yam festivals, Easter, Christmas and *Aju*[15] celebrations. Some of the social clubs have contributed to community development. A typical example of this is the Adu Social Club of Uburu, which is credited with building a headquarters complex at the cost of ₦350,000 (at 1980 prices), assisting in the building and equipping of Uburu Secondary School and a postal agency, and the grading of roads in the community.

In general, social clubs have become a useful instrument of social and infrastructural development in Ohaozara. Their participation in politics has been very limited. They are all apolitical, and prefer that partisan politics is discussed outside the club platform, though members may participate in politics as individuals.

SCHOOL COMMITTEES

Each of the primary schools has a committee composed of indigenes. Each committee caters for the needs of its school, in terms of provision of equipment and furniture, repair of buildings, and the settlement of teacher–teacher and teacher–pupil disputes, including the maltreatment of non-indigenous teachers. In effect, the committees complement the efforts of the local government management boards, and they report to their respective village development committees.

POLITICAL PARTIES

The NRC and the SDP, at the time of this research, had their offices at both the LGA and ward levels, and commanded considerable support. Details of their membership and activities are discussed in the section dealing with political empowerment.

Indigenous economic organizations

As the economy of the LGA revolves around land and agricultural resources, most indigenous economic organizations in the area relate to farming, credit, or both. They include *Isusu* clubs.

Isusu clubs

Isusu clubs are regarded as an indigenous system of saving in which a group of people come together, contribute fixed amounts at fixed intervals, and assign the total amount contributed to an individual member in rotation,[16] hence the alternative name of rotating savings club (ROTSAC).

But *Isusu* clubs are known to offer credit to members, and to share their accumulated savings at certain times of the year, rather than in rotation.[17]

These clubs are akin to the savings organizations found in rural communities in other parts of the world, such as the *Ketu* of the Negri Sambilian Malays, the 'Cheet' of the Mauritian Indians, the *Komiti* of the Maori Communities in New Zealand, and the *KE* societies in Korea. The clubs are known by various names among the different ethnic groups in Nigeria, namely: *Isusu* or *Otutu* among the Igbo, *Esusu* among the Yorubas, *Adashi* among the Hausas, *Dashi* among the Nupes, *Efe* among the Ibibios and *Oku* among the Kalabari Ijaws.[18] The operations of *Isusu* clubs in Igboland is well documented by Okorie and Miller.[19]

Isusu club membership is open or closed. Membership in open clubs is unrestricted, cutting across age, sex and occupational groups as well as socio-economic status. Such clubs have as members farmers, traders, motor mechanics and drivers, seamstresses, salaried workers of all categories, housewives and school children. On the other hand, the closed clubs are built around occupational groups such as teachers, hospital staff and local government staff, or religious groups such as women's guilds, or socio-economic classes such as *Ndi Onyibe* (*Ozo Oju* or *Ozo* title holders).[20] The clubs with restricted membership, especially among salaried workers, may be as small as four people. The total number of *Isusu* associations in the LGA is estimated at 400, with a total membership of 20,000.

Most of the clubs have by-laws, which set out the objectives, rules, regulations and penalties for breaches of any regulations. In some of the clubs the by-laws are written, in others they are implied. *Isusu* club officers provide the leadership required for the existence of the club. A typical club in Ohaozara has a chairman secretary, a treasurer and a provost. The more formal clubs have additional officers, such as the vice-chairman, assistant secretary and auditor. The club officers are compensated either in cash or in kind during the end-of-year meetings where savings and interests generated from loans are shared (if contributions are not collected in rotation). When contributions are saved for a year, the chairman/treasurer keeps the money and pays no interest on unborrowed funds, but members are satisfied that they have been compelled to save and that their savings have been kept safely. Club officers are rarely changed except when found guilty of some misdemeanour such as fraud, which is rare.

Most clubs are built around the founder/chairman. Club meetings are often held in the chairman's compound/home or in the home of the secretary. Frequency of meetings varies according to the type of *Isusu*. It may be monthly, weekly, fortnightly or every Igbo week (4 days). The days of the meetings are fixed to fall on less busy days such as a Sunday or *Eke* day (Igbo equivalent of a Sunday) for the convenience of most members. Time and place of meetings are decided by members through consensus. Most clubs hold their meetings either in the early morning or in the evenings to minimize interference with other daily work and household activities.

Although *Isusu* clubs in the area have a long history, predating the advent of the British colonialists, the life of an individual club may prove to be fairly short. Changes in leadership and/or membership, internal disagreement, or village developments external to the club may lead to the disbanding of a club or the formation of a new one.

The clubs serve as avenues for compulsory saving and obtaining credit without collateral (irrespective of gender) at low interest rates. They provide members with a lump sum of money to carry out tangible projects, which otherwise may not have been possible. Also, many members are able to obtain loans and default is almost non-existent, due to the use of indigenous sanctions and the existence of mutual trust and family bonds. Though the savings and credit functions of *Isusu* clubs are of primary importance, members regard the entertainment, fellowship and peace-making roles of the clubs as other reasons for their membership. Nonetheless, the clubs are non-political. There was no reported case of members using *Isusu* as a platform for political activities.

The success of *Isusu* clubs in rural savings mobilization and extension of credit with minimum default has led to the establishment of community banks (CB), whose philosophy is derived from the *Isusu* operations. Currently, there are over 1,500 community banks in Nigeria, with only one in Ohaozara LGA.

Non-indigenous economic associations

The non-indigenous economic associations of note in Ohaozara are (1) the different forms of cooperative societies, and (2) the Road Transport Workers' Union.

Cooperative societies

There are different types of cooperative societies operating in the LGA, including the Farmers' Multi-purpose Cooperative Society (FMCS); the Multipurpose Cooperative Society (MCS); the Cooperative Community Farm (CCF).

At the local government level, these cooperatives operate under the umbrella of a Divisional Cooperative Council, which is a secondary coordinating body. There were a total of 154 registered cooperative societies with a total membership of 6,446 in Ohaozara LGA as at 31 July 1993. It is significant to note that 95 per cent of all the registered societies are FMCSs. In addition to these, there are 11 other societies, with a total membership of 470, awaiting registration. Membership of the cooperative societies includes both genders, and the average membership strength of the registered societies was calculated to be 42.

The names of the cooperatives are indicative of their nature and objectives. Generally, cooperatives are formed to engender the spirit of cooperation among members and to render services at minimal cost to members. The basic cooperative principles are: open and voluntary membership; democratic control; limited interest on capital; patronage refund; cash trading at market price; and religious and political neutrality. These principles form the bond uniting cooperators the world over and serve to distinguish cooperative from non-cooperative enterprises.[21] Examination of these principles shows that they have social and economic dimensions which are indicative of the dual role of cooperatives. The cooperatives in Ohaozara operate within this general framework.

Each society has a set of officers (president, vice-president, secretary, financial secretary, treasurer, public relations officer, auditor and provost) as required by law. The officers are elected for two to three years. Officers can be re-elected as many times as members deem fit. The aspirations and activities of the societies are governed by their constitutions and by-laws. Breaches attract appropriate penalties: fines, suspension, denial of rights or expulsion. Their activities and operations come under the scrutiny of the supervising staff of local and state governments. This is one of the reasons why some indigenous organizations such as *Isusu* and age grade associations refuse to be registered as cooperative societies even when they have met all the statutory requirements for registration with the Cooperative Department of the state ministry.

Sources of funds for the cooperative societies are share capital, membership dues, fines, levies, interest on loans, members' savings (in the case of credit and thrift societies), and sales from products (in the case of consumer and production societies). A major source of funds for the societies is grants and loans from government. In fact, some members perceive cooperation as a means of obtaining grants, loans, farm inputs and essential commodities from the government.

The FMCS societies encourage members to engage in the cultivation of crops, assist in procuring farm inputs, especially fertilizers, improved seeds and seedlings, and reselling to members at reasonable prices. They also obtain loans and grants from the government, especially under the auspices of the BLP.[22] Members felt that they had gained in the past from belonging to the cooperatives, as they obtained fertilizers and other inputs; but they lamented that those gains are now things of the past.

The social principles of cooperation ensure open and voluntary membership, democratic control, and religious and political neutrality. The societies in Ohaozara behave true to type in these respects, and are not involved in any form of partisan politics as a group. Members are free to participate in politics as individuals. In fact, any attempt to engage in politics by a cooperative would involve withdrawal of registration by the appropriate authorities (the State Registrar of Cooperatives).

National Union of Road Transport Workers (NURTW)

The union, as the name implies, brings together commercial drivers. It has branches at Okposi, Akaeze, Ishiagu and Uburu. The Okposi branch, the biggest and busiest in the LGA, serves Ugwulangwu community as well. The community branches of the union are affiliated to the state and national bodies. The Okposi branch was established in 1985, and brings together commercial drivers and motor owners. The membership totalled 65 at the time of this research. Membership is compulsory for all commercial drivers, except those who opt out on religious grounds, such as members of the Jehovah's Witnesses sect.

The sources of funds for the union are load charges in the park and special levies for special projects. Ten per cent of transport charges on all cars loading in the park is deducted by the NURTW at source as each car loads. About a third of the amount realized from load charges is paid into the union funds while the rest (two-thirds) is shared among jobless drivers on duty each day.

Each branch is run by an executive committee made up of elected officers: chairman, vice-chairman, secretary, assistant secretary, treasurer, financial secretary, public relations officer, provost and auditors. Elections are held every three years, but officers with good performance can be re-elected as many times as members deem fit. Meetings are held once a month (every Sunday *Nkwo*) with refreshments and food.

The NURTW has a constitution adapted to the peculiarities of each branch. Each branch also has a set of by-laws guiding its operations and activities. Deviants are penalized in accordance with the constitution and by-laws. Stealing, fighting, inciting others to fight or quarrel, embezzlement of union funds, revealing union secrets, 'driving in opposition' (picking up passengers outside the park or attempting to load before your turn) are offences viewed seriously by the union; they attract stiff penalties on offenders. For example, embezzlement of funds and stealing attract suspension.

The union has been very useful to the members. They get ₦ 500 each at Christmas and there are social security arrangements to assist members in financial straits and their families in case of death. Members socialize and rejoice with other members at marriages, child naming ceremonies and other occasions. The union also assists members in settling cases with the police and minimizing police harassment on the roads.

The union is non-political. It has never participated in any form of politically motivated protest or demonstration. Members are free to participate in partisan politics on an individual basis, but are not allowed to discuss politics in union fora and meetings. Members believe that it is safer to keep off politics, to avoid antagonism and splits in the union.

Political empowerment

In 1993, the NRC and the SDP were well established in the LGA, with their secretariats located at the LGA headquarters at Obiozara. People in the area exercised their right to choose leaders within the parties at the three executive and legislative tiers of government. The NRC had a majority of seats in the local government council (seven to the SDP's five) and also represented Ohaozara in the state and federal assemblies, where the LGA had two seats and one seat respectively.

There seemed to be some gender-related obstacles in political participation in the LGA, as was evident from the gender distribution of leaders of the two political parties as well as elected representatives. The leadership of the two parties at the ward level was 80 per cent male. The elected members of the federal, state and local government legislatures were all men. The three local government council supervisors (appointed by the chairman) and about five senior political appointees at the state level (appointed by the governor) were also men. This bias indicated the political marginalization of women.

There was an absence of extreme rancour between members of the two political parties, among both the leaders and the led. There were various plausible explanations for this. One was to ascribe such maturity to the activities of MAMSER.[23] Another was to see it as collusion by the political class, especially the leadership, to compromise ideals and principles in order to get settled – by receiving financial benefits at the expense of the masses and their communities. Yet another explanation was to attribute the relative serenity at the LGA to the 'stabilizing effect' of the state governor. It was difficult to specify the exact reasons, but each explanation might have been partly true.

Unexpectedly, most social and economic organizations in the area were non-political and preferred to be insulated from politics, although individual members could engage in politics passively or actively. In the apolitical organizations, such as social clubs, cooperatives and traditional credit *Isusu* clubs, members could engage in politics (by contesting elective offices in the parties, for example) but were not allowed to discuss politics within the organizations' fora. Members of these organizations had never engaged in politically motivated strike actions, demonstrations or boycotts.

There were, however, exceptions to the norm. One of the social clubs in the Ishiagu community was regarded as a breeding ground for political aspirants. In the past, contestants backed by the club had been known to win elections. The town unions also had a link with politics to the extent that they were involved in the zoning of political offices in their communities to component villages in rotation. Attempts by individual political office aspirants to break such zoning practices were said to have resulted in political defeat.

Economic empowerment

In Ohaozara LGA, land is easily available and can be bought or sold, leased or inherited. Individuals have access to both patrilineage and matrilineage lands to varying degrees, depending on gender or position in the family. On the patrilineal side, the head of the family/household determines who gets what land from the communal land, with a preference given to men, while wives are given preference in order of seniority.

Employment opportunities are very limited, at the formal level. Although people are very reluctant to part with information about their total income, estimates of wealth (based on visible assets and types of homes owned) suggest that income is fairly distributed rather than skewed.

Gender-related obstacles are not pronounced in economic activities. Women are free to engage in any type of business, and especially farming, trading and crafts. Women in Ohaozara are known to be effective rice, yam, cassava and vegetable farmers. They also engage in the trading of assorted items (cloths, food items, shopkeeping). They are free to purchase different inputs such as fertilizers.

While women can farm the land, they cannot purchase land unless it is in association with men (husbands, brothers or other male relations). In the same vein, money lenders do not lend to women unless they are accompanied by men. The credit policies of formal organizations such as banks also place women at a disadvantage, as women are rarely accepted as guarantors for loans. Exceptions to this are loans from the *Isusu* clubs, cooperatives and other organizations which have female members.

The low wage rates for unskilled women's labour when compared with their male counterparts is another subtle gender-related obstacle. While men earned ₦ 60–₦ 80 daily from farm labour, women earned ₦ 15–₦ 20 during the survey period; and our investigations showed that such unjustifiable gaps exist throughout the year, irrespective of the fact that men and women have their exclusive niches and specializations in farm labour activities. For example, while men plough rice fields and make mounds for yams, women do all the weeding. The low wage rates translate to low economic empowerment for the women.

Accountability and transparency

Financial accountability

There is a bureaucratic arrangement to ensure financial accountability at the local government administrative level. All expenses are expected to pass through the internal auditor. In addition, auditors from the state Auditor-General's office are expected to audit local government accounts on a yearly basis and to examine expenditures by elected, appointed and employed local government staff. Such an audit team from the state were in Ohaozara to examine the accounts of the LGA for three weeks in July 1993, the time of field work for this study. The report of the audit was not made public, but there were rumours of irregularities with respect to payment for jobs never done or not completed, especially in connection with contracts for the sinking of 33 boreholes and the grading of LGA roads awarded to elected councillors. It may be difficult to confirm the veracity or otherwise of these rumours. The impression one got from talking to villagers was that the councillors hoped to share the federal allocation to the local government council among themselves. Councillors, most of whom were jobless prior to their election to the council, were known to have built houses, to have bought cars and to have built up substantial bank accounts within the first two and a half years in office.

The official sanctions for poor financial accountability for local government personnel might amount to dismissal, suspension or reprimand, but no one in a position of responsibility had been sanctioned in the previous two and half years despite widespread rumours of financial impropriety. Nor had any elected official in the LGA been sanctioned on the basis of poor financial accountability.

Political accountability

Political accountability is necessary to guide the actions of the elected and appointed officials. It engenders trust and respect in the democratic polity. To ensure political accountability at all levels (federal, state and local governments), some sanctions were outlined in the 1989 Federal constitution. These included the impeachment of elected legislative officers of the assemblies at local government, state and federal levels by members of the respective legislatures; the recall of elected members of the councils, the state assemblies and the National Assembly by the members of the ward, state constituency and federal constituency, respectively. Appointed political office holders could also be reprimanded or dismissed from office if found wanting in the performance of their jobs by the council chairman, the state governor or the president.

The leader of the local government council legislature in Ohaozara was prior to this research temporarily suspended on allegations of 'inability to perform' – in that he was unable to 'force' the council executive to render monthly accounts to the council legislature. The legislature thought that the council leader was collaborating with the executive. The leader, however, went to court, and the council executive intervened to have the case resolved out of court 'to avoid embarrassment both to the council and the state governor', or so we were told.

No other LGA official – elected or appointed – was sanctioned, despite rumours of financial impropriety and abandonment of their responsibilities. Perhaps ironically, the council chairman was selected for an 'international' award by the Nigerian-American Chamber of Commerce, for his 'excellent performance in community development'. The award was in recognition of the chairman's efforts towards the eradication of guinea-worm.[24]

Mechanisms for performance monitoring

Mechanisms for the monitoring of the performance of elected officials by the electorates do not exist. Elected officials do not go back to the electorates until their terms expire, when they may want to ask for fresh mandates from the electorates. The councillors are rarely re-elected for two reasons: the lack of performance and plundering of public funds; and the rotational arrangement for representation in the council within the constituent villages of a ward.

The Ohaozara local government promoted the idea of a so-called 'Ohaozara People's Forum'. The forum was said to be held at Obiozara (the council headquarters) on a monthly basis, during which the council chairman, vice-chairman, some supervisors and other key council staff would inform invited community leaders (including town union executives) of council activities. During such meetings, invitees were expected to ask questions and seek clarifications on issues, as well as pointing out shortcomings and making suggestions to improve council activities. The actual frequency of these meetings could not be ascertained, but between January and July 1993 only one forum meeting was held.

For the local government personnel, the normal civil service appraisal system, which relies on reports by superiors/supervisors on subordinates, is used. The effectiveness of this is questionable, given the general problems of corruption, nepotism and 'godfatherism', which have become endemic in the Nigerian public life, especially in the past ten years.

Lack of community-related data and reports also frustrates efforts to establish benchmarks for effective monitoring of the performance of both elected officials and local government personnel. For example, the provisional figures of the 1991 census at the community levels have not been processed. Furthermore, data on infrastructural development by previous council administrations are difficult to come by. This makes comparison of present and past administrations of the council difficult, if not impossible.

The structural deficiency arising from the lack of effective mechanisms for monitoring performance of both elected officials and local government personnel is indicative of the problems associated with financial and political accountability at the grassroots levels of democratic structures. It also makes it clear that it will be a herculean task to enshrine popular participation in the democratization process at the grassroots.

Government institutions

The Babangida administration, a military regime, created more structures and institutions aimed at enhancing popular participation than any previous administration in the country. These included MAMSER, the DFRRI, the NDE, the BLP, the People's Bank and the community banks.[25] Few of these had made any significant impact on Ohaozara LGA at the time this research was undertaken. In 1993, there was a MAMSER officer at the LGA to educate and enlighten the public on the government's two political parties. An advisory committee was inaugurated in the LGA in September

1992, as one of the strategies to explain the new presidential election process. In addition to political education in the LGA, MAMSER focused on the Food First Programme, aimed at improving farming techniques and the introduction of improved varieties; and at promotion of the formation of co-operatives to enable farmers to benefit from government grants and incentives. Mass literacy, which was one of the cardinal mandates of MAMSER, had been abandoned because of a lack of funds and purported conflict with the mandate of the Federal Ministry of Information.

When it started operations in 1989, the DFRRI, in conjunction with the local government council, provided materials for the construction of water boreholes in guinea worm endemic villages at a cost of ₦448,000, to improve the availability of drinking water, and reduce the incidence of guinea-worm disease. The DFRRI also claimed to have constructed 233.84 kilometres of earth roads in the LGA, but most of these roads had been in existence before its advent, although some might have been freshly graded. Also, the DFRRI was credited with assisting in the Ishiagu Electrification Project (Phase II) which involved 15.6 kilometres of high-tension cable and one sub-station. The project is generally regarded, however, as a form of self-help.

The BLP organized a series of enlightenment campaigns, seminars and workshops to create awareness among the rural women of Ohaozara. Some ward representatives were trained in soap and pomade making. In 1991, a domestic centre was established at Ishiagu for training and counselling newly married girls about to join their husbands. A cassava processing and bean grinding machine was given to Uburu Women's Guild Cooperative Society, although this had been out of use since the end of 1991 because of a technical breakdown. Also, a BLP mini supermarket was built and was functioning at the Obiozara headquarters. The BLP and the Cooperative Department of the local government administration jointly claimed credit for the registration of 45 new cooperative societies. The wife of the local government chairman was the chairperson of the BLP at the LGA, but the daily administration was done by the local government social welfare officer.

Conclusion

From our analysis, it is evident that despite significant community contributions, the physical infrastructure in Ohaozara LGA is inadequate and needs considerable improvement for enhancement of popular participation. The local administration needs to open and maintain more rural roads as well as to maintain school facilities. The state and federal administrations need to tar the potholed roads, provide pipe-borne water, electricity and other public facilities, and to upgrade communication links between the LGA, the rest of Abia State and other parts of the country. Rural physical infrastructures are *sine qua non* in the enhancement of the economic empowerment component of popular participation.

At the time of our research there was a visible presence of government institutions directed at enhancing popular participation in the LGA, but their level of effectiveness was questionable. The government institutions directed at popular participation seemed to have done more talking than acting. Government institutions aimed at popular participation in the LGA could be said to be well intentioned and capable of enhancing popular participation if well implemented. There was the need, therefore, for greater monitoring of the implementation processes to ensure the involvement of the people in project planning and financial accountability.

The local government administration and the local political class needed to show greater financial probity and transparency as well as political accountability. The apparent ignorance of the electorate about their powers over the elected officers at all levels was an indictment of MAMSER in its role of political education. Political education, either through MAMSER or any other organ, would need to emphasize the people's rights and obligations to those who are elected, as a means of ensuring accountability.

Most non-indigenous organizations such as the cooperatives and national NURTW in the LGA were found to be apolitical and of limited use as channels of political empowerment, although they were important sources of economic empowerment for the rural communities.

The indigenous socio-economic organizations, such as the town and village development unions/committees, participated in some limited manner in political office zoning, mobilization and candidate sponsoring, in addition to their major function in local governance. They displayed a desire to ensure equality and fair play in political representation and the sharing of the local, state or national 'cake', which Nigerian politics over the previous decade had come to represent. They also played an important part in the maintenance of peace and order within and among the communities.

Appropriate mechanisms for monitoring the performance of elected officials did not exist. The local people's leadership – *Ndi Uke*, town/development unions and the social club executives – could perhaps be persuaded to establish their own effective mechanisms and fora, building on their indigenous sanctions and moral institutions, to ensure political and financial accountability of the community's political representatives, as and when democratic institutions are re-established.

The low level of politicization of the grassroots organizations can be attributed to the separation of functions and powers. This raises an issue with respect to what the new direction and strategy might be. Could these organizations take a more active part in local and national politics? If yes, should political education be carried out through the existing organizations (indigenous and non-indigenous), or should new community-based organizations be established solely for that purpose'? Or did the organizations and societies perform well enough at their current level of political participation?

Whatever the answers to these questions may be, some salient lessons from this study need to be noted. These are:

- The dominance of the Igbo consensus approach, which does not require the counting of votes, in the electoral process of most indigenous grassroots organizations;
- The existence of self-sustaining community development bodies among the Ohaozara people;
- The existence of mutual confidence and trust between the leadership and their followers at both the organization and community levels;
- A strong emphasis on accountability and transparency in the indigenous systems (organizations and governments), in contrast to the lack of accountability and transparency in the 'modern' systems (organizations and governmental departments);
- The general tendency towards popular participation inherent in the indigenous systems; and
- The development, in Ohaozara, of hybrid organizations such as the social clubs, which rely on indigenous sanctions and rewards, while absorbing some 'modern' organizational structures.

There is a need to build on the progressive development of indigenous organizations, to absorb the complexities of modern society, without losing sight of the fundamental principles and essential ingredients of the indigenous systems. Our hopes for popular participation in the Nigerian development process are rooted in the principle of selective recourse to our indigenous practices, organizations and systems.

Notes

1 Adebayo Adedeji, *The African Alternative: Putting the People First* (Addis Ababa: ECA, 1990) p. 7.
2 *Ibid.*
3 *Ibid.*, p. 20.
4 See Victor Uchendu, *The Igbo of Southeast Nigeria* (New York: Holt, Rinehart and Winston, 1965), pp. 34–9; and A. E. Afigbo, 'Towards a history of the Igbo-speaking peoples of Nigeria', in *Igbo Language and Culture* (Ibadan: Oxford University Press, 1975), p. 15.
5 Ministry of Information, *ABIA in Brief* (Umuahia: The Government Printer, 1992), p. 2.
6. *Ibid.*, p. 12.
7 Onicha and Ukawu are communities in the neighbouring Onicha LGA.
8 The Igbo week consists of four days, namely: *Eke, Orie, Afor* and *Nkwo*.
9 The local salt industry at Okposi and Uburu sustained the Republic of Biafra during the Nigerian civil war. Since then nothing has been done by successive state and federal governments to develop the industry. The Onu administration (Abia State), however, has promised to develop the industry through the IBB Technology Village Project, which has not taken off.

10. M. M. Green, *Igbo Village Affairs* (London: Frank Cass and Co. Ltd, 1964), p. 26.
11 Marriage has special significance in Igboland, especially for a woman. Hence a woman is not regarded as having come of age until she is married.
12 See note 8 above.
13 G. T. Basden, *Among the Ibos of Nigeria* (London: Frank Cass & Co. Ltd, 1966), p. 256.
14 N. J. Nwese, and Aja Okorie, 'Traditional self-help organizations in agricultural development in Nigeria?', *Nigerian Journal of Rural Development & Cooperative Studies*, 1, 3 (1986), p. 89.
15 *Aju* is the traditional end-of-year festival in Ohaozara. It is celebrated every October in Okposi community.
16 F. A. Okorie and L. F. Miller, *Esusu Clubs and their Performance in Mobilizing Rural Savings and Extending Credit*, Technical Report AETR/26.1, Department of Agricultural Economics (Ibadan: University of Ibadan, 1976), p. 2.
17 *Ibid.*
18 See D. O. Ogunyemi, *Savings Facilities in Nigeria*, (Yaba, Lagos: The Pacific Printers, 1967), p. 7; and William R. Bascom, '*Esusu:* a credit institution of the Yoruba', in: *Journal of the Royal Anthropological Institute*, 82, 1 (1952), p. 66.
19 F. A. Okorie and S. F. Miller, *op. cit.*
20 *Ndi Onyihe* are the *Ozu* or *Oju* title holders. *The Ozu* or *Oju* title is the highest title in Ohaozara; this is called the *Oza* title in some parts of Igboland.
21 Enyeribe Onuoha, 'Cooperative development and the challenge of its humanism' in: M. D. Ijere (ed.), *New Trends in African Cooperatives: The Nigerian Experience* (Enugu: Fourth Dimension Publishers, 1975), p. 12.
22 Under the BLP, formation of a cooperative is a precondition for women benefiting from its activities.
23 MAMSER was established in September 1987 by the federal military government.
24 See *National Ambassador* newspaper, 17 July 1993, p. 2.
25 See Nigerian Federal Ministry of Information and Culture, *Foundations of Democracy* (Lagos: Government Printer, 1993), p. 283.

11

Grassroots Development and Male-centred Societies in Wurno, Sokoto State

NUHU YAQUB

Wurno town – and indeed the entire Wurno district – has symbolic spiritual importance not only to its residents but also to Sokoto State and, of course, the erstwhile Sokoto empire or caliphate. This is because after it was built in 1822 by Sultan Muhammadu Bello,[1] it served both as a *ribat* (fortress) to defend the imperial capital, Sokoto, and as the second capital to the caliphal socio-political formation, to which many actually repaired following the capture of Sokoto by the British in March 1903 .[2]

In addition, it is established that of the royal offices in the defunct Sokoto Empire, *Amir al-Sudan* or *Sarkin Sudan* (as the king of Wurno is variously referred to) was the senior title in the family of Muhammadu Bello.[3] Furthermore, Muhammadu Bello, who died in 1837, was buried in Wurno – thus making his resting place as much a revered place as the *Hubbare* of Sokoto.[4] Of course, these reasons are not the basis on which the LGA was selected for this pan-Nigerian research. Rather, the basic criterion of ruralness qualifies it for selection. Currently, the traditional ruler of Wurno is Alhaji Abubakar Chika Soro. He took over from Alhaji Shehu Malami – an industrialist and one of the best-known Sokoto princes.

Wurno town lies on the banks of the River Rima about 50 kilometres north-east of Sokoto. It is largely a rural settlement like the rest of the LGA, with the bulk of the population engaged in farming. The annual flooding from the Rima valley allows for rice cultivation. At present the dam constructed in the 1960s at Lugu, about five kilometres from Wurno town, is being canalized to assist in rice cultivation and food production in general.[5]

Wurno, from which the LGA derives its name, is also one of the two districts that constitute it. The other district is called Achida. Its main town, Achida, is about 25 kilometres from Wurno and it is situated at mid-point between the Sokoto metropolis and Wurno. As will be emphasized later, Achida is famous for its weekly (Wednesday) market which attracts buyers and sellers from Katsina and Kano states, Niger Republic, and other places within and outside the state. A major item of trade in the market is livestock.

The traditional head of Achida town is called *Dan Malik Achida*. Traditional rulers of both Achida and Wurno districts are subordinates of the Sultan of Sokoto, although they in turn have less important traditional title holders who assist them to carry out their functions in their districts.[6]

Methodology

Official permission for the conduct of our research was obtained from the Department of Local Government Affairs which is a unit in the office of the deputy governor of Sokoto State. This permission was invaluable as it authorized the Wurno local government officials to make available both the official records and their time. They also introduced me to other relevant persons. Research assistants were recruited for each of the zones that make up the LGA.

The questionnaires administered were an adaptation of what were used in the other six LGAs. They were designed to tap data, facts and nuances from the associations which were selected for research. Secondary materials included publications on the history, not only of Wurno LGA but also of the defunct Sokoto Empire, and newspaper articles. A series of visits was made to the Sokoto State Library and Sokoto History Bureau to consult and utilize other facilities.

A major factor that affected the rigour of the research was the timing: it was conducted during the rainy season and some of the respondents could not be persuaded to abandon farm work even for a short period of time. Sometimes, we were forced to get substitute respondents who, though still being members/officials of the sampled associations/clubs, were nonetheless second best. Another problem was the generally poor state of record keeping. Most of the clubs and even government offices unfortunately suffered from this problem.

In providing a close cross-section of a typical community in Sokoto State, this case study gives an indication of how social groups and popular organizations in rural areas of northern Nigeria can be assisted to attain or actualize their potential for self-reliance.

Basic socio-economic indicators

Demography

Based on the provisional figures of the 1991 population census, Wurno LGA has a total of 95,933 people: 45,988 or 48 per cent are males and 49,945 or 52 per cent are females. Other demographic details such as age distribution and the number of households were still being processed by the National Population Commission.

Education

Educational facilities in the LGA are provided under the auspices of the Local Government Education Authority (LGEA). In the 1992/3 session, there were 52 primary schools with an enrolment strength of 3,683 male and 1,217 female pupils (a male/female enrolment ratio of about 3:1). Within the same period, there was a total of 233 teachers for the primary schools, of whom only four were women. The LGEA has three area education offices and these are in Wurno, Marnona and Achida.

There is only one secondary school – for boys only – in the LGA. It has a student population of 1,016 with 22 classrooms. There are 22 teachers and a support staff of 25. According to the principal, the teaching staff strength is clearly inadequate.[7] There are no tertiary and vocational institutions in Wurno LGA.

Health

There are 14 health facilities which are mostly upgraded dispensaries and clinics. There are many patent medicine stores, mainly run by private individuals, and they are spread throughout the LGA. These health facilities, according to the director, partake in the drug revolving scheme, a national health policy.[8] There are 34 medical staff and 95 supporting (paramedical) staff.

There is a general hospital run by the State Health Management Board. It was upgraded from dispensary status (then managed by the LGA) in 1992. There are two doctors, 16 nurses, and 21 beds.

Potable water

In 1993, there were four boreholes functioning in Wurno town. An additional one was under construction. There is a tube well about half a kilometre from the town. A mobile tanker distributes water to individual houses (usually, residents converge at a particular point where they are all served). In Achida town there are three boreholes and a tanker brings water from the Sokoto metropolis for distribution to residents of the area.

Each zone of the LGA is provided with at least one borehole (in some areas, there are two). In other areas, there are low tower tanks as well as several local wells. In some hamlets, facilities such as hand pumps as well as local wells exist. Generally, these potable water facilities are quite close to centres of habitation.

Energy

In 1993, there was an ongoing contract to supply the main towns of the LGA with electricity. The towns to be linked included Wurno, Achida, Duinawa, Kwargaba and Alkammu.

Petrol and kerosene are available in Wurno and Achida. Firewood is the main form of energy used in most households in the LGA. The bulk of the firewood is obtained from the Gundumi forestry reserves, about 50 kilometres south-east of the LGA. Households also use farm waste and wood collected from their farms.

Transport and economic activity

A federal road traverses the LGA. It runs from the Sokoto metropolis to Sabon Birni, Isa, Kaura Namoda, Goronyo and Katsina. There are numerous feeder roads, most of which are not tarred. Bush paths, especially to the farms, are common.

There are two motor parks in the LGA, one each in Wurno and Achida. Both of them have perimeter fences with entrance and exit points. Commercial vehicles are required to load and unload within the parks and they are also required to pay a small fee for the use of the facilities provided. The peak periods for the use of the motor parks are the market days which are Wednesdays (Achida) and Fridays (Wurno). On their market days, Achida and Wurno are served by about 100 taxis and 50 taxis respectively. The heavy demand for transportation on those days has led to many instances of overloading of the available motor vehicles. The difficulties in the industry – scarcities of petroleum products, shortages of spare parts, and the general decrease in the number of available motor vehicles – may have accentuated this practice.

The markets are generally accessible to the bulk of the population by the pervasive use of donkeys and, to a lesser extent, camels to carry a sizeable portion of the wares bought and sold from the markets. The two main towns – Wurno and Achida – have both markets and shops.

Until recently, the LGA boasted of two relatively large-scale industrial undertakings. These were the Wurno Construction Materials Factory (WUCOMAT) and the Zaki Bottling Company. While the former produced building materials (particularly the red brick variety), the latter produced soft drinks such as the King Cola, the King Apple and Teem (lime) brands. Between them they employed hundreds of people in the LGA – thereby contributing to the economic well-being of the area.[9]

There is only one bank branch in the LGA. This is a branch of the United Bank for Africa (UBA) located in Wurno. In 1993 it was expected that more bank facilities would open in the near future.

Public facilities

There is one public library in Wurno which is a branch of the main state library. Achida is also served with a reading room. Of the 52 primary schools in the LGA, 14 are categorized as 'model primary schools' and each of these has a reading facility, akin to a library.

There is only one post office, offering the full range of postal services including an express mail service (EMS) facility. The post office is located in

Wurno. It had 100 functioning postal boxes in 1993, although it had a capacity of about 385. There is no public telephone in the local government secretariat. Although telephone receivers were seen in the LG secretariat during the field survey, they were all out of use. There is a radio link among the local government secretariats in the state and between them and the deputy governor's office, which is responsible for supervising the affairs of this tier of government.

There are two grades of judicial institutions in the LGA: the area and the upper area courts. The area court has two branches, one each situated in Achida and Wurno. The upper area court has only one branch and this is located in Wurno.

There are two police stations in the LGA: one each in Achida and Wurno. For the two stations there is a combined strength of 45 policemen and women, headed by a divisional police officer and assisted by an inspector.

Traditional and neighbourhood security organizations

Vigilante groups, popularly known in Hausa as *Yan Vanga,* have about 330 members, grouped in various towns in the two districts that make up the LGA.[10] The neighbourhood security group is meant to complement the security provided by the police and the restitutive functions of the courts. There is thus a high degree of cooperation between the neighbourhood organizations, the police and the courts. The vigilante groups are effective in preventing crime. The spokesman of the vigilante groups suggested that given the importance of their functions, a body such as the local government council should provide them with office accommodation.

Mass media

There are no local newspapers and news magazines published in the LGA, but the *Path,* a newspaper published by the Sokoto State Newspaper Company, was available in the LGA. It was published twice a week (Tuesdays and Fridays), with a circulation limited by the small size of the literate audience. The newspaper was a good source of information on the socio economic and socio-political affairs of Sokoto State and its sister state (formerly part of it), Kebbi State.

Another newspaper circulating in the LGA was *Gasikiya Tafi Kwabo,* a vernacular Hausa newspaper published by the New Nigerian Newspapers, Kaduna. Like the *Path, Gasikiya* is purchased in or supplied from the Sokoto metropolis. There are, of course, a few other national dailies and news magazines circulating in the Sokoto metropolis, and some of these find their way into the LGA.

The local (state) radio station, Rima Radio, is popular because it transmits most of its programmes in Hausa, as well as a few in English and Fulani. Next in popularity are the Hausa services of the Federal Radio Corporation of Nigeria (FRCN), Kaduna and those of the BBC. The Sokoto station of the Nigerian Television Authority (NTA) can be received in the LGA. Despite the establishment of TV viewing centres in Achida and Wurno, the problem of electricity supply does not allow maximum utilization. The state government has examined the possibility of setting up its own television station to cater for the cultural needs of its citizens.

The local government authority can use the traditional authorities to assist in disseminating messages through their own channels where other means do not exist. Specifically, if the message is about the collection of taxes, the channels of the traditional authorities are appropriate. In Wurno LGA, the *Sarkin Sudan* of Wurno and the *Dan Maliki* of Achida would summon their respective *Hakimai* (district/village heads) to brief them on the message to be disseminated. The Hakimai, in turn, would call on the appropriate authorities under them to spread the message. At this level, the town/village criers would be mobilized to disseminate the news. Apart from this means, important messages such as the sighting of the moon to commence or to end the Ramadan period can also be disseminated in the mosque, or in the Koranic schools whose sessions usually extend into the early hours of the mornings during the holy month.

Indicators of popular participation

Social and youth organizations

One estimate has it that there are up to 144 social organizations in Wurno LGA. In 1993, in Wurno District alone, 81 such clubs were said to be in existence; while in Achida District 63 were functioning.[11] According to the records on registered youth clubs, 70 were officially recognized by the local government Department of Social Development.[12]

Before discussing specifics, it is necessary to situate these social and youth clubs in the socio-cultural milieu of the Hausa-speaking people. Speaking generally, the Hausa social group is profoundly influenced by Islam, both as religious and cultural phenomena. Although, for example, the rights of women are duly recognized in Islam, these are circumscribed to the extent that men's rights take precedence over theirs whenever there is a clash. This point is very important in attempting to understand why youth and social groups are generally male-dominated. Membership is predominantly male, as females in the age bracket (16–40 years) tend to be in purdah marriage. Hausa society is not only a highly stratified society, but it is also one that is male-centred. This is especially so when the community which is selected for research of this nature is rural, agricultural and, in the language of the sociology of development, 'a periphery of the periphery'.

Social club leaders stress that they are non-political and are devoted mainly to the self-improvement of members in particular and the advancement of the community in general. This, of course, does not mean that members of the youth and social clubs cannot be members of the political parties, manifest political aspirations, or indeed express political preferences. Whatever may be the political disposition of any member is strictly his personal concern. Club names, emblems and other symbols are not used instrumentally for political ends. As a rule, too, the clubs try to live above ethnic and religious cleavages. This, their leaders argue, is because the social ideals of the community that they often promote would not be prosecuted effectively if divisive tendencies were allowed to manifest in their conduct.

The social clubs have a variety of social objectives. They may, for example, provide the manpower towards the monthly environmental sanitation campaigns in the LGA. Other tasks include the conduct of adult education classes (literacy campaigns); building of mosques or their maintenance; maintaining rural feeder roads and digging drains. The ability of the clubs to achieve set objectives is determined by the spirit of cooperation they exhibit.

Unlike the guild and craft associations, most of the social clubs have numerous executive positions: board chairman, club chairman, chief judge, divisional police officers (DPO), court clerk, chief protocol officer, chief legal officer, criminal investigation department (CID) officer, ombudsman, chief imam, usher, women's officer',[13] doctor, chief whip, muezzin and others. Indeed, some of the titled officers have no responsibility to perform. Others, however, are socially and functionally relevant. All clubs have provisions for the post of Imam, who is required to offer prayers for successful deliberations before the commencement of meetings, to offer thanks to God at the end of the meetings, and to lead the members in obligatory prayers if and when meetings coincide with times for such prayers.

One of the key explanatory factors in the effectiveness of the social clubs is the *esprit de corps* they generate. Because of the large number of clubs in the LGA, and the possibility of competition and conflict among them over available scarce resources, there exists a youth council, recognized by the local government authorities, which coordinates and moderates the clubs' activities.[14] The clubs are expected to send their chairmen and secretaries or treasurers to meetings of the youth council (YC). These representatives serve initially to constitute themselves into an electoral college for purposes of forming the YC executive council and later as the congress of the clubs. The officers of the YC include the chairman, vice-chairman, secretary, assistant secretary, treasurer, financial secretary, public relations officer and sports secretary. They have a renewable tenure of two years. The YC chairman has an office in the local government secretariat, although he is not a paid official.[15] Although the needs of individual social clubs can be forwarded directly to the local government executive committee, the YC usually serves as a useful link, and as a liaison body with YCs from other LGAs and also from other states.[16]

The most important function of the YC is the coordination of community development (CD) projects within the LGA. Any social club whose request to the local government authorities is not answered satisfactorily can call on the YC chairman or the entire YC executive to intercede on its behalf. The local government is obliged to assist the youth clubs in kind rather than in cash. Such assistance could come in the form of the provision of corrugated iron sheets, nails, tractors, or educational materials. The local government argues that it does not take over community development projects from the youth clubs as that could either encourage unhealthy competition or dampen popular initiatives.[17]

The Sokoto State government also assists in encouraging the development of the popular organizations. It annually reserves three seats for pilgrims to Mecca from the three LGAs which distinguish themselves in community development projects.

It would appear from the foregoing analysis that the social clubs are important instruments of mobilization and development. In 1992, local government records showed that social clubs in Wurno and Achida spent ₦ 362,137 and ₦ 285,583 respectively.

Provision has been made in club constitutions to ensure a regular frequency of meetings ranging from weekly to monthly and some degree of leadership turnover. During the research, a number of the social clubs (15 in all) had not had a change of leadership in the previous two years, while in a few others a change had been effected in the preceding year . The impression was that of social clubs where members were active, and the leadership role was regarded as an honour that should be accepted. Sanctions are also available in the various clubs. These ranged in 1993 from small fines of 20 *kobo* for laughing at meetings and 50 *kobo* for lateness at meetings, to higher fines for missing meetings and for not undertaking community development projects. There is also in some clubs the sanction of expulsion of members for serious misdemeanours.

Economic organizations

There are two credit schemes in the LGA. Both of them are modern. The *Asusu* credit institution, which is traditional and commonplace in southern Nigeria, does not appear to be in operation. People, particularly farmers, did not volunteer information in this regard. This does not imply, however, that such traditional credit institutions did not exist before, or that some of its features are not being utilized currently.

The principal scheme in operation works for the benefit of farmers.[18] It is described as a bank loan association and it involves four commercial banks. Since only the UBA has a branch office in the whole of the LGA, this means farmers seeking to borrow from the other banks have to travel to the Sokoto metropolis. Each bank lends to an association composed of 15 members. Twenty-two such associations were in operation as at the time of this research, and each had the required number of members. The minimum amount which could be granted to an association of the farmers was ₦ 45,000, while the maximum was ₦ 75,000. This meant that the average loan to a farmer in any association was ₦ 3,000 and the maximum was ₦ 5,000. UBA, as in all its loan agreements, insists on collateral, and two kinds are normally demanded: the joint and several guarantee of members; and a Central Bank of Nigeria (CBN) guarantee which normally amounts to 75 per cent of the approved loan.

The farmers are expected to pay the loans within 6–10 months of utilization. In 1993 the interest charged on the loans was 29 per cent. Although the repayment rate was encouraging, defaults were still numerous. To redress this, the UBA has been forced to go to court and sue 60 farmers from Wurno LGA. The bank manager explains that it is more cost-effective to go to court to have the loan liquidated for two main reasons: (a) the average local Hausa feels scandalized if dragged to court; and (b) although the CBN guaranteed the loan to the tune of 75 per cent, the process of getting it to redeem such a pledge is usually tedious. In spite of the seeming availability of this form of credit, the farmers complained that the loanable funds are inadequate, too bureaucratized, and that the interest rate on the loan is too high.

The other modern credit institution in the LGA was in its formative stage of development at the time of the research. The NDE, in conjunction with the Department of Agriculture of the Wurno LGA, was coordinating a new credit scheme. According to the directive from the NDE in Sokoto State, the LGA was obliged to prepare an area of farmland of about 5,000 hectares, which would then be shared and allotted to no fewer than 100 farmers. The LGA had not yet prepared the land but it had sent a proposal on the cost of preparing the land to the state government. It had not received any reply from the government at the time of this research. In anticipation of a positive response from the state government, two groups of farmers, numbering 126 and 108 persons respectively, had already been mobilized. The NDE loan scheme was intended to provide assistance in cash and in kind.

Political empowerment

At the time of this research, the nation's two political parties – the NRC and the SDP – both had branch offices in the LGA. The NRC had a membership of 8,172 compared with 2,804 in the SDP.

Only 7,822 out of the 25,145 total registered voters (about 31 per cent) of the registered voters were female. In some of the wards, women constituted less than one third of the total number of voters. This was the case in such wards as Dimbiso and Lahodu/Garin Bango where women are no more than 14.5 per cent and 19.1 per cent, respectively, of the total voters.

To extend the analysis further, if we assume that half of the population in the LGA was of the voting age (18 years and above) then 75 per cent of the male adult population, as compared with only 31 per cent of the female adult population, were registered as voters.

As elsewhere in Sokoto State, the LGA is NRC-dominated. Out of the ten councillors in the LGA, the NRC had nine while the SDP initially had one.[19] The two seats in the state House of Assembly, the only seat in the House of Representatives, as well as the senator representing the LGA and others in the senatorial district, were all occupied and represented by NRC members. Quite significantly, all elected political office-holders in and from the LGA were male.

At the time of this research, there were no reported cases of political activities such as demonstrations, strike actions and boycotts. Such incidents are indeed rare given the culture and structure of the society under study. Although we have already emphasized the hierarchical nature of the Hausa society, the absence of these forms of political expression should be seen in the light of sustained efforts to build consensus around local government policies and programmes. This approach is complemented by a high level of illiteracy which prevents the vast majority of the people from fully understanding their rights.[20] With the prevalence of a patron–client political tradition, people go into politics, join a particular political party or act politically in a particular way, not because of personal convictions as such, but simply because a relative, a friend or social superior has done a similar thing or has suggested it.[21]

Economic empowerment

People in the LGA have easy access to land as a means of production. Although there are only imprecise figures on the land mass of the LGA, within the context of the old Sokoto Province, it was said that land was plentiful:

> farmland can be said to be abundant for local needs, and individual households of a man and two or three wives usually cultivate as much as four to eight areas. In ... [some] areas the average area cultivated by each household is as high as nine acres.[22]

In contrast with the more densely populated area and land tenureship problems of eastern Nigeria, it is relatively easy in the LGA to acquire land for agricultural purposes. This is facilitated by the system of land inheritance guided by Islamic injunctions which stress equity and fairness in such matters.

The main problem of agricultural practice in the LGA is the restricted access of the people to adequate and cheap modern credit institutions, as explained above. Traditional forms of credit, which should be of great assistance to farmers, no longer thrive. Access to inputs such as fertilizers and seedlings is another difficulty. The problem created by the shortage of fertilizer is particularly acute. A high proportion of the state's allocation of fertilizer in 1993 was alleged to have been lost in transit.[23] As a result, a bag of fertilizer which officially sold for ₦ 80 fetched prices as high as ₦ 300 in local markets.

Another input that has become difficult to obtain is fuel. In view of the fact that the area is an arid zone and is therefore not endowed with adequate rainfall, farmers often resort to irrigation. Although large scale irrigation – particularly canalization – is under way in the LGA, farmers are still using rudimentary techniques. Most often, the farmers use mobile water pumps powered by small generating plants for this purpose. The acute scarcity and the attendant high prices of petroleum products, however, often render the machines non-operational.

We mentioned above that the LGA has not been able to prepare the land for the NDE scheme. One reason for this is the poor state of the tractor equipment for leasing in the LGA. The statewide tractor hiring scheme is not of much help to the peasants, who mostly cannot afford the cost.[24]

Traditional employment opportunities, like farming, tanning, buying and selling cows, cloth and food items, building, smithery and hawking water exist in the LGA. Most of them are carried out on a small scale and may not be highly remunerative. It may therefore be necessary to enhance the employment opportunities in the LGA by opening the area to investments that are environmentally sustainable.

The collapse of the two modern industries in the LGA was a setback for the local economy in Wurno. Ancillary employment opportunities could be enhanced if more post-primary institutions (particularly girls' schools) are built and the existing one expanded. Housing projects might attract some of the senior staff of the local government authority to reside in the area rather than travel from Sokoto, as is the current practice. Encouraging them to work and reside in the LGA could assist in enhancing its economic well-being.

Data on the pattern of income distribution in the LGA could not be obtained. In this rural setting, a wide differentiation of status is not very visible. For instance, residential buildings are generally made of mud and are unplastered, while the furnishings of the houses are simple and spartan throughout. In some cases, however, status is indicated by the clothes the residents wear. Even in this respect, however, not much differentiation could be observed.

Although, in theory, women have as much access to land, credit, inputs and technology as men, the cultural pattern and the socialization process of the area have some obvious disadvantages for women. For example, the practice of early marriage for girls usually does not allow them to acquire the relevant and necessary skills that can make them as economically productive as men. As a consequence, they are usually dependent on their husbands' material support for their well-being.

Accountability and transparency

If accountability is conceived as the process whereby people entrusted with positions of responsibility are periodically made to explain and/or report on their conduct in office, it can be said that reforms of the local government system over the past 15–18 years in Nigeria have resulted in the formulation of measures aimed at accountability and transparency. In Wurno LGA, the legislative arm of the council has considered and passed annual budgets and carried out other statutory functions, but has never reprimanded, sought the dismissal of any local government staff, or indeed attempted to impeach the chairman or his deputy.

Apart from mechanisms which are internal to the local government, external bodies – such as the office of Auditor-General of the Department of Local Government Affairs, the Public Accounts Committee of the State House of Assembly, and the appointed external auditors – also perform crucial roles in ensuring financial accountability. None of these bodies, however, has indicted the local government for financial misappropriation.

Recall was another instrument which could be applied by the political parties, at the time of this research, to discipline erring members by withdrawing support. The people themselves could discipline any elected official adjudged to be corrupt or unaccountable. The electorate could also refuse to re-elect an official even if his party continued to accord him support. Because this instrument had never been applied in the LGA, this researcher could not ascertain its effectiveness in ensuring accountability.

Mechanisms for monitoring the performance of social and economic organizations are reasonably exhaustive, although there could be some divergence between intentions and practice. This *caveat* is also relevant to the mechanisms for monitoring the performance of the elected officials.

Government institutions

A preliminary assessment of the effectiveness of federal government institutions such as MAMSER, the DFRRI and the BLP indicated that they were not active in Wurno LGA, probably because the government itself was no longer favourably disposed to funding them.

MAMSER was reported to have organized a series of enlightenment campaigns, general mobilization and political rallies, especially at the initial stage of party formation, to enable people to choose between the political parties in the LGA.[25] MAMSER was adjudged to be effective in such mobilizational efforts. As already indicated, people's party affiliations or participation in politics could have been adopted in spite of MAMSER's efforts. At the time of this research, MAMSER had been abolished and a new body – the National Orientation Agency (NOA) – formed in its stead.

The BLP was not operational in the LGA. It seems the people's religious background largely negated the aspirations of the BLP to mobilize women for the upliftment of their socio-economic status.

There was no branch of the People's Bank of Nigeria in the LGA. Plans were afoot to establish two community banks in Wurno and Achida. The local government had already paid the pre-registration fee for the proposed banks and promised to provide office space and the payment of staff salaries for between one and two years upon their coming on-stream.[26]

Among the federal government institutions only the NDE seemed likely to play an active role in the LGA, through its loan scheme, but this was still at an early stage of implementation.

Conclusion

Popular social and economic organizations have come to be regarded as catalysts of development, not only in Wurno LGA but throughout the state. Some of the organizations are well run with respect to record keeping; most are not. Accordingly, the internal machinery for the smooth operation of the organizations needs to be strengthened.

An important conclusion of this research is that gender-related obstacles to the economic and political development of women should be systematically dismantled, so as to ensure the full participation of all for the development of themselves and their communities.

Notes

1 According to Hogben, Muhammadu Bello is widely believed to have been the greatest of the sultans of Sokoto. He was indeed famous for his scholarship, administrative capability, piety and martial adroitness. For some accounts of his life see, among others, Ahmadu, Bello, *My Life* (Cambridge: Cambridge University Press, 1962); S. J. Hogben, *An Introduction to the History of the Islamic States of Northern Nigeria,* (Ibadan: Oxford University Press, 1967), p. 207; M. Last, *The Sokoto Caliphate* (London: Longman, 1977); ? Passion and M. Adamu, 'Introduction: a general history of the Sakkwato Caliphate', in: A. M. Kami and K. A. Gandi, (eds), *State and Society in the Sokoto Caliphate* (Zaria: Gaskiya Corporation Ltd, 1990), pp. 1–20.

2 Last, *ibid.*, p. 176.

3 *Ibid.*, p. 100.

4 *Hubbare* is the royal cemetery where past sultans as well as prominent members of the Sokoto royalty lie buried. It is sometimes a place of pilgrimage for important Muslim visitors to Sokoto.

5 Information gained from an official of Impresit Bakolori – the contractors handling the canalization project (August 1993). See also R. K. Udo, *Geographical Regions of Nigeria* (London: Heinemann Educational Books, 1981), p. 170.

6 Other traditional rulers in the districts include *Dangaladima* Achida, *Marafan* Sisawa, *Danbarara* Kwasare, *Galadiman* Gyelgyel, *Ubandawakin* Alkammu, *Sarkin Tundu*, *Lahodu* and *Bango* Gidan Bango for Achida District; and *Marafan* Wurno, *Magaryan* Wurno, *Dangladiman* Kwargaba, *Dangladiman* Chaco, *Sardaunan* Marnona, *Bunun* Dimbiso, *Sarkin Yakin* Dinawa and *Dangaladiman* Tunga for Wurno District.

7 Interview with the principal of the government secondary school, Wurno, 27 August 1993.

8 The drug revolving scheme is a cost recovery scheme introduced during the

tenure of Professor Olikoye Ransome-Kuti as Minister of Health. It is a national scheme whereby essential drugs are paid for and a separate bank account is maintained for the revenues generated which are meant for the re-supply of drugs.

9 The prolonged cessation of production by these two factories is not unconnected with the aftermath of the contest for the sultanship and the consequent removal of the immediate past *Sarkin Sudan* of Wurno – Alhaji Shehu Malami. He was the brains behind the setting up of the factories, 'to assist his subjects'. Other technical problems associated with the closure include raw materials availability and reliable electricity supply.

10 Interview with the leader of the vigilante group who is also the leader of the farmers' group, 17 August 1993. He stated that there were 28 and five branches respectively in Wurno and Achida districts.

11 Interview with the Chairman, Youth Council – an umbrella organ for all Youth Clubs registered with the LGA's Department of Social Development, 31 August 1993.

12 Information obtained while going through Wurno LGA Social Development Department's files, 9 August 1993 .

13 Although all of these clubs are male-dominated, having a women's officer in the clubs that have provision for it is aimed at mobilizing the free women, invariably unmarried women and prostitutes, to sing and dance whenever community development projects are to be executed.

14 Interview with staff of the Department of Social Development, Wurno LGA, 9–10 August 1993.

15 *Ibid.*

16 As at 31 August 1993, the YC chairman was busy making preparations for the impending visit of the youth council delegation from Jigawa State.

17 Interview with staff of the Department of Social Development, *op. cit.*

18 Information on this section was obtained from the Department of Agriculture, Wurno LGA, 17–18 August 1993, and the management of UBA, PLC, Wurno Branch, 1 September 1993.

19 According to the chairman of the LGA, the only SDP councillor attempted to decamp into the NRC in order to become an NRC councillor . As this was unconstitutional, the member was deemed to have lost his seat in the council.

20 Interview with Wurno LGA Chairman, 31 August 1993.

21 *Ibid.*

22 Udo, *op. cit.*, p. 170.

23 According to the Sokoto State Commissioner of Agriculture in a testimony to the state House of Assembly on this incident in August 1993, out of the 12,690 tonnes of fertilizer allocated to the state. 4,380 tonnes were diverted to unknown destinations. See the *Path*, 17–19 August 1993.

24 The LGA had two tractors which had broken down When they were functional, farmers were charged ₦ 25 per hectare (interview with staff of the Department of Agriculture, Wurno LGA, op.cit).

25 Interview with the social mobilization officer, Wurno LGA, I September 1993.

26 Interview with the chairman, Wurno LGA, *op. cit.*

III

Evolving a Way Forward

12

Looking Back to the Journey Forward: Renewal from the Roots?

ADEBAYO ADEDEJI

This final chapter is on perspective. It focuses on four strategic thrusts for moving forward and explores the prospects for renewal from the roots in the light of the analysis and the findings in the preceding chapters. There is also an attempt to identify the indicators for monitoring progress on the actualization of popular participation.

The four strategic thrusts which are to be explored are, first, fostering the integration of the dual system of grassroots peoples' organizations, thus putting an end to the uneasy cohabitation between traditional and indigenous social and political grassroots organizations and the non-indigenous modern organizations. The second thrust is putting in place a coherent forward-looking policy of restitution: how to look back to the journey forward. The third is finding a way to reconcile the growing individualistic image of change with the traditional, group-focused, communitarian image of change and, by so doing, to reconcile the demands of the market economy with the claims of the social economy. The final, imperative thrust is to devise an alternative system of governance for the grassroots level which will force the government to yield space to the people so that popular participation can become sustainable. In other words, we need to explore how nation states can evolve into genuine people's republics. But before exploring these four areas let us begin by highlighting some of the main findings and conclusions of the case studies.

The overarching theme

The seven different local government areas studied highlight the need to explain and compare the roles of both indigenous and non-indigenous forms of authority and association, as well as the need to consider the potential contributions, in both the short and the long run, of each mode of organization towards enhancing democracy, development, good governance and accountability in Nigeria. In virtually all the local government areas, people are confronted by the phenomena of minimum government and an irrelevant state. There is no doubt that the inability of civil society to assert itself *vis-à-vis* the state is a direct consequence of prolonged military rule. The vast majority of the people are not only apathetic to and alienated from the state, but have also been brutalized by its enormous coercive and extractive capacities.

This alienation of the people, particularly in the rural areas, has been extended to the democratization and development processes that have from time to time been introduced in Nigeria. The creation of a large number of new local governments since 1986, and the series of local government reforms undertaken since 1976, have failed to resolve the problem of popular alienation from politics and development. The over-centralization of power has accentuated the problem. There is no gainsaying the fact that as long as the state seeks a monopoly of the public-cum-political space and, by so doing, denies the legitimacy and liberty of non-state actors and organizations, the irrelevance of the state will persist.

In such circumstances, our battle cry must undergo a fundamental shift. It must move from *putting the people first* to *the people putting themselves first*, by asserting their sovereign power and claiming their inalienable rights. In other words, the people must empower themselves politically and economically. They must perforce seize the initiative. The ideal model for change is for government to yield space to the people by broadening the political, economic and social base of power. But in cases where such an avenue is unavailable, the people must assume their responsibility and face their historic challenge. Achieving a turnaround in any society is the primary responsibility of the people. The culture of public lethargy, perpetual grumbling and the dependence syndrome will have to be done away with if Nigeria is to undergo fundamental change and transformation, not just mere adjustment. Without doubt, the task of paving the way for popular participation in governance belongs squarely to the people and their organizations.

It is thus important for the state and society to be in a continuous process of engagement and disengagement. As one of the researchers has quite rightly asserted, the greater the interaction between the state and people's organizations, the higher the content of collective enhancement and the more outwardly political the organizations become. Wherever functioning popular participation organs exist, people tend to be better off and self-reliant. Even if the organizations are merely defensive or survivalist, important social and political learning processes are inevitable, implicit and, sometimes, unexpected. Thus, the organizations of civil society contribute in a crucial manner to the empowerment of an increasing, and often previously disenfranchised, body of citizens in economic, social and political terms.

The failure of governments to realize that they and people's organizations are two sides of the same coin is the underlying cause of the African crisis. Such a realization would have led inevitably to the maintenance of healthy relationships and to the development of the capacity to cope with the challenges not only of governance but also of public service delivery. We shall revert to this problem later. Meanwhile, let us map the journey into the future by looking back and down closely at the grassroots organizations.

Four strategic thrusts for moving forward

1 Integration of indigenous and non-indigenous social organizations

It is abundantly clear that in many parts of Nigeria traditional modes of social organization are very resilient. They continue to exist in spite of the deliberate effort to superimpose on them modern, non-indigenous socio-economic and political organizations. As we have seen in Chapters 5 to 11, social clubs, cooperative associations, craft and guild societies, road transport workers' unions and town and community development associations are the typical grassroots organizations in Nigeria (as indeed they are all over Africa, particularly in the English-speaking countries). They exist everywhere, albeit differing in forms and degrees of effectiveness and efficiency.

These modern institutions constitute part of the colonial inheritance and have evolved in many varieties. They are not always administered democratically, nor are they generally rooted in the tradition and culture of the society. Nevertheless, as the studies show, many of them, particularly the village development committees (VDCs) and the town development unions (TDUs), which are mainly post-independence creations, perform a vital role in the promotion of peace, unity and development in their communities. Their principal functions are (1) infrastructural development of the village or community; (2) settlement of individual and inter-village disputes; (3) promotion of community and government relations, as well as intra- and inter-community relations; (4) maintenance of community socio-cultural functions; and, (5) involvement in the overall local governance of the community.

In many respects, there is an overlap between their functions and those of the traditional social organizations, particularly the age grade associations which are peculiar to some communities. Like the TDUs and VDCs, these age grade associations perform social and economic roles but, unlike them, they also have political responsibilities. The age group system emphasizes popular participation by all in local affairs. People become gradually committed to the integrative roles enjoined by the system. Colonial dispossession and Africa's acculturative modernization, however, have undermined the age group system, with perhaps only one exception – Ijebu-Ode local government area – out of the seven that were studied.

The rapid and systematic organization of the age group society in Ijebu – the *Regberegbe* – throughout the nineteenth century was symptomatic of the era of progress, prosperity and stability which had prevailed in the pre-colonial Ijebu Kingdom. No one knows when the first *Regberegbe* was founded, who had initiated them, or for what purpose. Nor does anyone know why the three-year age group cycle was adopted, except that this coincides with the traditional family planning systems not only in Ijebuland but in many parts of pre-colonial Africa. The linkage between *Regberegbe* and the three-year interval considered desirable between the birth of one child and another by the same woman was partly to ensure that no two children of the same mother belonged to the same age group society, and partly to uphold the integrity of the family by ensuring that the younger ones did not rub shoulders with thier elders in the same societies.

In a strict sense, the *Regberegbe* were and still are people's organizations in civil society rather than institutions for governance, although in their heyday, during the 1870s, they enhanced their political position in the affairs of the state by successfully interfering in public affairs. The *Regberegbe* received their names by royal charters and such names are prefixed by the word *Oba* (King/Queen). They were therefore expected not only to obey but also to serve their liege loyally. Yet in the course of the past two centuries there have been many occasions when they have held opinions and viewpoints which have opposed successfully those of the Awujale (or King) of Ijebuland.

During the past decade, tremendous efforts have been made to revive and revitalize the *Regberegbe* as part of the deliberate policy of restitution. But a lot still remains to be done to turn these societies into agents of change required to meet the challenges of the twenty-first century. There is, first and foremost, the need to impose additional qualifications for membership besides age. Members should have shared values and a high sense of social responsibility which will encompass maintaining the moral integrity of the family system; strengthening the cohesiveness and unity of the community; providing humanitarian assistance to the needy; and assisting in protecting and ensuring a healthy environment.

It is crystal clear that in order to enhance the effectiveness of these grassroots organizations the present parallel arrangement must give way to integration. Every effort must be made to integrate the traditional societies with the modern interest groups so as to enhance their impact on the society and polity.

2 *Putting in place a coherent, forward-looking policy of restitution*

Such integration is only feasible, of course, within the context of a well-articulated policy of restitution and restructuring of Africa' s institutions. This requires the abolition of the 'acute disfunction between the history of the past and the history of the present, which was imposed by dispossessions and their consequences', and the renewal of the 'flow of history, of indigenous self-development, that was broken by the dispossessions'. And no solutions will endure unless they can make good 'the moral dislocations and the moral wounds inflicted on the fabrics of community, on vital dimensions of self-esteem and therefore self confidence'.[1]

It is because of this unwholesome legacy that ACDESS has been campaigning, since it was founded in 1991, for African countries to put in place the politics of material and non-material restitution. Without doubt, Africa has much to gain in experience, in self-confidence and in vision if it looks back in order to look forward. Therefore there must be a coalition, if not a merger, between the VDCs and TDUs on one hand, and the age group societies on the other hand, for the optimalization of the impact of these grassroots popular participation organizations. Parallel existence weakens the capacities of both and impedes the forces of democratically-determined development.

It is also vital for economic interest groups, such as trade unions, farmers' associations, consumer groups and business associations, to have national membership and orientation so that they can direct their demands towards the national political centre. But first these organizations need to re-establish their autonomy, for the state has succeeded largely in subjugating them. Consequently, most of them are ineffective in advancing the interests of their membership and in motivating them to popular action.

What is urgently needed is the creation of a new legitimacy and the evolution of new traditions. If this 'cutting across' between traditional modes of social organization and modern ones can be accomplished, adequate capacity would have been developed at the grassroots for revitalizing the economic, political and social systems in the rural communities of Nigeria. It is imperative to put in place structures of genuine participation which, while having the qualities to address the challenges of today, draw inspiration from the wisdom of the past. In other words, Africa needs to restructure its institutions and, by so doing, to reinvent itself.

3 Restoring the social economy

The effect of marketization on popular participation in general and on democratically-determined development in particular has been addressed in Chapter 1. A number of questions were posed. Will the market allow the people to participate effectively in the development process? Are there people-friendly markets? What is the impact of the market on economic empowerment? Are markets really free? From our discussion, the importance and usefulness of the market in meeting certain human needs is not in dispute. The progressive dominance of domestic markets is largely as a result of conscious political decisions because, at the domestic level, marketization has meant reduced state interventions, reduced subsidization and increased privatization. Unregulated and uncontrolled, the forces of marketization even at the domestic level are the forces of inequity and marginalization. Hence, in all industrialized market economies, governments protect the people from the excesses of the market.

Indeed, the market economy best serves the interest of the people when it functions in tandem with a robust social economy founded on values of cooperation, sharing, trust and mutual obligation. It is the totality of the values, norms, attitudes and beliefs of a society which determine the dynamics of its social economy by shaping its political and economic organizations. It guides the general feeling towards development.

The social setting consists of the social organization of production, its associated patterns of ownership and distribution, forms of social differentiation and the cultural milieu. The core of this setting is the social organization of production which determines the scope and cycle of production and reproduction as well as the broad social system in terms of relationships among groups and individuals.

Unfortunately, the Nigerian social economy is currently undergoing severe strains and stresses due to long and persistent political crisis, uncontrolled urbanization, the virtual disappearance of social sanctions, and imitative modernization. Today, the country's social fabric is in danger of collapse.

More than ever before, we need urgently to search for economic policies that will strengthen the already weakened social economy. It is imperative to find holistic approaches to dealing with poverty, unemployment and social disintegration with a view to restoring community bonds. There is no doubt that the market economy will be supportive of the social economy under the following circumstances: (1) that the market is primarily local in character, augmented but in no way dependent on trading relationships with more remote localities; (2) that capital is locally owned and most production is carried out by small enterprises; (3) that a strong, democratically accountable government sets the goals and provides a regulatory framework for the market's socially productive function; (4) that appropriate policies in support of gender equity are put in place to ensure that men and women share responsibility for the functions of both the social and the market economies; and, (5) that a strong and politically active civil society exists to mobilize the community and ensure public accountability.

When all these conditions are satisfied, the market economy and the social economy become complementary and the market forces of inequity and marginalization are ameliorated and kept under control. Needless to add, human security consequently is enhanced. The globalization of marketization, however, tends to negate all of these conditions as there are no global governments and institutions to play the ameliorating role of the local grassroots institutions at the domestic level.

4 Search for an alternative system of governance at the grassroots level

Given the perennial nature of the Nigerian political crisis, solutions at the national level may take quite some time to come by. We need not fold our arms and leave the millions of people in the rural areas who are trying hard to survive through their popular grassroots organizations hapless and without hope. The studies have shown beyond doubt what has been known for a long time: the resilience of the rural population and their undaunted survivalist culture. In order to give a fillip to this spirit, therefore, and provide the enabling environment for renewal from the grassroots, it is imperative to search for an alternative innovative system of governance at the grassroots level. Such a system will be a symbiosis of the traditional and modern systems of governance as it will bring together the local government, popular and participatory grassroots organizations, and traditional institutions of governance in each community.

It will be left to each community to work out the specificities and details of this alternative governance system. Without the approval of the state and federal governments it will no doubt be difficult to embark on this experiment. There is therefore an urgent need to sensitize state functionaries and traditional leaders alike. They need to yield space to the citizen by involving people's organizations from the start in decision making and in the implementation and monitoring of programmes and projects. Exclusionary structures – against women, youth or non-indigenes – must be avoided.

Renewal from the roots?

There is no doubt that renewal from the grassroots holds the key to the economic liberation and political transformation of Nigeria in particular and of the whole of sub-Saharan Africa in general. In the light of the overwhelming evidence from communities in all parts of Nigeria, it is clear that the state has failed the people. The various tiers of government – federal, state and local – have not only failed to deliver an acceptable level of core social services and functions which fall under their authority, but they are also unresponsive towards the aspirations and appeals of the people. This failure, together with intensified economic decline, has increasingly forced local community efforts to act in lieu of the state, in order merely to survive and maintain a minimum standard of social services for the next generation. Needless to add that they embark upon this task with meagre and insufficient means.

Such instincts, spirit and determination give a lot of hope for the future of Africa – for its renewal and regeneration and for its transformation and liberation. A new African transformation ethic which incorporates rather than alienates the present and future African realities – political, social, cultural, environmental and economic – seems to be in the making. This new African transformation ethic is developing quite satisfactorily from the grassroots. It is not only human-centred but it is also predicated on the fundamental proposition that change and development have to be engineered and sustained by the people themselves through their full and active participation, and that these cannot be undertaken on their behalf but rather have to be an organic outcome of a society's value system, its perceptions, its concerns and its endeavours. We must nurse the entire evolutionary process of this transformation ethic until it blossoms.

There are two major, but not insuperable, difficulties in the way of the grassroots renewal. The first is their lack of leverage. Grassroots people's organizations have yet to make much significant impact at local and national levels. It must be admitted, however, that the indirect impact of these organizations is often much wider than their direct contribution. The second difficulty is that these grassroots organizations have many constituencies – donors, beneficiaries, policy makers and the public – which have conflicting expectations. There is a need, therefore, for these organizations to develop mechanisms for multiple accountability so as to enhance both their effectiveness and their democratic credentials.

Because of this multiple accountability, these organizations are generally suspected of being mere mirrors of the Northern NGOs which assist in funding their activities. Since the northern NGOs are themselves funded by their governments, there is the suspicion of manipulation. This has provoked new debates about the desired relationships and division of labour between northern NGOs and their southern counterparts. There is a genuine concern, particularly in Africa and even more so in Nigeria, lest indigenous grassroots organizations become the new source of dependence on the industrialized countries. The northern NGOs have all that their African counterparts lack: education, skill, information and, above all, financial resources. They now often employ or commission specialists to undertake studies and produce campaign materials and strategies for their use. These northern NGOs are extremely well provided for by their governments, particularly when they are operating in Africa.

In less polite circles, northern NGOs are accused of representing establishment interests more than those of the poor, and of not being in full support of endogenous African political and economic development paradigms. Their operations are characterized as anachronisms from another era, still focused more on relief than on development, negligent in the creation and strengthening of indigenous capabilities to replace themselves and unmindful of the growth of indigenous grassroot people's organizations that are rapidly developing much-needed operational capacities.

There is no doubt that some of these criticisms are exaggerated, if not inaccurate, but a few are true and valid. Many non-African NGOs have gone a long way in promoting North/South partnership and some are even helping in the development of African NGOs, including the funding of such NGOs. But there is no doubt that the influence of non-African NGOs as donors is often detrimental to ensuring genuine partnership and this adversely affects the enabling environment for popular participation. To minimize such conflict and avoid the impression of domination, the African Charter has laid down the following ground rules for cooperation between non-African NGOs and VDOs and their African counterparts:

1. Cooperation in all forms must be transparent and reflect African priorities;
2. Non-African NGOs should give due recognition to African NGOs and the participatory, self-reliant initiatives launched by African grassroots organizations;
3. Non-African NGOs should utilize African expertise to the maximum

extent possible with regard to their development work in Africa and advocacy and campaigning work at the international level; and

4 Cooperation and dialogue should be strengthened to increase the effectiveness of their interventions at the community level.

The African Charter also gives due emphasis to the need for the creation of national fora for undertaking honest and open dialogue between governments and grassroots organizations and NGOs.

Unfortunately, African governments have yet to address seriously the issue of how to fund their people's and community-based organizations. Even more fundamental is the fact that many of them have yet to come out with well-articulated policies on NGOs and grassroots people's organizations. There is an urgent need for clarity and coherence in public policies and attitudes toward these organizations by their governments. They should not merely be tolerated as long as they are of 'good behaviour', adhering to and supporting the policies of the government of the day, or as long as they act as alternative conduits for foreign aid. It is not uncommon for people's organizations in Africa in general and in Nigeria in particular to be looked upon as being anti-government because they champion the cause of the destitute and play an advocacy role against the profligacies of the powers-that-be.

The relationships between people's organizations and the state are characterized by positions of unequal power, making it very tempting for the state to dictate the conditions and terms of such relationships. The relations are usually very complex – sometimes cooperating, sometimes in conflict, sometimes dominating and compliant, and sometimes in true cooperative partnership. The attitude of the government to people's organizations is dependent on the nature of the state itself and on the social base of power. A people's government, enjoying their full confidence, cannot fail to be responsive to popular demand. Conversely, a government with a narrow social base of power is most unlikely to be willing to yield space to the people. Such a government will fail completely to motivate people and galvanize and tap their energy and commitment. In such circumstances, giving support to people's organizations hardly arises as an option. Rather, they will be the object of constant harassment. Such a government will want to control and monitor these organizations with a view to marginalizing them. Thus, only a government with a broad social base of power, accountable and responsive to popular demand, will provide an enabling environment for grassroots people's organizations.

When and wherever the conditions are conducive, there are three levels of interaction between governments and people's organizations: national, departmental and local. At the national level, in addition to formulating national policies towards grassroots organizations, national fora will need to be established to enable honest and open dialogue between the government and these organizations in order that the experience of grassroots participatory development may come to inform national policy making.

These organizations also need to establish relations with departments/ministries of government along the line of their own special interest. Such interactions will facilitate intervention and impact by the NGOs on sectoral public policies; they will also enable the government department concerned to include the grassroots activities in its programme.

The local government level is perhaps the most difficult, as we have seen in the preceding section where we propose, as a means of enhancing co-operation, the search for an alternative system of governance at that level. In addition to everything else, grassroots organizations often challenge the local power structure, traditional as well as modern. Hence we have proposed an innovative system that brings together all concerned – local government leaders, grassroots people's organizations, and existing pre-colonial traditional institutions of governance. Where the local power structure is élitist and oppresses the poor, however, this arrangement does not deny the right of grassroots people's organizations to seek a fundamental change.

In all these interactions, the overarching objective of the grassroots people's organizations is to ensure community empowerment and self-development and the guarantee of fundamental human rights. The attainment of equal rights by women in the social, economic and political spheres must become a central feature of a democratic and participatory pattern of development. Only then will renewal from the roots not only become a dynamic reality but also lead to the fundamental transformation of the society, the economy and the polity.

Indeed, the greatest challenge and herculean task of grassroots people's organizations is how to play the multiple roles required of them: as advocates, educators and catalysts; as monitors and whistle blowers; as mediators, conciliators and bridge builders; and as implementers of projects and programmes. This is what popular participation is all about: *the empowerment of the people to effectively involve themselves in creating the structures and in designing policies and programmes that serve the interests of all as well as effectively contributing to the development process and sharing equitably in its benefits* (the African Charter).

Monitoring progress in the journey forward

The task of achieving an increasing measure of popular participation is therefore formidable, even if it is exciting and challenging. As we have argued in Chapter 1, it encompasses political democracy, the democratization of the development process, governance and public service delivery. It is a four-in-one process. The journey to its full realization is a long and tortuous one. It is full of ups and downs. While there can be no doubt about the imperative of measuring progress in the forward movement, it is very difficult to work out a quantitative and objective basis for such measurement.

The African Charter was quite courageous in articulating the indicators to use in the measurement of progress. Nine such indicators were identified as follows:

1 *Literacy rate:* This determines the capacity for informed popular participation in public debate and decision making. An illiterate society is not likely to be a participatory society. It is more likely to suffer from public apathy, perpetual grumbling and the dependence syndrome. To build the environment for popular participation, therefore, a high rate of growth in literacy is essential until illiteracy becomes a matter of the past. This is why education for all (EFA) is a fundamental requirement of popular participation. Among Third World countries, Nigeria has one of the lowest adult literacy rates – 52 per cent in 1994 – when countries like Mauritius, Botswana, Kenya, Zambia and even Zaire have 80, 75, 71, 75 and 74 per cent respectively. In terms of the EFA target, Nigeria has reached only 78 per cent as compared to Ghana's 88 per cent, Zaire's 91 per cent and Zambia's 90 per cent.

2 *Freedom of association:* To what extent are fundamental human rights respected? In particular, how much freedom exists for the formation of any association – political, economic, social and cultural – without official interference or sanctions? What guarantees are there for constitutional rights? And how is the situation evolving? The persistent demand by successive military governments in Nigeria and elsewhere that political associations should be registered and approved by them contradicts the freedom of association.

3 *Elected representation:* Is there a pervasive system of democratically elected representation in national bodies, or are representatives in such bodies predominantly nominated?

4 *Equality before the law:* Is the rule of law supreme? Do people arrested by the police have the right of *habeas corpus*? Is there a relentless movement towards social and economic justice and equitable distribution of income? Is there a deliberate policy of equality of opportunities?

5 *Human, ecological and legal environment:* How well protected, over time, are these?

6 *Press freedom:* Is there a culture of press and media freedom?

7 *Number and scope of grassroots organizations:* Is there a large and growing number of grassroots organizations which are democratic and self-reliant in all spheres of human endeavours?

8 *Decentralized decision-making processes:* How centralized are the decision-making processes and the institutions? How pervasive and internalized is the four-dimensional administration of deconcentration, delegation, devolution and decentralization?

9 *Public accountability:* Ensuring public accountability at all levels of leadership is an essential requirement of popular participation.

These indicators, which are very essential in developing the enabling environment for popular participation, need to be supplemented by others that are more specific and directed. In so far as the domain of political empowerment is concerned, the following additional monitoring indicators will be required:

1 *Democratic political culture:* This encompasses assessing how pluralistic the political party system is and, as already indicated, the freedom to establish political parties or associations; how free and fair elections are when they take place, and whether anyone can tamper with the outcome of such elections. In other words, how effective, real and genuine is the sovereignty of the people? How are the people succeeding in putting themselves first, in occupying the driver's seat of the political machine?

2 *Independent and democratic political organizations and machineries:* Nowadays, particularly in industrialized market economies, political party machineries have been seized by an oligarchy. There is no doubt that this development is undermining the democratic process. For new democracies such a development will be catastrophic. In addition, unless political organizations have independent sources of funding, they will be vulnerable to manipulation. Therefore the monitoring of the extent of self-reliance of these institutions is very important for the vitality of the democratic process.

3 *Nature of the political process:* Is politics a zero-sum game, a winner-take-all, rule-or-ruin endeavour? Or is it a game fostering inclusion, unity, participation and consensus building?

4 *The politics of restitution in place?* Progress towards the abolition of the acute disfunction between the history of the past and the history of the present through the cutting across between the traditional and the modern modes of social and political organization.

With regard to economic empowerment, the following additional special indicators will be useful in monitoring progress:

1 *Access to the means of production:* Measurement of the access of the masses to land, credit and extension services and, in particular, the enhancement of the role of women as agents of change and transformation, especially in the food production sector, must be constantly monitored. Indeed, all the nine instruments of economic empowerment discussed in Chapter 1 under the section on *Democratically determined development: a second sub-set of popular participation* must be kept under constant surveillance.

2 *Dominant development paradigms:* The monitoring of the dominant development paradigms that determine socio-economic policies is imperative. Are they holistic and human-centred, based on the new African transformation ethic, or are they externally crafted, donor-driven, focusing on macro-economic aggregates and things rather than on people?

3 *Optimal mobilization and efficient utilization of resources:* This includes measuring constantly the degree of efficiency in optimal domestic resource mobilization (through increased domestic savings and investment), maximizing the rate of expansion and diversification of the productive capacity, improving human resources capacity and strengthening the scientific and technological base.

4 *Ensuring a just and egalitarian society:* There is a need to monitor the acceleration in the improvement in the level of income and the pattern of its distribution, as well as the pattern of expenditure, for the satisfaction of people's basic needs.

5 *Monitoring of the marketization process:* The effect of marketization on the democratically determined development process must be kept under constant watch and the evolution of the social economy, including employment promotion, will need to be monitored constantly.

Finally, there are the all-important issues of governance, public service delivery and accountability which we discussed at some length in Chapter 1 and which feature in all the case studies. These, too, have to be monitored very closely.

It is needless to add that monitoring requires the establishment of appropriate machineries at all levels, culminating in the setting up of an independent national monitoring body which will publish an annual report on the state of popular participation in Nigeria.

Note

1 Basil Davidson, 'For a politics of restitution', in Adebayo Adedeji (ed.), *Africa Within the World* (London: Zed Books, 1992), p. 24.

APPENDIX I

Constitutional Means of Ensuring Accountability at Local Government Level

If accountability is conceived to be the process whereby people who hold or are entrusted with positions of responsibility are supposed to explain and/or report on their conduct in office, it can be said that the headlong reform of the local government system of administration over the past two decades in Nigeria has resulted in the enunciation of a number of measures aimed at achieving accountability and transparency. The mechanisms for achieving accountability that prevailed in 1993 are described below.

In specific terms, the institutional mechanisms governing local government accounting procedures are contained in:

1 The provisions of the Financial Memoranda of the 1977 Local Government Edict;

2 The Local Government (Basic Constitutional and Transitional Provisions) Decree No. 25 of 1989;

3 The implementation guidelines on the Application of the Civil Service Reform in the Local Government Service 1989;

4 The Local Government (Basic Constitutional Provisions) (Amendment) Decree 1991;

5 The establishment of the Directorate of Projects Monitoring and Evaluation, in the office of the Auditor-General of Local Government Affairs, the Public Accounts Committee, etc.

These institutional mechanisms prescribed specific roles for: the local government chairman, who was the chief accounting officer; the secretary; the supervisor for finance; the treasurer and the internal auditor – all of them being internal officers of the local government.

The legislative council of the local government was also intended to perform some watchdog roles. It was charged, among other things, with the responsibility of examining and debating monthly statements of income, the annual budget (which though subject to the chairman's veto could be overruled by a two-thirds majority of councillors) and expenditure rendered to it by the executive arm. It also had the power to impeach the chairman whenever his/her conduct violated constitutional provisions.

Apart from the above mechanisms, which were internal to the local government, there were external bodies, such as the office of auditor-general of the Department of Local Government Affairs, the public accounts committee of the state House of Assembly, and appointed external auditors. These bodies were supposed to perform crucial roles in ensuring financial accountability.

Recall was another instrument which could be applied by the political parties to discipline erring members by withdrawing support. Section 304 of the 1989 Constitution provided for the recall of elected officials including the local government chairman and vice-chairman. It was also implied in the 1989 Constitution that the people themselves could discipline any elected official adjudged to be corrupt or unaccountable, although the mechanisms for achieving this were not widely explained.

In the final analysis, the electorate could refuse to re-elect an elected official even if his/her party continued to accord him support.

Researched by Nuhu Yaqub

APPENDIX II

Federal Government Institutions Designed to Encourage Popular Participation, Mobilization and Employment

MAMSER

The Directorate for Social Mobilization, Self-Reliance, Economic Recovery and Social Justice (MAMSER) was formally inaugurated in September 1987. It was established to mobilize the citizenry for effective participation in the political process and to elicit positive changes in the people's attitude to politics. It was expected to realize its objectives by a systematic political education of the people through seminars, lectures, debates, drama presentations and the mass media.

MAMSER was also directed to explain to the people the emerging political system: the constitution, strategies and channels for participation (such as voters' registration and voting procedures), as well as the consequences of participation or non-participation in politics. MAMSER was to operate at the three tiers of government: the federal, state and local.

The MAMSER programme was scrapped early in 1993 and efforts were made to streamline its activities under another agency to be called the National Orientation Agency (NOA).

BLP

The Better Life Programme for Rural Women (BLP) was inaugurated in September 1987 by the former first lady (1985–93), Maryam Babangida. It was specially targeted at rural women to encourage their active participation in the economic life of their communities and to help them expand the scope of activities aimed at self-generated income and economic empowerment in a male-dominated society. It was intended to be implemented at the local, state and national levels.

The stated objectives of the BLP were: to stimulate and awaken the consciousness of women who live in the rural areas about their rights and their social, political and economic responsibilities; to bring women together for better resolution of their problems through collective action; and to mobilize women for concrete activities towards achieving specific objectives, including seeking leadership. Women were also to be taught simple skills such as palm oil processing, soap making, cloth weaving, etc.

In some areas, the BLP has been highly effective in breaking down barriers to women's economic progress, while in many areas the developmental objectives have been lost, and considerable amounts of money have been wasted on poorly planned projects and purely social gatherings.

The Better Life Association became the organizational forum of the BLP, with the first lady as the national chairperson, wives of state governors and local government chairmen as the chairpersons at the state and local government levels. Each LGA had a Better Life Association encompassing Better Life Societies organized on a community basis.

DFRRI

The Directorate of Food, Roads and Rural Infrastructures (DFRRI) was established in 1986 by the federal military government as an agency with the purpose of aiding food production, constructing feeder roads for the transportation of agricultural inputs and products between the rural and urban centres, and providing basic infrastructural facilities (such as electricity, water, radio and television sets) in the rural areas.

It was intended that the DFRRI would help to open up the rural areas for social and health services, including clean water, education, light and decent accommodation, increased and improved agricultural inputs and easy evacuation of farm produce for increased income, and that it would ultimately discourage rural–urban drift.

The cost of approved projects was shared among the three tiers of government, in the ratio of 60 per cent federal, 30 per cent state and 10 per cent local. The identification, planning and execution of projects was usually done by DFRRI officials in collaboration with local government officials.

Local communities in project areas were rarely involved in the conception or planning of the projects. Only in the execution of a few of its projects did the DFRRI enlist the participation of local communities, as for example in the construction of deep wells in the villages, where the DFRRI asked the villagers to dig the wells while it supplied the necessary materials and machines both for the construction of the wells and their operation.

NDE

Set up in 1986, the National Directorate for Employment (NDE) was charged principally with providing young school leavers with opportunities for self-employment. Other aims of the programme as originally designed were the reactivation of public works, the promotion of direct labour, the organization of artisans into cooperatives and the encouragement of a culture of maintenance and repair.

For the purpose of creating jobs, the NDE might obtain from an LGA land which would then be allocated to unemployed persons who had enrolled with it. Loans would be provided at low interest rates to assist the recipients to buy inputs and meet operational costs. Alternatively the NDE would enter into agreement with established craftsmen and women for the training of selected individuals.

The NDE did not establish a presence throughout the country as was intended, nor did it make a significant impression on the problems it was designed to resolve. A major problem faced by the NDE was its inability to recover loans. In the course of the research undertaken for this volume, NDE officials were generally found to be unable to disclose details of their financial operations.

People's Bank

The People's Bank was established by the federal government in October 1989 and the first branch was set up at Ajegunle in Lagos. It drew some of its original inspiration from the Grameen Bank of Bangladesh and the Badam Kredit Kecamatan of Indonesia. It is unconventional in that its capital base is wholly provided by the government and it is exempted from a number of banking act regulations.

The People's Bank is intended to provide specialized services to the rural and urban poor who do not have access to the credit facilities of commercial banks. It also aims to encourage self-employment for Nigeria's unutilized and under-utilized manpower resources, and to help cushion some of the painful effects of the structural adjustment programme on the poor sectors of the economy. Its other objectives include: complementing government efforts to improve the productive base of the economy; raising rural employment and income; halting rural–urban migration; and inculcating banking habits at the grassroots level.

The bank lends money to its clients at a very low interest rate (5 per cent per annum in 1993) and without collateral, beyond a guarantee of the loan by two persons considered by the bank as creditable and responsible. Anyone who has maintained a deposit account with the bank for at least six months while making periodic deposits is entitled to apply for a loan, the amount of which is partly determined by the size of the deposit in his/her account at the time of application. The amount granted as a loan also depends on the project or business for which the loan is needed. Loans granted by the bank during 1993 generally ranged between ₦ 500 and ₦ 25,000.

Community banks

Community banks have been established throughout Nigeria since the first one, the Alhari Community Bank in Kaduna opened in 1990. By 1993, a total of 175 such banks had been established throughout the country. The objectives of the community bank system is to:

- Promote rural development by providing financial and banking services as well as other facilities to the communities, hitherto inadequately supplied with such services;
- Enhance productive activities in the rural areas, and hence improve the economic status of rural people and rural areas;
- Promote the emergence of an effective and integrated national financial system that responds to the needs of the whole economy at all levels: from the community, the local area, the state and the nation.

Each community bank is an independent, self-sustaining financial institution owned and managed by its own community, whose interests it serves, though it can do business with others which do not own it. The initial capital, of a minimum of ₦1 million, must be contributed by registered socio-economic organizations and individuals within a particular community from which the bank takes its name. At least half of the initial capital must be contributed by socio-economic organizations, with the remainder contributed by individuals within the community to a maximum of ₦50,000 per individual. After take-off, the federal government contributes ₦500,000 to augment the share capital. A federal government agency, the National Board for Community Banks (NBCB), supervises the banks' operations to ensure that they operate according to their guidelines.

A community bank provides credit facilities to its customers at concessionary interest rates and without stringent collateral.

APPENDIX III

Grassroots Comments on and Reactions to the Scientific Findings

Report of ACDESS POPART Workshops

In order to review and expand upon the results of the seven empirical case studies by its research fellows, the *ACDESS Research Workshop on Popular Participation in Rural Communities in Nigeria (POPART)*, was held from 7–9 December 1994. The Workshop, also providing an opportunity for evidence and analyses contributed by academics and practitioners who participated in it, was followed by a *Training Workshop on Popular Participation in Development in Nigeria: How Can Popular Development Organizations Become More Effective in Influencing Policy-Making?* (9–11 December 1994). In spite of varying environmental, cultural, economic and political conditions in the communities studied and represented, the conclusions reached by the participants of both workshops was that notwithstanding internal and external limitations of organization, there can be no doubt that wherever they exist people tend to be better off and more in control of their lives. Even if organizations are 'merely defensive' or 'merely survivalist', important social and political learning processes are inevitable, implicit, sometimes unexpected, and often unwanted by the powers-that-be. In other words, in spite of all the obstacles grassroots organizations face in Nigeria, they have been contributing in a crucial manner to the empowerment of an increasing, and often previously disenfranchised body of citizens, in economic, social and political terms.

1 The issues

In the circumstances and in order to build on existing foundations, the Workshops explored the scope and structural prerequisites for expanding popular participation in all aspects of development and based on the premises that only the broad involvement of the people can engender socially, economically as well as environmentally and politically sustainable structures. In the light of such an exploration, proposals as to how to increase the effectiveness and influence of civil society organizations at all levels of policy making, implementation and monitoring were put forward. Finally, some areas requiring further investigation and proactive research and strategic studies were identified.

With regard to the exploration of the scope and structural prerequisites for expanding popular participation the following cardinal questions were raised:

On civil society, the state and external support

- Which respective roles do traditional and modern organizations of civil society and the state play in development and what are therefore meaningful general strategies? For example, if the state is perceived to be weak in the delivery of services, possibly little or no resort to it may be taken and society may build up surrogate structures from below. Traditional governance can function in support of such efforts but can also be a static and stalling element with its own vested interest.

  How could the state and its institutions, but also international donors (including NGOs) be made more responsive to people's real needs and aspirations, i.e. support initiatives without dominating and instrumentalizing them for their own aims?

  How can the interaction with various tiers of government be made more productive in the design, implementation and monitoring of development policies and efforts?

  (i) How should civil society organizations present their cases to various tiers of government (lobbying and advocacy strategies, skills in conducting negotiations and dialogue)?

  (ii) How should they respond to initiatives and actions taken by governmental agencies? How can the responsiveness and sensitivity of state agencies and in the final analysis the respect of the individual civil servant, for people's concerns be developed?

  (iii) How can the 'right to knowledge' on development programmes and projects – basic data and information, accounts, evaluation results – be claimed in practice?

  (iv) How can the capacity to analyse and utilize information be improved and a two-way flow of information be implemented?

- How can education and the cooperation with the media be developed in the promotion of popular development?

Building internal strength

- Which are the obstacles internal to popular participation organizations?

- How can civil society organizations be strengthened?
- How can they be made more representative, more effective, more transparent and accountable?
- How can cooperation between and among organizations of civil society – be it within localities, regions, the nation or the continent – be encouraged and made more efficient?
- How can it be avoided that organizations duplicate efforts, reinvent the wheel, amass frustrations and peter out as their energies and resources are being drained?
- How can networks be set up which allow the fast, effective and cheap exchange of information – given that most NGOs are hardly, if at all, reachable by phone or fax?
- How can the dearth of knowledge about each other's operations at local and national levels, and in particular as far as modern versus traditional organizations are concerned – be overcome (particularly important in a very heterogeneous entity like Nigeria with its many cultures and languages, where mutual understanding, respect and recognition is essential in fostering social cohesion)?
- How can mechanisms be developed to strengthen coordination among the organizations at various levels, be they modern or traditional?

II Summary of conclusions and recommendations

In the light of overwhelming empirical evidence from communities in all parts of Nigeria, there can be no doubt that the post-colonial state has bitterly failed the people. This is no insight confined to the ivory towers of the universities but wide-spread and experienced as a daily reality. The state, i.e. various tiers of government at federal, state and local levels, not only fails to deliver an acceptable level of core social services and functions which fall under its authority, but it is seen as unresponsive, even irresponsible, towards the aspirations and appeals of the people. Coupled with intensified economic decline, this has increasingly forced local community efforts to act in lieu of the state, albeit often with meagre and insufficient means, in order to merely survive and maintain, for example, a minimum of education for the next generation. While often operating under extreme duress in an environment hostile to any change of the power structures, many of these people's organizations well understand the implicit political nature of even the most mundane effort at survival.

Suggestions on the way forward therefore ranged from fundamental changes to the state's structure and mode of operation to the need for establishing autonomous networks from the local to the national levels where experiences can be shared and successful endeavours widely communicated.

The need to sensitize state functionaries and traditional leaders about the imperative of 'yielding space' to the citizenry and involve people's organizations from the start in decision-making, implementation and monitoring of programmes and projects was emphasized. Exclusionary structures – be it against women, youth, non-indigenes or on the basis of class – should be scrutinized and efforts made to replace them with non-discriminatory ones. It was recognized that women often had informal communication linkages which made them extremely effective – even if they were hardly visible to the outsider. They were thus playing more crucial catalytical roles than was commonly acknowledged.

In order to coordinate the broad range of activities – and to organize for a much larger gathering of organizations of civil society in a year's time – a group of volunteers from amidst the participants who had signed up to constituting a loose network (NETPOP) pledged to diligently work towards the objectives formulated by the participants. Of particular importance was the replication of such gatherings not only at the national but also at the regional, e.g. ECOWAS, level.

A. Governance

The workshops identified two types of structure of governance, the formal and the informal. A tentative working definition was adopted where formal refers to the state institutions of governance, while informal refers to the non-state institutions of governance, or to associations. At the level of LGAs, *formal* refers essentially to the local government council. Under a democratic system, the council consists of two arms, the executive and the legislative. But under the military, there is a caretaker committee, appointed by the military administration. Informal structures can be sub-divided into two – viz. the indigenous and the non-indigenous.

The indigenous include the following:

- Age grade
- Kinship
- Community leaders
- Titled chiefs
- Secret societies.

The non-indigenous include:

- Community Development Associations
- Religious groups
- Economic groups

- Farmers' organizations
- Welfare associations etc.

The Workshops proffered the following recommendations in order to enhance governance at the community level:

1 While the group accepts the existing structures identified above, it recommends a *village assembly* in addition. Members of the village assembly should be elected in a village general meeting. Within the village committee, there should be sub-committees of occupational and interest groups. Finally, there should be an Assembly of Villages comprising the various village committees within the local government area.

2 The principle of trust in reaching decision, which has proved very useful among the informal groups, should be strengthened. It is also recommended that women must be fully integrated in the decision making process.

3 The process of monitoring and control of the local government should be in accordance with constitutional provisions and not be based on decrees and edicts. The village assembly should also be incorporated into the monitoring of the local government. The present methods of monitoring among the informal groups (i.e. moral sanctions) should be strengthened.

4 Resource mobilization at the village level should be through households rather than from individuals. The group also recommends that the allocation to the local governments should now be 15 per cent from federation accounts and 15 per cent from the state's accounts. But more importantly, local governments should endeavour to enhance their internally-generated revenue – as a way of discouraging the present dependence syndrome.

5 Accountability of the local government should be strictly enforced and those found guilty of corruption should be brought to book.

B. State and civil society

The identification of the relationship between the state and society is central to the discussion on the future of development and democracy.

Civil society organizations exist throughout Nigeria in a multitude of forms, in large numbers and with substantial membership. In their relationship *vis-à-vis* the state they can be classified into two groups, the non-autonomous ones and the autonomous ones.

1 THE CURRENT CHARACTER OF CIVIL SOCIETY ORGANIZATIONS

The *non-autonomous* ones tend to have strong linkages to state authorities or depend on the state for support. Organizations in this group are not only dependent on the state, but are also propped up by the state in its (and their) own interest. One can therefore not expect them to pursue drastic reforms of the state apparatus. The issue is to examine under which conditions they would free themselves from the control of the state. The relationship between the state and these traditional organizations is often quite intricate and bi-directional: people holding positions of authority in the state are in fact recruited by the traditional leadership of the society. In this sense, the state and traditional society can therefore be seen to be 'working in partnership'.

The *autonomous* ones, such as the village unions, town unions etc., are inward-oriented and focus on communal development and welfare; they are rarely explicitly political.

Given this interweaving of interests and dependencies, ultimately and most often power is therefore controlled by a very tiny segment of the Nigerian society. With the limited perspectives of both of these groups of civil society, neither one is capable of confronting the state with a view to correcting its excesses and to making it functional in the interest of the vast majority of the people.

2 THE TASK AHEAD

The task ahead can therefore be defined as follows:

(a) Strengthen civil society organizations in order to make them independent of the state;

(b) Undertake capacity-building of the popular traditional organizations so that they will be strong enough to resist the state;

(c) Encourage networking of the organizations, involving the linking up of many of the organizations, thereby broadening their base of operation;

(d) Undertake a close analysis of the judicial system with a view to proposing ways and means of ensuring an effective operation of the rule of law and providing a basis for accountability;

(e) Undertake a study on the relationship between poverty and empowerment;

(f) Study the value system in order to enhance the integrity of the members of the traditional organizations.

III Proposals for further research and strategic studies

The following proposals for further research were made:

1 Popular participation and capacity-building: the role of indigenous cultural organizations.

2 In-depth study of the political and economic power of traditional orga-

nizations with potentials for popular participation.

3 The role of civil society organizations in reforming and reconstituting the educational system.

4 People-centred leadership training and political education for village associations and the citizenry.

5 Concepts for ameliorating communication flows among grassroots organizations from the local to the national level.

6 Individualism versus communalism in Nigerian society – towards a renewal of the value-system.

7 Alternatives to the current local government system: the potential contribution of popular participation organizations and traditional systems to governance in modern times.

8 Laws and rules enforcement within traditional groups: a larger lesson to be learnt?

9 Code-of-conduct for civil society organizations.

10 Local government and international resources provided to NGOs and their use.

11 The use of radio for mass communication and education.

Bibliography

Adedeji, Adebayo, 'Economic Reform and Democracy: An Alternative for Africa', in: *Journal of Democracy*, Vol. 5, No. 4, October 1994 .

Adedeji, Adebayo, (ed.), *South Africa and Africa: Within or Apart?*, 1996, London: Zed Books; CapeTown: SADRI Books; Ijebu-Ode: ACDESS.

Adedeji, Adebayo, Sadiq Rasheed, & Nelody Morrison (eds), *The Human Dimension of Africa's Persistent Economic Crisis*, 1990, Hans Zell Publishers, London, UK.

Adedeji, Adebayo, *The African Alternative: Putting the People First,* 1990, ECA, Addis Ababa, Ethiopia.

Adedeji, Adebayo, 'Nigeria Shivering and Hovering on the Brink', text of public lecture delivered in Lagos on 8 July 1994.

Adedeji, Adebayo, 'Africa and the Africans and their Historic Challenge', Convocation Lecture of the Eight Convocation Ceremony of the University of Calabar, Nigeria, 3 December.

Adedeji, Adebayo, (ed.), *Africa Within the World: Beyond Dispossession and Dependence,* 1993, ACDESS and Zed Books, Ijebu-Ode and London.

Adedeji, Adebayo, 'The Rehabilitation and Restitution of the Nigerian Political Recovery as a Prerequisite for a New Economic Order', lecture delivered in Lagos on 14 January 1994 at the 12th Delegates Conference of the Chartered Institute of Bakers of Nigeria.

Afigbo, A.E., 'Towards a History of the Igbo-speaking Peoples of Nigeria', in: *Igbo Language and Culture*, 1975, Oxford University Press, Ibadan, Nigeria.

Ake, Claude, 'The Limit of Pluralism in Nigeria', in: *Nigerian Journal of Critical Social Science*, Vol. 1, No.l, January, 1988.

Ake, Claude, *The Feasibility of Democracy in Africa*, CREDU Occasional Publication, No. l, 1992.

Ake, Claude, *Political Economy of Africa*, 1981, Longman Group Ltd., Ibadan, Nigeria.

Akeredolu-Ale, E.O., Lagos Zone Report, Preliminary Draft, in: *DFRRI Survey of NGGA's in Nigerian LGAs*, 1991 .

Akingbode, Funso, *Selected Nigerian Popular Organisations and their Opera-*

tional Dynamics, paper presented in Rus Communication Ltd National Workshop on Mobilisation of Popular Organisations Towards The Success of the Transition Programme, Jos, 1994.

Amuwo, 'Kunle, 'Transition Planning in Nigeria: A Critique of the Civil-Military Transiting Variant', in: *Africa Development*, Vol. XVIII, No.l, 1993.

Amuwo, 'Kunle, 'Treetop Politics versus Grassroots Democracy in Nigeria: Some Theoretical and Methodological Queries', in: *Africa,* Vol. XLVII, No.4, Dec. 1992.

Badejo, Bamidele, *Ijebu-Ode in Perspectives*, 1992, Fairweather Books, Ijebu Ode, Nigeria.

Barkan, Joel D., Michacl L. McNulty and M.A.O. Ayeni, '"Hometown" Voluntary Associations, Local Development and the Emergence of Civil Society in Western Nigeria', in: *The Journal of Modern African Studies*, Vol. 29, No. 3, 1991.

Bascom, William R., Esusu: 'A Credit Institution of the Yoruba', in: *Journal of the Royal ,Anthropological Institute*, Vol. 82, Part 1, 1952.

Basden, G.T., *Among the Ibos of Nigeria*, 1966, Frank Cass & Co. Ltd, London, UK.

Bayart, J.F., A. Mbembe and C. Toulabor, *La Politique par le bas en Afrique Noire*, 1992, Ed. Karthala, Paris, France.

Bello, Ahmadu, *My Life,* 1962, Cambridge University Press, Cambridge, UK.

Bevan, Anuerin, *Democratic Values*, 1950, Fabian Tract, No 282, London, UK.

Bratton, Michael, 'Beyond the State: Civil Society and Associational Life in Africa', in: *World Politics*, Vol. XII, No.3, April 1989.

Chazan, Naomi, 'Patterns of State-Society Incorporation and Disengagement in Africa', in: Donald Rothchild and Naomi Chazan (eds), *The Precarious Balance. State and Society in Africa*, 1988, Westview Press, Boulder.

Davidson, Basil, 'For a Politics of Restitution' in: Adedeji, Adebayo, (ed.), *Africa Within the World. Beyond Dispossession and Dependence*, 1993, ACDESS and Zed Books, Ijebu-Ode and London.

ECA, Afican Charter for Popular Participation in Development, ECA, February 1990, Addis Ababa, Ethiopia.

ECA, Underlying principles for enhanced dialogue, cooperation and interface between governments and peoples' organisations, in: *Studies in Participatory Development*, No. 4.

Ekeh, P.P., 'Colonialism and the Two Publics in Africa: A Theoretical Statement', in: *Comparative Studies in Society and History*, 17(1), 1975.

Ekeh, P.P., 'The Constitution of Civil Society in African History and Politics', in: Caron, B. et al, (eds), *Democratic Transition in Africa,* 1992, CREDU Documents in Social Sciences and Humanities, Ibadan, Nigeria.

Ekeh, P.P. and G. Ashiwaju (eds), 'Nigeria Since Independence: The First 25 Years', Vol. VII, *Culture*, 1989, Heinemann Educational Books Ltd., Ibadan, Nigeria.

Eteng, I.A., Popular Organisation in Transition Mobilisation, Some Participatory Models, paper presented at National Workshop on Mobilisation of Popular Organisation Towards the Success of the Transition Programme, Hill Station

Hotel Jos, 20–22 July 1993.

Evans-Pritchard, E.E. and M. Fortes, *African Political Systems*, 1940, Oxford University Press.

Federal Ministry of Information and Culture, *Babangida Administration: Foundations of Democracy*, Lagos, July, 1993.

Foucault, Michel, *La Volonte de Savoir*, 1976, Gallimard, Paris.

Fukuyama, Francis, *The End of History and the Last Man*, 1992, Avon Books, New York.

Fukuyama, Francis, 'The End of History', in: *The National Interest*, No. 16, Summer 1989.

Gboyega, Alex, *Political Values and Local Governments in Nigeria*, 1987, Malthouse Press, Lagos, Nigeria.

Graft, William, African Elite Theories and Nigerian Elite Consolidation: A Political Economic Analysis, in: Barongo, Yolamu, *Political Science in Africa. A Critical Review*, 1983, Zed Press, London, UK.

Green, M.M., Igbo Village Affairs, 1964, Frank Cass & Co. Ltd., London, UK.

Hogben, S. J., An Introduction to the History of the Islamic States of Northern Nigeria, 1967, Oxford University Press, Ibadan, Nigeria.

Imam, A., 'Democratisation Process in Africa: Problems and Prospects', in: CODESRIA Bulletin, No. 2, 1991.

Iwayemi, Akin, *Oil and the Macroeconomics Policy Issues in an Open Developing Economy: A Case Study of Nigeria*, Vol. I, National Centre For Economic Management, Ibadan, Nigeria.

Last, M., *The Sokoto Caliphate*, 1977, Longman Group Ltd., London, UK.

Lemarchand, Rene, 'Uncivil States and Civil Societies: How Illusion Became Reality', in: *The Journal of Modern African Studies*, Vol. 30, No. 2, 1992.

Lipset, Seymour, 'Reflections on Capitalism, Socialism and Democracy', in: *Journal of Democracy*, Vol. 4, No. 2, 1993.

Mafeje, Archie, 'On "Icon" and African Perspectives on Democracy: A Commentary on Jibrin Ibrahim's Views', in: CODESRIA Bulletin, No.2, 1993.

Maravall, Jose Maria, 'The myth of the authoritarian advantage', in: *Journal of Democracy*, Vol. 5, No. 4, October 1994.

Marx, Karl, Communist Manifesto, 1848, KMSW.

Milbraith, Lester W. and M. L. Goel, *Political Participation: How and Why Do People Get Involved?*, 1977, University Press of America, New York.

Mills, C. Wright, *The Sociological Imagination*, 1959, Oxford University Press, New York.

Mitchell, Timothy, 'The Limits of the State: Beyond Statist Approaches and Their Critics', in: *American Political Science Review*, Vol.85, No.1, March 1991.

Nigeria, Federal Republic of, The Report of the National Inventory of Community-based Infrastructural Facilities in Afijio LG area of Oyo State, 1991, The Presidency, Lagos, Nigeria.

Nigerian Ministry of Information, ABIA in Brief, 1992, The Government Printer, Umuahia, Nigeria.

Nnoli, O., 'Values and Political Development: Towards Achieving a Participatory Political Culture', paper presented in National Orientation Agency Workshop on

National Mobilisation, 1994, Enugu, Nigeria.

Nwese, N.J. and Okorie, Aja, 'Traditional Self-Help Organisations in Agricultural Development in Nigeria', in: *Nigerian Journal of Rural Development & Cooperative Studies*, Vol.1, No. 3, 1986.

Nyong'o, Peter Anyang, 'Democratization Processes in Africa', in: *CODESRIA Bulletin*, No.2, 1991.

Nyong'o, Peter Anyang, 'Democratisation Processes in Africa', in: *AAPS Research Agenda*, No. 1, 1992.

Nzimiro, I., *Studies in Ibo Political Systems*, 1972, University of California Press.

Odugbemi, O. O., *Nigerian Culture and Space Utilization with Special Reference to Yorubaland*, in: O. Y. Oyeneye and M. O. Shoremi (eds), *Nigerian Life and Culture*, 1985, Department of Sociology, Ogun State University, Ago Iwoye, Nigeria.

Ogunyemi, D. O., *Savings facilities in Nigeria,* 1967, The Pacific Printers, Yaba, Lagos, Nigeria

Okorie, F. A. and Miller, L. F., 'Esusu Clubs and their Performance in Mobilizing Rural Savings and Extending Credit', Technical Report AETR/26.1, Department of Agricultural Economics, University of Ibadan, Ibadan, Nigeria, 1976.

Okumagba, M.P., *A Short History of the Urhobo*, 1982.

Olaitan, Wale, 'Democracy and Democratization in Africa: Not Yet the Glorious Dawn', in: B. Caron, A. Gboyega and E. Osaghae (eds), *Democratic Transition in Africa*, 1992, CREDU, Ibadan, Nigeria.

Onimode, Bade & Richard Synge (eds), *Issues in African Development – Essays in honour of Adebayo Adedeji at 65*, 1995, Heinemann Educational Books (Nigeria) Plc, Ibadan; ACDESS, Ijebu-Ode.

Onuoha, Enyeribe, 'Cooperative Development and The Challenge of its Humanism', in: M.O. Ijere (ed.), *New Trends in African Cooperatives. The Nigerian Experience*, 1975, Fourth Dimension Publishers, Enugu, Nigeria.

Otite, O. 'On the Concept of a Nigerian Society', in: *The Nigerian Journal of Economic and Social Studies*, No. 13(3), 1971.

Otite, O. (ed.), *The Urhobo People*, 1982.

Otite, O., 'Continuance and Change in an Urhobo age grade organisation in Nigeria', in: *Cahiers D'Etudes Africaines*, Vol. 12, 1971.

Otite, O., *Ethnic Pluralism and Ethnicity in Nigeria*, 1990, Shaneson C.I. Ltd, Ibadan, Nigeria.

Oyediran, O. and E. A. Gboyega, 'Local Government and Administration', in: O. Oyediran (ed.), *Nigerian Government and Politics Under Military Rule*, 1979, Macmillan, London, UK.

Passion and M. Adamu, 'Introduction: A General History of the Sakkwato Caliphate', in: A.M. Kami and K. A. Gandi (eds), *State and Society in the Sokoto Caliphate*, 1990, Gaskiya Corporation Ltd., Zaria, Nigeria.

Stephan, Alfred, *Rethinking Military Politics: Brazil and the Southern Cone,* 1988, Princeton University Press, Priceton N.J., USA.

Touraine, Alain, *La voix et le regard*, 1978, Le Seint, Paris.

Uchendu, Victor, *The Igbo of Southeast Nigeria*, 1965, Holt, Reinhart and Winston, New York.

Udo, R. K., *Geographical Regions of Nigeria*, 1981, Heinemann Educational Books Ltd, London, UK.

UNDP, *Human Development Report* 1993, New York & Oxford.

Weber, Max, *Theory of Social and Economic Organization*, 1947, Oxford University Press, New York.

Yahaya, A.D., 'The Developmental State in the Process of Transformation: The Implication for the Political Science Discipline', First Annual Lecture of the Nigerian Political Science Association (NPSA), 1989, Ibadan.

Index